MONUMENTAL
SEATTLE

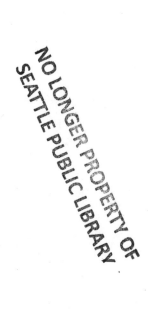

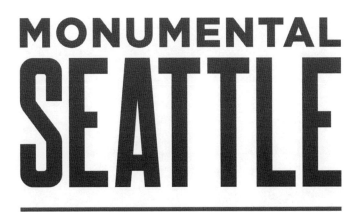

MONUMENTAL SEATTLE

THE STORIES BEHIND THE CITY'S STATUES, MEMORIALS, AND MARKERS

ROBERT SPALDING

WSU PRESS

Washington State University Press
Pullman, Washington

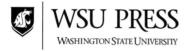

WSU PRESS
WASHINGTON STATE UNIVERSITY

Washington State University Press
PO Box 645910
Pullman, Washington 99164-5910
Phone: 800-354-7360
Fax: 509-335-8568
Email: wsupress@wsu.edu
Website: wsupress.wsu.edu

Library of Congress Cataloging-in-Publication Data

Names: Spalding, Robert, 1968- author.
Title: Monumental Seattle : the stories behind the city's statues, memorials,
    and markers / Robert Spalding.
Description: Pullman, Washington : Washington State University Press, [2018]
    | Includes bibliographical references and index.
Identifiers: LCCN 2018015302 | ISBN 9780874223590 (alk. paper)
Subjects: LCSH: Monuments--Washington (State)--Seattle--Guidebooks. |
    Historical markers--Washington (State)--Seattle--Guidebooks. | Public
    sculpture--Washington (State)--Seattle--Guidebooks.
Classification: LCC F899.S465 A27 2018 | DDC 917.9704--dc23 LC record
available at https://lccn.loc.gov/2018015302

Maps by Chelsea Feeney, www.cmcfeeney.com

In memory of my grandfather, Oscar Spalding; he was a student of history and taught me to appreciate the many wonderful stories our past provides.

CONTENTS

ILLUSTRATIONS & MAPS

ACKNOWLEDGMENTS

First, thanks to the many reporters at Seattle's daily newspapers who over the years captured the life of our city and its people. Without their contributions, many of these stories would be lost.

Thanks to the following for reviewing my initial drafts and making insightful comments and thoughtful suggestions: Irene Geisner, Greg Gartrell, Lorraine McConaghy, and my mother, Grace Spalding.

Thanks to the reviewers for Washington State University Press for their helpful comments, and to Beth DeWeese for her advice, guidance, and thoughtful care in editing this book, and to the entire WSU Press staff. Thanks to the librarians in the Seattle Room of the Seattle Public Library for their time and assistance.

Thanks to the following for answering questions and being generous with their time: George Blomberg, Port of Seattle; Hayley Chambers, Ketchikan Museums; Ron Chew, local writer and historian; Debra Cox, Seattle Public Library; Scott Davies, Pike Place Market; Jeff Day, artist of the Jimi Hendrix bust; Laurie Dunlap, Seattle Parks and Recreation; Sandy Esene, Public Art Program, Seattle Office of Arts & Culture; David Eskenazi, sports author, historian, and collector; Robert Gallagher, Seattle Public Schools; Kristin Halunen, Museum of History & Industry; Kate Hodges, Seattle Public Schools; Lissa Kramer, Southwest Seattle Historical Society; Stephen Langdon, University of Alaska at Anchorage; Phillip Levine, local artist; Stephen Lundgren, local historian; Jeremy Mattox, local maritime historian; Lynette Miller, Washington State Historical Society; Cathy Stanford, Assistance League of Seattle; Elizabeth Stewart, Renton History Museum; Vicki Stiles, Shoreline Historical Museum; Galen K. Thomaier, historian, Seattle Fire Department; Erica Thompson and Jessica Albano, University of Washington.

I am grateful to Washington State University Press for the opportunity to bring the stories of Seattle's monuments to print and preserve them for future generations, even as the city's landscape will surely change and these monuments, memorials, and markers may be relocated, set aside, or lost.

Finally, thanks to my children, Kate and Ava, for driving all over Seattle to hunt for statues and plaques; and to my wife Kim whose support and love makes all this possible.

Robert Spalding

PREFACE

Heritage markers found all around Seattle indicate sites of historical memory and communicate perspectives on the past. People often take no notice as they pass by these monuments, memorials, and markers. At times the markers provoke debate over their meaning and who or what they celebrate. Throughout the city's history local leaders wanted to influence who and what would be remembered, create a particular version of history, and construct memories for the public to consume. Creators of the monuments hoped that future generations would recognize the importance of events, people, objects, and places they deemed worthy of preservation.[1] Some of the heritage markers have disappeared, gone with demolished buildings or stolen; others have been vandalized. Those that remain reflect the past but continue to influence our present.

Beyond the words chiseled into granite or embossed in bronze are opportunities to understand the deeper meaning of the monuments in the context of their creation. This book surveys many of Seattle's heritage markers to consider what story is presented, why some stories were selected over others, and who funded and erected them. Each of these monuments exists within three time periods: first, the historical event commemorated; second, the confluence of events which led to the creation of the monument itself; and last, the state of the monument in contemporary times. The public can learn what a memorial meant at the time of its creation and think about what it means now.

The process for placing a monument in a public space in Seattle has not changed much in the past century. The city itself does not usually fund monuments but instead evaluates the gifting of public art from private individuals or groups. There are a small number of exceptions in which the city did pay for monuments: the Chief Seattle statue, and the Second World War memorials at Victory Square, Memorial Stadium, and Memorial Plaza at the Public Safety Building. Today an individual or group presents a proposal for a potential monument to the mayor, who consults with the city department responsible for a location and maintenance; usually this is the parks and recreation department. The mayor may also ask the Seattle Arts Commission for their recommendation as to the artistic suitability of a monument. With limited public and park space, the bar to place a statue, monument, or memorial is much higher now than in decades past.

Primarily, the heritage markers in this book were funded by private donations and public fundraising drives called "subscriptions," with large numbers of individuals donating to a particular statue. Civic groups often led fundraising and design. The Seattle Chamber of Commerce, immigrant groups, commercial clubs, veterans groups, the Daughters of the American Revolution, Yukon Club, and Propeller Club all developed heritage markers for Seattle.

People often use the terms monument and memorial synonymously, and this book also uses the terms interchangeably. Monuments are defined as objects of public remembrance; the word comes from the Latin *monere*, meaning "to remind" or "to warn." A monument is a structure, statue, or a building which honors an individual or a notable event and contains both a herald and a form. The herald is the message inscribed on the structure, and the form is the physical object placed in the location. A form can be a statue, boulder, fountain, or plaque. A memorial is a structure or a statue built to specifically remember a dead person or a group of individuals who died in a major event.

Monuments were a regular feature in ancient Greece and Rome and widely erected in European cities, but were slow to be accepted in the United States. In 1781, the U.S. Congress reviewed plans for a column to commemorate the Revolutionary War victory at Yorktown, Virginia. A proposal for a bronze equestrian monument to George Washington was submitted to celebrate the end of the war. Although the plans for both monuments were approved, the funds to construct them were not. John Quincy Adams, the sixth president of the United States, famously observed that "democracy has no monuments." Many of the founding fathers agreed that the combination of democracy and a literate population made monuments obsolete, relics from a time when monarchs and royalty used statues to remind the people who their leaders were.[2]

As the country celebrated its centennial in 1876, attitudes toward monuments began to change as "statue mania" swept across the United States. Americans erected hundreds of statues and monuments to help repair the divisiveness that split the country during the Civil War. Statues of Christopher Columbus, pioneers, and Revolutionary War heroes helped people remember a time before the nation was divided. In an attempt to reframe the national narrative away from the war, many statues portrayed ideas of manifest destiny, American exceptionalism, and Anglo-Saxon supremacy.

Late nineteenth-century statues were typically figurative and vertical. Male subjects were placed high on a pedestal and dominated the physical space below. Artists intended monuments to be permanent public fixtures, crafted from enduring materials like marble, granite, or bronze.

What's In and Out

The sheer number of heritage markers in Seattle and King County required some limits on the research and subject matter for this book. Geographically, present-day Seattle city limits form the boundary for inclusion. While there are many other public monuments around western Washington—the Pioneer Mother Memorial in Vancouver, Winged Victory in Olympia, the Peace Arch in Blaine, and many others—the city of Seattle is the focus of this book. While not always an easy distinction, monuments whose primary purpose was public art are not included. This approach meant excluding famous Seattle statues such as Waiting for the Interurban, the Fremont Troll, Lenin, and others. While offering their particular perspective, they do not necessarily represent a connection to Seattle's past. Memorials currently located in cemeteries were limited to those monuments that were first located in public spaces. An example of this is the Doughboy statue from World War I. For the sake of telling a coherent narrative, some decisions were required about what stories to tell and which statue and markers to reference only in the appendices. Appendix I lists statues that are monuments or memorials; appendix II lists the historical markers.

The Great Depression and Second World War ended decades of statue mania as both funding and enthusiasm for monuments waned. Erika Doss, author of *Memorial Mania*, wrote that as much as these earlier statues were "timeless vessels of permanent national values and beliefs," their turn-of-the-century notions became irrelevant as progressive ideas prevailed in the latter half of the twentieth century.[3] Developments in women's rights, modern art, and the peace movement were at odds with the principles represented by many previous monuments.

Seattle erected its first monument, the Pioneer Square totem pole, in 1899. In the following ten years, the city dedicated only one other monument, the Birthplace of Seattle at Alki. The Alaska-Yukon-Pacific Exposition in 1909 brought nationally known sculptors to Seattle, and they created three imposing statues: George Washington, James J. Hill, and William H. Seward. This exposure to national artists also helped local sculptors James A. Wehn and Alonzo Victor Lewis develop skills and launch their careers. Beginning with the Chief Seattle statue in 1912, other statues, medallions, and plaques were placed around the city until 1932, when the Doughboy would become the last major statue erected for many years.

During the Great Depression, less expensive plaques became the preferred method to promote histories and memories. The Second World War prompted an intense civic debate about how to memorialize the sacrifices made by Seattle citizens. Nautical commercial clubs placed maritime historical plaques every year between 1957 and 1985. Ethnic groups sponsored statues to explorers like Leif Erikson and Christopher Columbus. Other groups used plaques to help preserve and celebrate historic neighborhoods and locations like Pioneer Square and the Pike Place Market. Historical markers for "firsts" were sponsored all over the city: first airfield, first cabin, first hospital, first service station, and many others.

Heritage markers reflect how particular groups in Seattle wanted to remember their city's past. They represent the events, people, objects, and places that at one time were determined to be worthy of preservation and respect. Pacific Northwest historian Carlos Schwantes described the *heroic nature—heroic men* approach, which had been prevalent in the presentation of the region's history. Past generations of historians created a framework for thinking about how the area was settled; since nature assumed heroic proportions in the far northwest in people's minds, the area required heroic men to conquer it.[4]

This *heroic man* concept set the stage for Seattle's first statues, which primarily honored the men who settled Puget Sound. While early twentieth-century statues were dedicated to white businessmen like James J. Hill in 1909, John H. McGraw (1913), and Thomas Burke (1930), later memorials honored Martin Luther King Jr. (1991), local musician Jimi Hendrix (1991), and Sadako Sasaki (1990), a young girl killed by the atomic bomb dropped on Hiroshima, Japan. In 2001 the city of Seattle added two plaques to the Birthplace of Seattle monument. These new markers honored the original women settlers and the Native Americans present at the landing of the Denny Party in 1851.

Statues are often considered heroic at the time of their dedication; however, the meanings of a monument continually change and are therefore always unfinished. Art historian Kirk Savage wrote, "no matter how much a monument may pretend to be eternal and unchanging, its meaning always evolves as its viewers bring new concerns and understandings to it."[5] This book tells the creation stories of Seattle's heritage markers and how both the stories and the markers have changed throughout the years.

Commemoration and Controversy

Some Seattle monuments sparked controversy. Disagreements arose over artistic decisions, placement, or the subjects of certain memorials. The *Seattle Daily Times* took the *Seattle Post-Intelligencer* to task for its support of the stolen Pioneer Square totem pole, more from competitive spirit than concern for the Tlingit tribe from which it was stolen. In the 1920s, the Chief Seattle statue was thought by some to be too "native" for a modern city. The Doughboy memorial was controversial for its artistic representation of a First World War soldier. It took until 2001 for plaques recognizing the Denny Party women and the native Duwamish to be added to the Birthplace of Seattle monument. The often vandalized Christopher Columbus statue has been removed from the waterfront and placed in storage.

xvi   Monumental Seattle

More than 150 years after the Civil War ended, the Confederacy is memorialized in statues and memorials spread across the United States. The majority of these memorials were sponsored by a civic group, the United Daughters of the Confederacy. Their primary objective was to honor the Confederate generation and support the "lost cause" mythology of the Civil War, which claimed that the war was about states' rights, slavery was a benevolent institution, and that while the war was lost it had been a just cause in which the soldiers who fought were heroes.[6]

A chapter of the United Daughters of the Confederacy was active in Seattle. In 1909 they dedicated a large tree in Ravenna Park to Confederate General Robert E. Lee. The women who sponsored the ceremony comprised a who's who of Seattle socialites. In 1926 the group erected a ten-ton granite monument in Seattle's Lake View Cemetery at a plot where the remains of Confederate soldiers had been buried since 1911. Nearby is the Grand Army of the Republic Cemetery, where Union veterans from the Northern states are buried. Like other areas of the country, the Pacific Northwest saw an upsurge in white supremacy in the 1920s, marked by continuing support for removal of Native Americans to reservations, Ku Klux Klan rallies, and discriminatory neighborhood restrictions.

A national debate is now underway about the meaning of the memorials. Supporters of the Confederate monuments say they represent the history of the South and honor its heritage. Opponents say the statues are bitter symbols of a time in America's past when millions of Africans were kept in bondage, and that their presence continues to reinforce a racist message. Some cities are removing their Confederate statues, or moving them to less prominent locations, but some southern states adopted legal restrictions to prevent cities from removing them. A number of historians have advocated for the addition of monuments next to the Civil War memorials to explain the perspective of African-Americans, or the removal of the monuments to museums where historical context could be added.

Seattle also finds itself in the middle of this debate. In 2017 Mayor Ed Murray recommended the removal of the Lake View Confederate memorial as well the Vladimir Lenin statue in the Fremont neighborhood. He stated that they represent "historic injustices" and are symbols of hate, racism, and violence. Both monuments are on private property and have been defaced. Representing another perspective, local historian Tim Wright suggests the removal of the Confederate memorial will make the local history of white supremacy easier to forget, while adding an interpretative sign can explain its proper place in Seattle's history. At the time of this writing, no decision has been made as to the future of these two monuments.

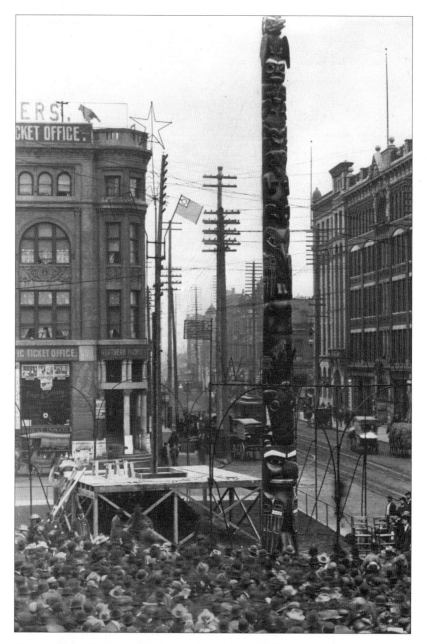

Pioneer Square Park on October 18, 1899. Seattle's first monument was a totem pole stolen from a Tlingit native village in Alaska. *Courtesy of the Seattle Municipal Archives #29981*

CHAPTER ONE

THE PIONEER SQUARE
TOTEM POLE

The 1897 arrival of the steamship *Portland* in Seattle with more than a ton of gold from the banks of the Klondike River in Canada's Yukon Territory spurred the rush north for gold, and marked Seattle's emergence as the primary economic connection to the far north and Pacific Rim.[1]

Two years later, Edward Harriman, a director of the Union Pacific Railroad, organized a Seattle to Alaska expedition of more than a hundred people, including scientists. A common view held by scholars at the time was that the Native cultures of Alaska would soon disappear in the face of modern civilization, and the expedition's scientists wanted to preserve what they thought were the final remains of Tlingit culture. Harriman chartered the steamship *George W. Elder*, which was remodeled for the voyage and featured lecture rooms, a library, a stable for animals, taxidermy studios, and luxurious cabins. Newspapers around the world ran front-page stories about the trip, and cheering crowds saw the ship off from the Seattle waterfront.

Southeastern Alaska includes hundreds of islands separated by a vast network of watery channels and inlets. The largest island in the area, Prince of Wales Island, was home to scores of totem poles or *Kooteeyaa*, as Native Alaskans call them. The village of Tuxecan alone was home to 125 totem poles with striking, elaborate imagery. While decorative carving was characteristic of all the tribes of the North Pacific coast, only the natives of western British Columbia and southeastern Alaska carved totem poles. As the Harriman expedition returned to Seattle, they stopped at Cape Fox, near Ketchikan, Alaska, and visited a temporarily deserted Tlingit community. The inhabitants had moved to the nearby village of Saxman in 1894 to attend a Presbyterian Church and school. Members of the expedition took totem poles and other items and loaded them onto their ship. Harriman donated thousands of Cape Fox items to museums across the country. One totem pole went to Harvard's Peabody Museum, another to the Bronx Zoo, and one to Cornell University. (All three have since been returned to the Tlingit.)[2]

After the success of the Harriman expedition, the *Seattle Post-Intelligencer* newspaper organized a follow-up excursion on the steamship *City of Seattle* in September of 1899. The Chamber of Commerce sent a special delegation of some of its most prominent members representing many of the city's leading businesses. The delegation visited Skagway and Sitka, toured the Treadwell mines near Juneau, and took a trip on the White Pass & Yukon Railroad. The businessmen hoped that beneficial economic results would follow for both Seattle and Alaska. They also purchased crate loads of mementos from Natives, and as the ship turned south to return to Seattle, someone suggested that a totem pole would be the ultimate souvenir.[3]

The *City of Seattle* detoured to the island of Tongass, home to a small Tlingit community. To the expedition members—like those in the Harriman party—the village appeared nearly deserted. The men of the community were away salmon fishing, and the women were working in the nearby canneries. Only the elderly and small children remained behind. To the visitors, the totem poles standing around the village looked weathered and decrepit.

The tallest pole belonged to a Tlingit lineage of the Raven clan, known in English as the Kininook family. It stood to honor a woman called "Chief-of-All-Women," who drowned in the nearby Nass River while traveling to visit her sick sister. As was customary, her siblings and other lineage members planned a memorial for her. They hired a carver and told him the stories they wanted to be shaped on the totem pole. This pole is one of only a few dedicated to a woman; most honored deceased chiefs, traditionally men.[4]

The carvings represent stories of the Kininook family. On top, Raven the trickster holds the crescent moon in his beak, referring to his gift of light to humankind. Below Raven, a woman who married a frog perches atop her frog husband and holds their frog child. Next is Mink, often Raven's helper, followed again by Raven standing atop a whale holding a seal in its mouth. Raven's grandfather, from whom

Raven stole the light, stands at the base of the pole. These depictions reflect the Kininook family's Raven cultural group; the frog and whale stories were clan stories.[5] Totem poles were a vital part of village life, and the Alaska Natives regarded them as beings and relatives. Often, mortuary poles had human remains interred within, and the Natives considered them sacred. Anthropologist Stephen Langdon explained, "Their disappearance would have caused great despair, sense of loss and deep anxiety."[6]

Disregarding the village's ownership of the totem pole, members of the excursion went ashore, sawed it down, cut it into two pieces, and floated it out to the waiting ship. In the process, they broke the beak off of the bottom Raven. In Seattle, workers unloaded the pieces and transported them to the Denny Hotel. There, a team of carpenters repaired a few decaying spots, reassembled the separate pieces by attaching them onto a new, durable cedar back, which was built up with cedar and tin to restore the original appearance of being carved from a solid log. They painted the totem pole and prepared it for presentation to the Seattle City Council.

On the morning of October 18, 1899, the clouds cleared as people gathered in Pioneer Place for the dedication of the totem pole as the first public monument in their city. The crowd filled the street and cheered as the group from the Chamber of Commerce arrived. The neighborhood was a busy commercial area and the noise from street traffic made it difficult for the people on the edges of the crowd to hear the speakers. The organizers placed the large totem pole near the apex of the little grassy triangle of the park. Each carved figure on the totem pole faced towards First Avenue, looking northwest, in the direction of Alaska and their former home on Tongass Island.

The day's speeches noted that the monument provided excellent color and interest to the business center of the city, thereby "lifting [Seattle] forever out of the commonplace." James W. Clise, a prominent real estate developer, reinforced Seattle's economic connection to Alaska in his introductory speech: "I believe that this pole will be an object of most intense interest to visitors and strangers, that it will be illustrated in hundreds of publications, and that it will be regarded by our own people with loyal appreciation. It is eminently fitting that it should be located in Seattle, the gateway of commerce of the north."

William H. Thompson, an attorney for the Great Northern Railway, presented a similar logic to the crowd, noting that since the earlier Harriman expedition had removed native artifacts, it made sense for Seattle to rescue and preserve a totem pole from Alaska as well. He stated that other visitors had removed nearly all the small totem poles, and the remaining large ones were decaying as the original coats of paint had weathered away. The memorials crafted by the Native Alaskans were disappearing more rapidly than the Natives themselves. Thompson spoke, " We who are to be the last neighbors of these swiftly vanishing tribes, owe a duty to civilization and to education to take the lead in preserving for coming men the history and traditions of the red men." With this, Thompson provided the stamp of approval for the appropriation of Alaskan Native culture by the Seattle men.

The attorney then addressed the rumors spreading around town, mainly instigated by the *Seattle Daily Times*, that they had stolen the totem pole from its rightful owners. "A few fragile folk of over delicate sensibilities have feared," Thompson said, "that this monument is here as the result of grand larceny." The crowd laughed as he further asserted neither the tribe nor the clan currently claimed control or ownership of the village from where they had retrieved the totem pole, and the inhabitants had deserted the village years ago. Removing the totem pole was "not different from that of removing a carved and valuable panel from an old derelict (ship) being beaten to pieces by the waves of the sea," Thompson continued. "We have brought it here as a present to Seattle, not as a headstone torn from a grave, but as a rude, strong piece of sculpture carved by a savage, but steady hand. It will here voice his deeds with surer speech than if lying prone in moss and fern on the shores of Tongass Island."[7]

In spite of the persuasive speeches and the fanfare of the unveiling celebration, many in Seattle were unsure whether it had been appropriate for their city leaders to have removed the Alaskan totem pole. The *Seattle Star* reported that, "an avalanche of criticism descended on the heads of the committee members."[8] A rival newspaper insulted the *Post-Intelligencer* with the headline, "Sackers and Looters of Indian Villages, Desecrators of Graves, Destroyers of Tombstones."[9]

To defuse the situation (and reframe the narrative into a more humorous story), a member of the committee who brought back the totem pole suggested it would be a good joke for the members of the excursion to sue themselves for the sum of $20,000. For the joke to work, they needed to recruit an actual plaintiff. The committee decided on a local Indian, Cheshiahud, who was called "Lake Union John," and who lived on his property on Portage Bay. (In 2008 the city and the Seattle Parks Foundation created a multi-use loop trail around Lake Union and named it after Cheshiahud.) To provide the appearance that Cheshiahud was related to the northern tribes, he was nicknamed "Salmon" and given the last name of Tolstoi, the Russian novelist, for the appearance of Russian-Alaskan heritage. The conspirators selected two local lawyers to act as attorneys for both the plaintiff and defendants while a false complaint was drafted and papers served in a municipal court.

People in Seattle were not the only ones reading the inflammatory headlines in the *Seattle Daily Times*. Alaskans also read the articles and became so angered by the injustice of the cultural theft that a federal grand jury from Alaska indicted eight members of the excursion. It was one thing to participate in a fraudulent lawsuit in a local Seattle court; facing a real federal indictment was a much more severe matter for several leading citizens of Seattle.

The accused citizens nominated Thompson to return to the scene of the incident, and make peace with the wronged Native Alaskans. He drafted both a bill of sale and an apology, and each member of the excursion donated money for the trip and the restitution. After making the journey north, Thompson returned to Seattle accompanied by two Tlingit, George and William Kininook, grandsons of Chief-of-All-Women. Initially, the family asked for the sum of $20,000. However, the newspapers reported that the two grandsons stated that restitution for the theft could be settled by the amount of $500.

By this time the U.S. government had appointed a new federal judge for Alaska, who stopped over in Seattle as he journeyed to his new assignment. City leaders honored him at the Rainier Club and explained the incident from their perspective. They convinced him that they had saved the monument from decay and had paid the Natives. Soon after taking his seat on the bench in Alaska, the judge set the indictments aside and considered the matter resolved.

The dedication of additional totem poles around Seattle added to the importance of the iconic symbol linking Seattle to the north. Natives moved to the city from British Columbia and Alaska and carved hundreds of totem poles for tourists, primarily selling them from the Ye Olde Curiosity Shop on Seattle's waterfront. Local carvers such as William Shelton at Tulalip and Joseph Hillaire at Lummi produced Coast Salish-style story poles in the 1920s and 1930s.[10] A totem pole carved in 1901 by the Bella Bella tribe of British Columbia was placed at Belvedere View Point Park in West Seattle in 1939.

The stolen totem pole from 1899 stood tall over Pioneer Place for many years, watching impassively as the economic center of the city moved northward. By the early twentieth century, all of Seattle's banks had relocated north of Yesler Way, which became a dividing line between the new downtown on one side and a skid row area on the other. By the 1930s, hundreds of unemployed men occupied the area looking for food at the missions and lodging in the many cheap hotels and shacks south of Pioneer Square.

On the evening of October 22, 1938, witnesses in a nearby tavern saw a man furtively approach and place a burning newspaper at the base of the totem pole. Then he ran down the street and disappeared. The flames grew and burned from inside the totem pole as firefighters responded. They tried to hack a hole at the bottom of the pole in which to spray water, but were unsuccessful. Not daring to place a ladder against the pole in case they knocked it over, they used an aerial ladder from a fire truck instead. A firefighter chopped the beak off the upper Raven and sprayed water into the pole through the opening. One thousand people looked on for over an hour, as first smoke, then flames, and finally water poured forth from the eyes of the legendary figures on the totem pole.

Within a day, the *Seattle Daily Times* published an editorial encouraging the restoration of the burnt monument. "Since other cities of the Puget Sound basin also have totem poles of more or less authenticity, Seattle's distinction is not unique. But our totem pole has stood for so many decades that it would be sorely missed if destroyed or removed," the editorial argued. "Of the totem pole, it may be said we first desired, then pilfered, then endured. But it has become a landmark, and the site would seem empty without it. Let's try to save the totem pole."[11] After firefighters extinguished the fire, an inspection revealed eight-foot long cracks up the sides splitting the carving apart. Dry rot had set in among the pole's more complicated features. As a result of the fire, several noses from figures on the totem pole fell off, and even if it survived the winter, the city would probably need to replace the beloved monument.

Locals swamped the Seattle Board of Parks Commissioners with suggestions and offers of assistance. A committee of Alaska Yukon Pioneers suggested the statue of a sourdough miner recently completed by sculptor Alonzo Victor Lewis be placed in Pioneer Park as a replacement. Others suggested casting the replacement pole in concrete, rather than wood. Joseph Edward Standley, the proprietor of Seattle's Ye Olde Curiosity Shop, knew several Alaskan Natives who would carve a pole for $3,000. The Indian communities at Neah Bay and Queets submitted bids as did Swinomish carvers from La Conner. Dr. Gus Knudson, curator of the zoo, offered to find a local Indian to carve a replacement in Woodland Park, where visitors could watch. The park board interviewed a pair of Suquamish Indians but raised issues regarding their ability to carve an accurate copy since they had no experience and were unfamiliar with the history of the Tlingit.

Professors from the University of Washington supported the acquisition of a traditional Alaskan totem pole rather than an example carved by local Natives. Melville Jacobs, head of the anthropology department, urged the park board to protect the old totem pole from unskilled hands. He stated that Viola Garfield, a professor of anthropology and an expert on Alaskan totem poles, could "express an uncommercialized, disinterested scientific and artistic judgment," of the Seattle landmark.[12] Garfield pointed out totem carving was never an art form practiced among Puget Sound tribes, and, since the totem pole was priceless, it was important to undertake the project correctly.[13]

Meanwhile, the U.S. Forest Service in southeastern Alaska was leading an effort for Native artisans to restore and carve totem poles. When the regional supervisor in charge of the Tongass National Forest heard about the damage to the Seattle totem pole, he proposed that carvers in the program duplicate the pole. Seattle shipped the damaged pole in January 1940 to the Forest Service shop in Saxman, two miles from Ketchikan, Alaska. There, Kyam and Kininook Natives, members of the Tlingit community where the totem pole had been carved decades earlier, created a duplicate in three months under the direction of Charles Brown, a skilled tribal craftsman. They carved and painted the new pole to resemble the original at the time of its removal to Seattle.

The remnants of the original totem pole were in four sections and remained in the workshop in Saxman for two years. The Forest Service was planning to create a model Native village north of Ketchikan at a location called Totem Bight. It was suggested that the remnants be transferred there, but the District Supervisor indicated that only one of the remaining pieces was considered worthy of keeping and the other three pieces were so rotten that they could not be repaired and should be destroyed. In 1945, all of the totem pole remnants were burned at Totem Bight with the permission of the original owners since a copy of the memorial had been made.[14]

A special act of Congress transferred ownership of the new totem pole from the Forest Service to the city, and on July 27, 1940, Seattle dedicated it in Pioneer Place. In the early 1970s, the city repaired the totem pole after decades of exposure to the weather. The Park Department removed it to the Seattle Center where it was refurbished by John C. Hudson Jr., a member of the Tsimshian tribe of British Columbia and Alaska. The totem pole "restates the significant role played by the Indian in the life of our city," Mayor Wes Uhlman said at its rededication on August 21, 1972. Bernie Whitebear, chairman of the United Indians of All Tribes, said the totem pole "symbolizes the reemergence of an Indian nation and the part we are going to play in the future of our city."[15] Whitebear, who passed away in 2000, is memorialized with a sculpture of a Native American dreamcatcher, erected by the Leschi Community Council at the corner of Yesler Way and 32nd Street.

The totem pole still stands in Pioneer Place. Tourists, office work-ers, nearby residents, and the homeless all pass by its carved faces. Still facing north, it continues to provide a connection between Seat-tle and Alaska—the original intent of the Seattle excursion members who stole the totem pole. It was the city's first memorial, but within a decade, another monument and series of historical markers would tell the earlier story of Seattle's founding by white settlers from the east.

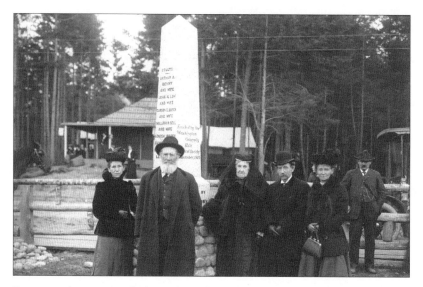

Present at the 1905 Birthplace of Seattle monument dedication were five of the original pioneers. From left to right: Lenora Denny, Carson Boren, Mary Denny, Rolland Denny, and Mary Low Sinclair. *Courtesy of University of Washington Libraries, Special Collections, Theodore E. Peiser, photographer, TEP0002.*

CHAPTER 2

FOUNDERS, FIRSTS, AND A STATUE OF LIBERTY

Birthplace of Seattle Monument

The temperature on Puget Sound was crisp on the afternoon of November 13, 1905, as 1,000 spectators pressed close together, straining to catch a glimpse of a flag-draped pylon on the beach at Alki Point. It was Founders' Day—the annual holiday to remember the founding of their city—and a new monument, Birthplace of Seattle, was about to be unveiled. Nearby, a single foundation post from the original first cabin remained; property owners had demolished the rest of the cabin in 1892. Earlier in the day, the crowds watched as city leaders placed six bronze tablets around Pioneer Square across Elliott Bay to mark historical sites of early Seattle.

While the Founders' Days of the late 1800s were discrete remembrances, beginning in 1905, they turned into larger celebrations and presented the popular Anglo-American narrative of the founding families' triumph over nature and the creation of modern Seattle.[1] Knute Berger, a local journalist, reflecting on the early settlers, said "In [their] twilight decades, they were honored, lauded, and memorialized incessantly."[2] They were a rapidly disappearing generation of founding settlers whose experience most could only read about in books.

Dignitaries attending the ceremonies that day included a U.S. senator, judges, military and civic leaders, and a few of Seattle's original settlers. Many people watched from the front lawn and veranda of the Stockade, a summer resort owned by Alfred Smith, who donated the land for the monument. The smell of cooking clams wafted through the air as volunteers prepared a celebratory dinner to enjoy after the speakers completed their remarks.

Five of the original group of two dozen settlers from the Denny Party attended that day: Carson Boren, Mary Denny, Lenora Denny,

Rolland Denny, and Mary Low Sinclair. Boren, uncomfortable with the attention from the crowd, remembered the rainy, gray day fifty-four years earlier when he came ashore as a young man. Mary Low Sinclair was nine years old when she landed on the beach with her family. She glanced over to where the original cabin had stood and recalled the rank, acrid smell where sea and land met; they had come ashore at low tide and struggled to unload their possessions through the mud. Rolland Denny, son of Arthur Denny, had been born only two months before. His mother Mary had carried him ashore.

Members of the Denny Party

Arthur Armstrong Denny (29), Mary Boren Denny (29), and their children Louisa Catherine (7), Margaret Lenora (4), and Rolland Herschel (2 months)

David Thomas Denny (19), brother of Arthur Denny

Louisa Boren (22), sister of Mary Boren Denny

Carson Dobbins Boren (27), Mary Boren (20), and their child Gertrude Lavinia (1)

John Nathan Low (31), Lydia Culborn Low (31), and their children Mary (9), Alonzo (7), John (4), and Minerva (2)

William Nathaniel Bell (34), Sarah Ann (36), and their children Laura Keziah (9), Olive Julia (5), Mary Virginia (4), and Lavinia (10 months)

Charles Carroll Terry (21) and his brother Lee Terry (19)

The speeches recalled November 13, 1851, when the sailing schooner *Exact*, on its way from Portland, Oregon, to the Queen Charlotte Islands in Canada, stopped at a forested point located on the eastern shore of Puget Sound. Three members of the group, John Low, Lee Terry, and David Denny had arrived earlier and scouted the area. They claimed the entire point for a jointly owned town site and named it Alki, a local Chinook word meaning "by-and-by" or "eventually." The point where the Denny Party went ashore was about 130 acres of land standing ten feet above the tidal high water mark. Behind it, at a slight elevation, was a plateau covered with timber. The

Natives who regularly wintered at the point watched curiously as the new settlers scrambled ashore.

After spending the first winter at their original claims, Arthur Denny, Boren, and Bell explored the shoreline of nearby Elliott Bay and discovered a low point of land connected to a slightly higher mound next to the deep water on the east side of the bay. So, while the Low and Terry families remained at Alki, the Dennys, Borens, and Bells each staked their claims of 320 acres along the eastern shoreline of Elliott Bay on February 15, 1852.

Over the next few years, Alki and Seattle competed to see which settlement would dominate central Puget Sound. At first Alki was clearly the most important settlement on Elliott Bay.[3] However, as time passed, Seattle won out and even Charles Terry, Alki's most successful resident, eventually admitted defeat and moved to the Seattle side of the bay.[4] By 1900, Seattle's population grew to 80,000. West Seattle, which includes Alki Point, incorporated in 1902 as a town of only 1,000 residents and voted for annexation by Seattle in 1907.

So, why was the 1905 Birthplace of Seattle monument placed on Alki Point instead of Pioneer Square? In 1853, when the Dennys, Borens, and Bells surveyed their new home sites and laid out a plan for their new city, they would not have thought of Alki as their new city's birthplace; indeed, they were glad to be rid of that windy, uncomfortable stretch of beach. However, years of perspective gave the surviving settlers a sense of nostalgia, and affected how they wanted to preserve their memories of Seattle's founding. They formed a committee in the 1880s to determine who qualified as a "founder" and to select a proper location to memorialize the city's birthplace. The committee consisted of four of the original founders, Arthur and David Denny, William Bell, and Carson Boren; plus Henry Yesler, a prominent citizen who arrived in Seattle in 1852; and Henry Van Asselt, a homesteader from the Duwamish Valley (the current site of Boeing Field) in 1851.

As they evaluated Pioneer Square, the location of their first claims, members of the committee observed what thirty years of progress had done to what they remembered as a simple, quaint, pioneer town. Seattle had become a waterfront boomtown, hastily built and characterized by industry and vice. They stood surrounded by a large saw-mill, railroad trestles, brothels, gambling and dance halls, saloons, and large coal bunkers covered in grimy black dust, where workers loaded coal onto waiting ships. The dirty, noisy, industrial character of Seattle didn't reflect the heroic stories the committee wished to commemorate about their city's founding. Arthur Denny, even after commerce and business occupied most of his original Seattle claim, still kept his house with a barn, orchard, and animals as the city grew up around him.

Alki, in comparison, remained peaceful and unsullied over the decades. It was nearly unpopulated, with a lovely, clean beach and a sweeping view of Puget Sound and the Olympic Mountains. The surviving Denny Party members felt their arrival at Alki represented their founding story more appropriately than dingy Seattle, so they drew up plans to place a monument there. Arthur Denny's daughter Lenora donated the marble pylon and paid for an engraver to chisel the text. The inscription obfuscated where Seattle originated, with the words "Seattle—New York—Alki" all carved onto the face. The name New York was originally proposed by Lee Terry but was eventually dropped and people called the area Alki.

The 1905 Founders' Day crowd cheered as Edmond Meany, a professor at the University of Washington, was introduced. His speech highlighted and supported the narrative of western conquest that was popular at the time. Seattle's creation, similar to the national narrative of Manifest Destiny, was the story of predetermination. In local mythology, the arrival of Seattle's settlers was deliberate, planned, and preordained.[5] Meany said in part:

> From this portal of the western sea, we gaze back over the broad expanse and marvel at the magnitude of what our people have wrought in three centuries. From Jamestown to Seattle has been one long series of struggles by a nation triumphant over every form of obstacles. It is especially appropriate for our own community to undertake this work while there still remains with us some of that noble pilgrim band who laid the foundations of this thriving, throbbing metropolis of a commonwealth.[6]

After praising the accomplishments of Seattle's first settlers, Meany ended his speech with a special tribute to their wives. He spoke of their heroism and fortitude in leaving their comfortable homes, and urged the audience to consider the monument as a memorial to the courage of both the men and the women who created a great and prosperous city. While he honored the wives in his speech, the granite shaft listed only the names of the male settlers, their children, and Louisa Boren as the only unmarried woman. The married women were engraved into stone as "And Wife."

Edmond Meany

Edmond Meany was a historian, educator, collector, and prolific writer as well as a prominent and popular civic leader who played a pivotal role in the history of the University of Washington and the region. He documented the historical past, often in collaboration with pioneer societies. Meany was a driving force and participant in many of the city's memorial projects: the Birthplace of Seattle, Chief Seattle, George Washington, William Seward, John McGraw, World Flyers, and the Arthur and Mary Denny homestead.

Meany and his family arrived in Seattle in 1877. He graduated from the Territorial University as valedictorian of the class of 1885 and received a master's degree in science in 1889. By 1897, the university appointed him full professor and head of the history department. Keenly interested in local history, Meany wrote many books and articles, and delivered countless speeches on the subject. On April 22, 1935, as he prepared for a class, he suffered a stroke and died. Before the funeral, his body lay in state on campus in Meany Hall before a service attended by thousands of mourners.

Later that year, the man who was the driving force behind so many of Seattle's memorials received one of his own. The Pioneer Association of Washington State honored him on September 9, 1935, when they unveiled a memorial tablet at the Washelli Cemetery pool and renamed it the Meany Memorial Pool. The bronze tablet on the granite marker features a relief plaque of Edmond Meany created by sculptor Richard Brooks, with whom Meany worked to commission the statue of William H. Seward. The memorial is still there.

The names inscribed on the monument represented a snapshot of time from 1851. Not all the original settlers had an impact on Seattle's history, while others not listed on the monument—like David "Doc" Maynard and Henry Yesler—arrived only a year later and contributed enormously to the city. Of the original founding group, Lee Terry stayed only for the first winter and then returned to New York. John Low left after seventeen months, moved to Olympia and then California, but returned years later to Snohomish, a town northeast of the city. William Bell left after the Indian attack in 1856 with his invalid wife, yet returned fifteen years later to develop real estate in the current neighborhood of Belltown. Carson Boren sold his entire claim and lived as a recluse in the woods. Charles Terry was extremely successful and became one of the town's richest men, but lived only sixteen more years before dying at age thirty-seven. David Denny settled south of Lake Union but went bankrupt in 1893. Arthur Denny inspired numerous plans and businesses in Seattle and died wealthy and respected in 1899.[7]

The Birthplace of Seattle monument was altered and updated over the years. In 1926, the city moved it to the beach side of Alki Avenue SW, and the Automobile Club of America brought a piece of Plymouth Rock across the country from Massachusetts in a transcontinental caravan of cars. The club mortared the rock into the side of the pylon, and added an additional plaque describing the journey. During the Seattle centennial celebration of 1951 another plaque was attached with details of a nearby buried time capsule to be opened in 2051.

In 2001, the 150th anniversary of the landing, descendants of the city's five founding families gathered to reflect on the price paid by the indigenous people who welcomed their ancestors. On a rainy day, similar to the weather in 1851, a re-enactment of the landing took place with the sailing ship *Yankee Clipper* substituting for the *Exact*. Organizers added two more plaques to the monument. One of the new plaques specifically honored the wives whose names were not included on the original engraving: Mary Ann Boren Denny, Lydia Culborn Low, Mary Kays Boren, Sarah Ann Peter Bell, and Louisa Boren.

The other plaque praised the Native Americans who helped the original settlers survive their first winter. Cecile Hansen, chairwoman of the Duwamish, called the 2001 celebration bittersweet, but acknowledged the historical significance of the landing of the *Exact*. She said she was heartened to know descendants of Seattle's founding families were expressing an interest in helping the tribe's effort to gain federal recognition. With fewer than six hundred registered members and no defined land, leaders say recognition as a political entity is necessary to ensure the community can continue.[8] The Duwamish, whose leader the city of Seattle was named for, have not yet been recognized by the U.S. government.

A separate plaque celebrating the first home site was placed across the street at Sixty-third Avenue and Alki Avenue Southwest on April 24, 1962. The West Seattle Rotary Club installed the marker on the side of an apartment building located on the site where David Denny and Lee Terry built the first log cabin.

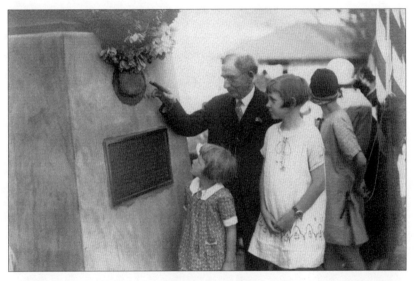

Rolland Denny visited the Birthplace of Seattle monument in 1926. Here he is pointing to the piece of Plymouth Rock added that year. *Courtesy of University of Washington Libraries, Special Collections, POR1424.*

Pioneer Square Markers

The 1905 Founders' Day afternoon unveiling of the Birthplace of Seattle monument was preceded earlier that day with the unveiling of six historical markers around Pioneer Square. The Washington State Historical Society, Washington State Pioneers Association, and *Seattle Daily Times* sponsored the plaques and created the text engraved onto

A Small Statue of Liberty

Near the Denny Party's landing site on Alki Beach is an eight-and-a-half-foot replica of the Statue of Liberty. To celebrate the fortieth anniversary of the Boy Scouts of America and to "strengthen the arm of liberty," Jack Whitaker, a longtime scout enthusiast from Kansas City, led a campaign to place copies of the Statue of Liberty across the country. More than two hundred scout troops in thirty-nine states raised funds to have statues shipped to them and placed on pedestals. Two thousand local scouts unveiled Seattle's copy of the statue on Alki Beach in 1952. Organizers sealed a metal box containing the names of 5,000 scouts and other souvenirs in a vault in the statue's base, to be opened in the year 2000.

Vandals targeted the statue over the years. They pulled the entire statue off its base with a car in 1975. In the 1980s, they removed her crown and ripped the torch from her hand. At the time, Joanne Richey, whose family ran the Seaside Pharmacy across the street, said, "It's been knocked down, pulled over, painted and damaged a number of times. Once it was even removed, and they found it again in some warehouse."[9] On April Fool's Day in 1996, the arm carrying the torch was ripped off. In 2003, the torch was broken off again and found in the wet sand nearby at low tide.

The scouts removed and opened the time capsule underneath the base as planned to celebrate the millennium in 2000. Unfortunately, days before the ceremony, the city performed some excavation work and damaged the vault, allowing water to seep in. Many of the paper items were severely saturated, but some of the souvenirs were recovered: manuals, badges, and insignias.[10]

The Seattle Statue of Liberty Plaza Project, a citizens' committee from West Seattle, led an effort to recast and repair the statue in 2007. They replaced the original square concrete base and asphalt lot with an improved plaza and pedestal. Two dozen scouts, who attended the first dedication, wore names tags stating, "I was there." A new time capsule was placed in 2009 by the Southwest Seattle Historical Society and will be opened in fifty years.

the bronze tablets. At each unveiling, a speaker provided a brief history, and a city official accepted the plaque on behalf of the city.

First Post Office

Nearly two hundred people watched as officials attached the first bronze tablet to the wall of the Stevens Hotel on the corner of First Avenue and Marion Street, the location of Seattle's first post office in 1853. Arthur Denny was the first postmaster, operating the post office from his cabin. A postal carrier brought Seattle's first mail—twenty-two letters and fourteen newspapers—by canoe from Olympia. Orion Denny, one of Arthur Denny's sons, unveiled the tablet; historian Thomas Prosch provided a history of Seattle's postal service, and Postmaster George Stewart accepted the tablet. The marker is currently located on First Avenue on brickwork in front of the Henry Jackson Federal Building.

First School House

The crowd walked down the street and stopped at the Sullivan block on the east side of First Avenue between Cherry and Columbia Streets. This was the site of Bachelor's Hall, the building that housed the first school. The school opened in January 1854 with fourteen pupils. Catherine Blaine, the first person to teach school in Seattle, unveiled the tablet. Dillis Ward, a former student and then teacher, remembered attending school when First Avenue was just a trail and Indians camped on the nearby beach. Professor Frank Cooper, Seattle Schools Superintendent, accepted the plaque on behalf of the city.

Developers eventually demolished the Sullivan block and constructed the Right Hotel on the site. They reinstalled the marker on the new building, but by 1951, yellow paint covered the plaque. When the Bank of California demolished the hotel building in 1958, they removed and restored the plaque and installed it on their new parking garage, in approximately its original location, where it remains today.

The Blockhouse

The procession moved on to Kennedy's Drug Store at the foot of Cherry Street. Here a blockhouse was erected before the 1856 Battle of Seattle, when natives from the Klickitat and Yakama tribes attacked the small settlement. Walter Graham, one of the men who helped defend the blockhouse, unveiled the tablet. Judge Cornelius Hanford presented the tablet to the city. As a child, his parents had carried him into the fort during the battle. Colonel George Lamping accepted the plaque on behalf of the Washington National Guard and used the opportunity to thank the volunteers who had departed a few years earlier to fight in the Philippine-American War (1899–1902), and to eulogize those soldiers who did not return. In 1922, the tablet was removed when the building was remodeled, and disappeared.

Yesler's Sawmill

The crowds then walked one block south to First Avenue and Yesler Way, the site of Henry Yesler's sawmill, the first steam-powered mill on Puget Sound. Lumberman John R. Williamson unveiled the tablet on the Mutual Life Building and reminded the crowd that while they were honoring the great deeds of the past, the future still offered the opportunity for everyone to make their mark in the city. "Do you men and women," he asked the audience, "regret that you were not here at the beginning of things? You are here today at the beginning of things," suggesting that it was still the early days of Seattle's great commercial future.[11]

Great Northern Railway executive Samuel Hill (son-in-law of Great Northern owner James J. Hill) presented the tablet, and former Governor John McGraw accepted it on behalf of the city. The *Seattle Daily Times* noted in both 1951 and 1972 that the marker was missing. A few days after the newspaper published the second article, an unidentified person dropped off the missing plaque at the newspaper's office. The *Seattle Daily Times* donated it to the Museum of History and Industry where it remains today.

Second Blockhouse

Hundreds more joined the crowd as they walked through Pioneer Square toward the intersection of Main Street and Occidental Avenue. At about the same time the first blockhouse was constructed, settlers erected a smaller blockhouse where the Schwabacher Building now stands. A wooden stockade connected this fort to the larger blockhouse at First Avenue and Cherry Street. John Blaine unveiled the tablet; as an infant, his parents placed him aboard the U.S. Navy warship *Decatur* for protection during the Indian attack. Historian Clarence Bagley presented the plaque and gave a speech about the positive interaction the settlers had with the Natives and pointed out that many friendly Indians from the Duwamish and Suquamish tribes lived along the shores of Puget Sound. The plaque still appears in its original location.

First Cabin

Finally, the crowd stopped in front of the Hoge Building at Second Avenue and Cherry Street, the former site of Seattle's first cabin. Eighty-year-old Carson Boren himself—who built the cabin in April 1852—unveiled the last tablet of the day. Soon after staking his claim, he sold off parts of his land and then later disposed the remainder for only $1,100. He retired as a recluse, living in the forest, and died in 1912 at his ranch near present-day Woodinville.[12] Judge Thomas Burke presented the marker to the city and spoke of the self-reliance and fortitude of the settlers that led to the creation of Seattle. The tablet remains on the Hoge Building today.

The Birthplace of Seattle monument at Alki Point and the six plaques in Pioneer Square dedicated on the 1905 Founders' Day were the city's first historical monuments. Judge Burke declared in his closing speech that the seven sites set apart on that day were being "marked for all time."[13] Historians and civic boosters used these stories about the founding of Seattle to establish a history which supported its status as a prominent and successful city.

The narrative of the story of Seattle was about to change. Part of that transition was reflected by a changing perspective about monuments and who and what should be memorialized and commemorated. As the founders' number dwindled, the newcomers who arrived in the 1890s and 1900s took front and center in civic leadership. For them, Seattle had always been a place of banks, steamships, railroads, and tall buildings, all connected to Alaska and the North Pacific. The original settlers' quaint past of log cabins and friendly co-existence with the local Natives was now often ridiculed by the newcomers who displaced them. The new perspective at the dawn of the twentieth century was one of trade and the accompanying riches that would flow into Seattle.

Other Plaques Celebrating Early Seattle

First Settlers in King County

Markers placed in 1940 at Boeing Field honor four settlers who preceded the Denny party. The first marker is a large rock with a plaque memorializing Luther M. Collins, Henry Van Asselt, and Jacob Mapel and his son Samuel, who staked their claims in this area. The four men paddled up the Duwamish River in canoes and settled here on September 16, 1851. The ashes of Jacob and Samuel Mapel were reinterred under the marker, and the family placed an additional marker next to the original.

Arthur and Mary Denny Homestead

Rolland Denny, the only living son of Arthur Denny, unveiled a bronze tablet on May 21, 1933, on the northeast corner of Second Avenue and Union Street. Attached to a wall of the Rhodes Department Store, the plaque marked the original site of the Denny homestead.[14] Developers demolished the building in 2003 for a new skyscraper and Seattle Art Museum expansion, and the plaque is now missing.

Old Central School

A plaque marks the location of the Old Central School on Third Avenue between Madison and Spring Streets. Built in 1870, the school enrolled one hundred students in its first year. Twenty former students attended the 1940 dedication ceremony.[15]

First Hospital

The Seattle Historical Society placed a marker on the location of Seattle's first hospital in 1967. The Sisters of Charity of the House of Providence established the hospital in 1878 on a parcel of land on Fifth Avenue. An old house served as the hospital until the sisters constructed a seventy-five-bed building in 1882; the hospital relocated to its present site at 500 Seventeenth Avenue in 1911. The plaque remains on a wall along the steps of the courthouse on Fifth Avenue, across from the Seattle Central Library.

Louisa Boren

Louisa Boren was the last surviving member of the original Denny Party. Two years prior to her death in 1916 at the age of eighty-nine, the Washington Women's Pioneer Auxiliary honored her with a park and monument. Louisa's life typified the early settlers' experiences: she made moccasins, hunted game, chopped wood, and raised eight children while feeding horses, milking cows, and trading with the Duwamish.[16] The boulder with the attached plaque is still located on Interlaken Boulevard on the south side of the road just to the west of Nineteenth Avenue East.

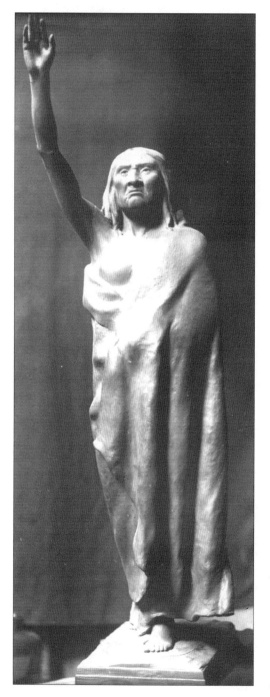

James A. Wehn created this three-foot-high study of Chief Seattle to use as the basis for crafting the larger statue which would be placed at Tilikum Place in 1912. *Courtesy of the Seattle Municipal Archives #30405.*

CHAPTER 3

IMAGES OF CHIEF SEATTLE

The Birthplace of Seattle monument and historical plaques unveiled during the 1905 Founders' Day celebration scarcely mentioned the role that Natives played in Seattle's founding story. The bronze tablets offered no information about the assistance provided to the Denny party by the Duwamish during the first winter. Nothing in the text indicated how integrated daily life was for both settlers and Natives in the city's first decades.[1] The only references to Native people were on the two blockhouse plaques describing the fortifications and the Indian attack of 1856. The markers instead focused on the establishment of the school, post office, first cabin, and sawmill—early buildings that displaced a ruined longhouse and other structures from an abandoned Native settlement on the site known as Little Crossing-Over Place.

As the years passed, even the early settlers started to overlook the contributions of the Natives. The death of Chief Seattle in 1866 on a reservation across Elliott Bay received little notice in the city that bore his name. Puget Sound newspapers did not cover his passing, and he faded from prominence in Seattle's civic consciousness. Residents pushed the Natives to the city's outskirts and off to reservations, even though they had been an integral part of early Seattle life and contributed much of the workforce for the first industries.

By the early twentieth century, the economic center of the city moved northward, away from Pioneer Square. City engineers removed and flattened Denny Hill, which stood between the new downtown and Queen Anne Hill, to facilitate the city's development and growth. A regrading project at Fifth Avenue and Denny Way marked a historic spot where the old boundaries of the David Denny, Carson Boren, and William Bell claims intersected. Architect Roy D. Rogers thought that the location would be perfect for some kind of a statue. Some funds were left over from the street work, so he met with historian Clarence Bagley, the chairman of the Board of Public Works, and proposed a marble statue of the Roman god Mercury bringing riches from the Orient. Business leaders would use a statue to support a new narrative of Seattle's economic and financial dominance.

Clarence Bagley arrived in Seattle in 1860 as a young boy. He worked in printing and journalism and collected the journals of early settlers. In 1899 he was appointed the chairman of the Board of Public Works but maintained his interest in Seattle's history. He became aware of James A. Wehn, a twenty-one-year-old sculptor who had created a bas-relief plaque entitled "Seattle Girl" and a bust of Chief Seattle's eldest daughter, Princess Angeline (Kikisebloo). Bagley telephoned Wehn and asked him to visit his office and discuss Rogers' proposal for the Mercury statue. The young artist suspected the public would not accept the proposed classical figure. "What we want here in Seattle is something typical," he argued. "We can't start out right at the first with Greek art. We want to start the people off right; with something they will appreciate it and then gradually bring them up." Bagley agreed with him, "The city fathers will never go for a thing like that."

As Wehn stood up from his chair, preparing to leave, an idea inspired him. "To heck with this winged Mercury," he said, "How about a statue of old Chief Seattle after whom Seattle is named?" Bagley had long admired and respected Chief Seattle. "Now you've got something Wehn; now you've got something!"[2] The artist soon returned with a drawing of Chief Seattle raising an arm in greeting. Bagley was pleased with the concept and submitted it to the *Post-Intelligencer* for publication on July 31, 1907.

The response to Wehn's drawing was mixed. The *Post-Intelligencer* noted that news of the statue "provided the general public with a new summer topic." Some people did not believe that the city council should pay for public art in any form. Old-timers who remembered Chief Seattle wanted to speak with the sculptor before he created the face of the statue. One of them, Samuel F. Coombs, said that Mr. Wehn drew "a very pretty face for Chief Seattle, but not the face I so well remember." He provided the artist with a letter discussing his memories of the chief's face. Judge Thomas Burke and other members of the art committee of the Rainier Club said they would quickly approve a statue of Chief Seattle.[3]

First Sculptor of Seattle

James A. Wehn created many of the city's most recognizable statues in the early to mid-1900s. Born in Indianapolis, he moved to Seattle in 1889 with his family at the age of six. As a child, he began to sketch, paint, and work with clay. After an apprenticeship in a Chicago studio, Wehn returned to Seattle and created his first portrait medallions.

His sculpture of Angeline, the daughter of Chief Seattle, led to his first major commission in 1907, a sculpture of the chief. His work on that project led to a friendship with Edmond Meany, who advised Wehn on historical accuracy as the artist sculpted numerous local figures. Wehn also helped teach a new generation of local artists as the founder and first instructor of sculpture at the University of Washington's College of Fine Arts. Over the course of his career, Wehn created more than three hundred medallions, medals, statuary, and other works, including the first official design for the seal of the City of Seattle. His work can be seen today across the city. James A. Wehn died October 2, 1973, at the age of 91.

By July of the following year, the *Post-Intelligencer* published pictures of the clay models for the monument's side panels. The text referred to the chief as "Sealth, Chief of the Nisquallys." Several prominent and respected scholars disagreed with the words Wehn had selected. Thomas Prosch, a journalist and historian, wrote a letter stating that the chief was not from the Nisqually tribe and that no one referred to him as "Sealth." Edmond Meany, in a separate letter to the mayor, stated that the name of the chief should be written as "Seattle" not Sealth, and the text should identify the tribe as the Suquamish rather than the Nisqually. Clarence Bagley said Seattle was the pronunciation accepted by the settlers who knew him.[4] (The current understanding is that Seattle's name as spelled using the International Phonetic Alphabet is "siʔal" and pronounced "see-ahlsh.")

Later that month, a committee appointed by the city council agreed on the inscription based on changes suggested by Prosch, Meany, and others. It read:

Seattle, Chief of the Suquamish, A Firm Friend of the Whites,
For Him the City of Seattle Was Named by Its Founders.

Wehn worked on the statue for thirteen months. He wanted to send it to a foundry on the East Coast for casting, but public opinion persuaded him to use a local company, the Phoenix Art Bronze and Iron Foundry. To squeeze the statue into their only available mold, the local workmen sawed off the plaster model at the knees and chest. Unfortunately, their lack of experience in casting larger statues showed; details of the sculpture were lost and the seams were clearly visible with large gaps between pieces. Examining the disastrous results and contemplating the lost months, an irate Wehn loaded the misshapen plaster parts of Chief Seattle in a wheelbarrow and dumped them in Elliott Bay.

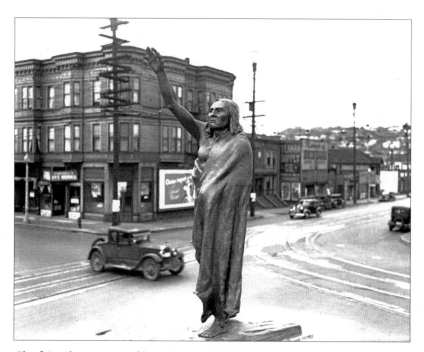

Chief Seattle statue at Fifth and Denny Way. *Courtesy of the Seattle Municipal Archives #10654.*

Wehn told the committee, "I'm starting over. I'm going to make a damn good statue, and I'll have the best foundry in the United States." He used the opportunity to craft a better representation of Seattle. To create a more realistic figure, he first observed and then tried to convince Natives to pose for him or at least be photographed.

One of the first Indians who would talk to Wehn was known locally as "Snoqualmie Jim." The artist showed an Indian-head penny to him which led to a discussion about great local chiefs, but Jim initially refused to be a model. After Wehn completed the Seattle statue, Snoqualmie Jim eventually posed for the artist and his likeness was featured on a 1915 medallion.

The artist eventually located a Suquamish Indian who agreed to take the ferry to Seattle and pose for fifty cents an hour. During the first session, Wehn asked him to stand with his hand outstretched. After the first modeling session, he grew tired of posing and he left. Wehn never saw him again. Several years later the artist received a letter from a woman who said proudly, "every time I pass the statue of Chief Seattle I think of my father because that is his arm."

Meanwhile, Wehn shipped the completed statue to Rhode Island where the Gorham Company took nine months to cast it in bronze. When it arrived back in Seattle, the sculptor rushed down to the railroad station and helped uncrate it. He remembered, "A gem emerged from the crate. The bronze was smooth, rich and seamless, everything the sculptor could have wished for."[5] Originally budgeted for $3,000, the final cost was $12,000. The statue was complete and ready to be placed on the pedestal that had been empty and waiting since 1910.

On November 8, 1912, a new civic group, the Tilikums of Elttaes, submitted a petition to the Park Board to officially designate the triangle park at Denny Way and Fifth Avenue North as Tilikum Place. Tilikum was a Chinook Jargon word for "friend," and "Elttaes" was Seattle spelled backward, which apparently sounded "native" to the Tilikums. Made up of many of the city's most influential men, the group's goal was to expand Seattle's business opportunities north to Alaska and across the Pacific to Asia. They played a visible role in the public unveiling of the Chief Seattle statue.

Founders' Day November 13, 1912, was the sixty-first anniversary of the Denny Party's arrival at Alki and the coming out party for Wehn's statue. Arthur Denny might have been Seattle's founding father, but Chief Seattle had become its patron saint.[6] *The Seattle Daily Times* exclaimed, "The occasion will be one of grateful acknowledgment of the debt of gratitude owed to Chief Seattle for his friendship to the earliest Pioneers of the city which bears his name."[7] Coll Thrush noted in the book *Native Seattle* that songs, poems, brochures, and stories revealed little about the real man, but instead presented "little more than a character from central casting" Hollywood-style, and appropriated his life to tell the creation story of white Seattle.[8] The statue was another prop to tell that story.

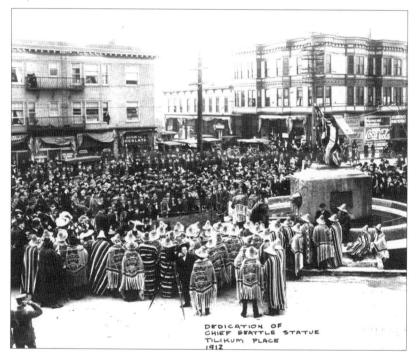

Spectators crowd around the flag-draped Chief Seattle statue in Tilikum Place in 1912. Members of the civic group Tilikums of Elttaes dressed in "Native" costumes for the unveiling ceremony. *Courtesy of the Seattle Municipal Archives #30406.*

The celebration began in the early afternoon with a parade up Second Avenue from the Alaska Building to Tilikum Place. Police officers led the procession, followed by a marching band and a battalion from the fire department. Next came Mayor George Cotterill and the statue committee riding in cars, members of the city council, and a few of the surviving settlers. Finally, one hundred leading citizens—the Tilikums of Ettlaes—painted and wearing an approximation of Native costumes and blankets in a "riot of color and silent savagery" stalked along in feigned ferocity as the crowd cheered them on.[9] The imagery and actions of the marchers attempted to depict the ferocity of the Haida tribes located in coastal British Columbia, in contrast to the more peaceful Duwamish from the central Puget Sound area.

In Tilikum Place, officials roped off the vicinity around the flag-covered statue and erected a stand with seats for the remaining settlers and speakers. Several thousand people packed the surrounding area. The crowd cheered the city officials and Tilikums as they rounded the corner and entered the area. The biggest cheer was for Sir Thomas Lipton, the city's honored guest when he appeared on the platform. He was the founder of the Lipton Tea Company and a famous sportsman, especially in yachting, rowing, and soccer. He was visiting Seattle on his way to San Francisco when city officials persuaded him to take part in the celebration.

Myrtle Loughery, a seventeen-year-old great-great-granddaughter of Chief Seattle, pulled the cord, and the American flag draped around the tall, bronze figure fell away. The crowd stood quietly for a moment and then exploded with a long and loud cheer. Mayor Cotterill accepted the statue on behalf of the city and noted that the location for the monument was between the original homesteads of David Denny and William Bell. At that time, this land was far beyond the northern edges of the newly settled Seattle, but after sixty years now the location was almost at the center of a large, modern metropolis.[10]

Wehn stood behind the podium and expressed a sense of pride at what he was able to create for the community and thanked those who helped him. "Brother Tilikums, I wish to thank you for the honor that you have extended me today, in accepting my humble labor—the modeling of this statue of Chief Seattle, the city's first great Tilikum."[11] The artist had produced a life-sized portrait of Chief Seattle, and according to critic-at-large Robert Haslach of the *Seattle Argus,* "endowed it with authenticity and grace."[12] Many of the settlers attending the ceremony that day remembered the chief, and while the artist created an idealized representation of the figure, they acknowledged it did represent realistic aspects of the Native leader. The statue stood with one foot only half resting on the ground, his right hand raised, and the palm extended in peace, "with his face lifted and expressing courage, kindness, and supreme power," praised the *Post-Intelligencer*.[13]

The city placed the pedestal for the statue in a circular pond with two bronze bear heads on either end of the base acting as fountains with water pouring from their mouths. One plaque described Chief Seattle; on the opposite side was a pictorial representation of Chief Kitsap as he first observed British Admiral George Vancouver's ship arriving in Puget Sound in 1792. A small, triangular plaque placed on an end of the pedestal was the sign of the Tilikums of Elttaes. The figure gazed down Cedar Street toward a narrow view of Elliott Bay.

The Chief Seattle statue exemplifies an artistic perspective that developed after the conclusion of the Indian Wars and white conquest of the American West. Several monuments erected during this era created images of peace and friendship portrayed by the heroic figure of an Indian offering a sign of peace or welcome. Wehn developed his statue at the same time as other statues of welcoming Indian chiefs were created, such as those of Chief Mahaska and Chief Keokuk in Iowa and Chief Oshkosh in Wisconsin. These works supported a particular public memory of the recent western expansion.[14]

The pageantry of that celebration and the public's adoration of the statue were forgotten by the mid-1920s. Editorials in the *Seattle Daily Times* stated that Seattle had grown to "metropolitan proportions" and suggested the quality of the statue and the subject of Chief Seattle himself was no longer appropriate for a modern city. The editorial board was not kind to the chief, "Artistically, the aboriginal Siwash [savage] does not yield readily to treatment by the brush or by the chisel. He is far from being the ideal subject either for the painter or the sculptor. Nature cast him in an unheroic mold." The city no longer maintained the monument, its cracked and dingy sides loosely supported the two bronze plaques; a pool of dirty water surrounded it with a collection of debris including old tires and pieces of wood.[15] The *Times* further suggested Seattle should remove such "relics of barbarism" and replace it with something more modern and thoroughly representative of Seattle.[16]

In 1936, the West Seattle Legion Post and commercial clubs proposed relocating the statue to Duwamish Head in West Seattle, but the city turned them down. Other groups suggested what they thought were more appropriate locations. In the late 1950s students at Seattle University wanted to relocate the statue to their namesake campus. They proposed that student donations would cover the cost of the move. An editorial in the student newspaper stated, "The statue of the leader who welcomed our founders to Alki Beach is virtually inaccessible. What was meant to be an attraction for tourists is today a public eyesore."[17]

The Teamsters' Union proposed to move Chief Seattle to an area two blocks east on Denny Way. They offered to pay for the move and construct a new pylon for the statue. The Teamsters' suggestion echoed the students' claim that the figure was too hidden in its location. The Seattle Historical Society suggested that the memorial move to the grounds of the brand-new Museum of History and Industry in Montlake. "It seems fitting and proper that those interested in Seattle history, particularly the schoolchildren of Seattle, should have the opportunity of viewing this important piece at close range," Horace W. McCurdy, president of the society, wrote in a letter to the city. The city also considered the possibility of placing the statue at the new Civic Center (the current Seattle Center).[18]

In the face of all the suggestions, the statue remained in its original site as the city prepared for the Century 21 World's Fair in 1962. The location of the monument was now lauded as "an increasingly appropriate spot," with the new Space Needle towering over his shoulder and the new monorail passing directly overhead. Chief Seattle welcomed visitors to Seattle as the city attracted tourists to the World's Fair.[19] The Park Board revitalized the monument; they removed the parking spaces around the statue, restored running water to the fountain and pool, and planted shrubs and trees. Crews removed the statue to Woodland Park where they gave it a good cleaning before returning it to its pedestal.

In the mid-1970s, the city made additional improvements to Tilikum Place and revitalized the Denny Regrade area. They removed the statue for six months while crews expanded and rehabilitated the park. Improvements included enlarging and lowering the pedestal at the center of a granite pool, closing a section of Cedar Street, and adding new benches and a drinking fountain. Seattle sculptor

Richard Beyer shaped two twelve-ton granite boulders to fit within the rim of the pool. Workers planted eleven sycamore trees to match the trees that lined the monorail route. With the work completed, a crane returned the statue to its pedestal.

A marching band and cheerleaders from Sealth High School performed for a crowd of more than one hundred people on December 8, 1975. Opened in 1957, the school's name represented a closer English pronunciation of the Suquamish leader's actual name. The guest of honor was once again Chief Seattle's great-great-granddaughter Myrtle Loughery Larsen, then age eighty-one, the same Myrtle who unveiled the statue in 1912. Observing the smaller crowd, she remembered, "There were more celebrities then."[20] Several attendees said it seemed as though the statue had shrunk during its brief absence from the park. They were relieved when city officials reassured them that the statue only appeared smaller since they had lowered the pedestal and expanded the size of the surrounding park. In 1989, the statue received an unexpected cleaning that led to a sparkling discovery. Mario Scott, a thirty-year-old cab driver, often passed by the memorial as he drove his customers around the neighborhood. He thought the grungy green coating reflected a lack of respect for Native people. He scrubbed the statue with an acidic cleaning solution hoping to restore its former glory. "The Indians in this area need to know that the Whiteman cares…that someone cares about their heritage," said Scott. "No one gave me any permission to do this. I wanted to do something for Seattle, and for the Indians."[21]

For seven hours he cleaned the bronzed statue from top to bottom, finishing off with a coat of polish. Bystanders, including police, thought he had permission to do the work. Unfortunately, his well-intentioned cleaning severely damaged the statue. The acid he used stripped the green patina from the statue and began eating away at the bronze beneath. Seattle's face was soon pitted and streaked with brown coloring; his clothes turned a mottled green. Patricia Leavengood, a conservator working with the Seattle Arts Commission, said the statue needed to be professionally cleaned to leach out all of the acids and then covered with a temporary protective coating. Before they could replace the patina, they needed to strip the statue down to the bare metal.

As the restoration began, the conservation crew discovered a long-hidden secret. Under the many layers of dirt, grime, and corrosion that covered Chief Seattle, was a very fragile layer of gold leaf. "We started stripping and found it," said Patricia Tuttle, who was performing the restoration work. "It was a real surprise."[22] Fissures and cracks in the gold leaf had allowed the bronze to come to the surface and cover the statue with a green patina. Records at the Washington State Historical Society Museum and Library at Tacoma referenced the gilded finish that was present when the foundry delivered the statue. So, Mario Scott may have done the city a favor; if there had been no acid cleaning, there would have been no discovery of the gold leaf. Today, the gold leaf has again turned to a bronzed, green patina.

Chief Seattle Busts

As a part of the process of creating his statue, Wehn also completed a bust of Chief Seattle. He referred to it as a "sketch" that allowed him to practice his skills for the larger figure. The city was impressed with the quality of the bust and placed an order for three of them to be cast in bronze. They mounted these on three large drinking fountains that served horses, dogs, and people: one dedicated at Pioneer Square on July 4, 1910; the second placed at Tilikum Place, but later relocated to Westlake and Fourth Avenue; and the third at the intersection of Occidental and King.

During the Great Depression, the city wanted to dispose of the horse watering fountains for scrap. One was sold to the Renton Fire Department for $300. The firefighters placed it at Renton's central fire station, now the Renton History Museum. The city of Seattle scrapped and melted down the bust from Westlake and Fourth. However, John Royle, the Streets and Sewers Department shopkeeper, saved the Pioneer Square bust. "The chief doesn't eat anything, he is all paid for, and besides, we might want him sometime," he said.[23] During the Second World War, Charles Thorndike, chairman of the Washington State Pioneers' Association, proposed that the bust be placed on a new drinking fountain. The city council streets committee turned down his proposal and the Parks Department planted flowers in the old horse trough instead.

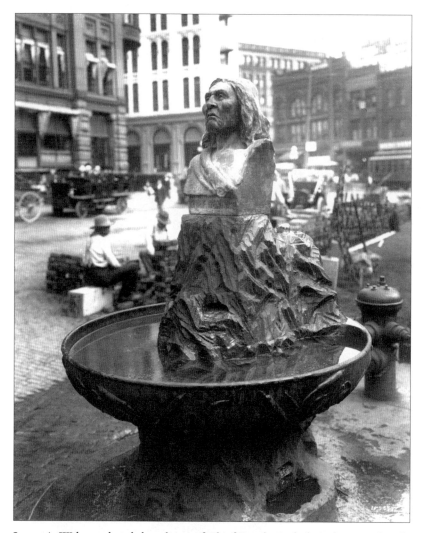

James A. Wehn sculpted three busts of Chief Seattle, including this one placed in Pioneer Square Park in 1910. *Courtesy of University of Washington Libraries, Special Collections, Asahel Curtis, photographer, CUR659.*

The Pioneer Square bust disappeared from its pedestal in 1974; an anonymous caller said they would return the statue only after Mayor Wes Uhlman shaved off his mustache. The mayor refused to concede to the extortion. An anonymous tip led police to a party in the Capitol Hill neighborhood. Four policemen entered the house and saw the bust placed on top of a piano in the living room. They arrested the owners of the house, a young couple, as they tried to grab the stolen goods and flee. Police held the statue as evidence until officers returned it to Pioneer Square.

And that is where it remains today, in a paved, urban park located in Seattle's first neighborhood. Nearby are a 1909 wrought-iron pergola, the Native Alaskan totem pole, and an art installation by Edgar Heap of Birds. Created for Washington State's 1989 centennial celebration, the piece was dedicated to the city's homeless Indians and remains as a counterpoint to the idealized Chief Seattle bust.[24] Two panels showcase Native Lushootseed symbols on one side with an English translation on the other, and according to author Mildred Tanner Andrews, "convey a sense of loss and struggle, but with it a sense of ongoing pride and determination to survive."[25] The surrounding area had changed over the years from Duwamish village, to a business district of gold rush period merchants, to a skid road populated again by Indians, and then to a historic district catering to tourists. The panels read:

Chief Seattle, Now the Streets Are Our Home
Far Away Brothers and Sisters, We Still Remember You.

A Bust for Seattle University

James A. Wehn crafted a separate bust of Chief Seattle in 1958 for the Broderick Memorial Fountain at Seattle University. According to Wehn biographer Fred Poyner, this likeness is markedly different from the earlier sculptures. Seattle's face seems less a strict interpretation of the man, but more angular and stern, conveying a sense of authority rather than welcome and greeting.[26] It currently stands next to a pedestrian entrance to the university off Broadway Avenue.

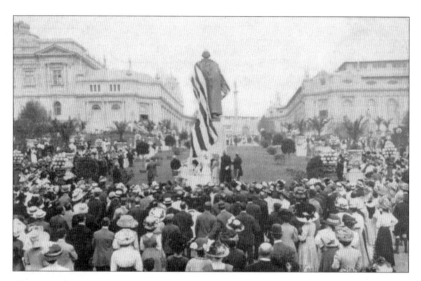

The June 1909 A-Y-P opening featured the unveiling of a large statue of George Washington by Lorado Taft. *Courtesy of University of Washington Libraries, Special Collections, AYP969.*

CHAPTER 4

MONUMENTS OF THE ALASKA-YUKON-PACIFIC EXPOSITION

The Alaska-Yukon-Pacific (A-Y-P) Exposition brought more than three million visitors to the University of Washington campus in Seattle between June 1 and October 16, 1909. A group of Alaska gold rush pioneers and the Seattle Chamber of Commerce provided vision for the fair, and people came from around the world to view hundreds of exhibits and enjoy the games on the Pay Streak midway. Building upon the successful promotion of their city as the departure point to the Yukon gold fields, Seattle used the A-Y-P to further solidify itself as the gateway to the resources of Alaska and Asia.

The A-Y-P was preceded by other large expositions and fairs in the United States that provided a template for the local organizers. The Centennial International Exhibition of 1876, the first official World's Fair in the United States, was held in Philadelphia to celebrate the hundredth anniversary of the signing of the Declaration of Independence. Organizers exhibited a selection of statues that inspired a number of American artists to travel to Paris to continue their studies.

Within two decades, these artists returned from abroad and displayed their craft on a scale that would have been unimaginable in 1876. The Chicago World's Columbian Exposition in 1893, attended by some twenty million, had a profound effect on architecture and the arts. Dozens of up-and-coming artists produced more than two hundred massive outdoor sculptures made from "staff," a temporary mixture of plaster and fibrous materials such as hemp fiber and straw. Sculptures of marble, bronze, and plaster by 150 American artists were displayed inside the various buildings. These artists provided leadership for the sculptural programs of upcoming expositions: the 1901 Pan-American Exposition in Buffalo, the 1904 Louisiana Purchase

Exposition in St. Louis, and the 1915 Panama-Pacific International Exposition in San Francisco.

Seattle's Alaska-Yukon-Pacific Exposition was not as large or well-attended as other world fairs. Still, architecture, arts, and sculpture played a prominent role there. Numerous artists and their assistants traveled to Seattle to produce large temporary sculptures to adorn the fair's buildings and fountains. Exposition officials unveiled a few permanent statues, including a large statue of George Washington that was a nod to the past and the state's namesake. While this particular statue was not connected to the commercial purpose of the fair, its sponsors felt the A-Y-P provided an ideal opportunity to unveil their memorial. Statements of Seattle's new vision of trade with Alaska, the Yukon, and the Pacific were showcased in statues of former Secretary of State William H. Seward and railroad magnate James J. Hill. A memorial to Norwegian composer Edvard Grieg indicated the importance of the region's large population of Scandinavian immigrants. These monuments provided the city prominent statues that remain in Seattle today.

George Washington

The Daughters of the American Revolution (DAR) was founded in 1890 and grew out of the late-nineteenth-century interest in the Colonial Revival. The 1876 Centennial Exposition and the hundred-year anniversary of the signing of the Declaration of Independence sparked an interest in the art, architecture, and stories from America's colonial past. Although primarily dedicated to historic preservation and patriotic education, the DAR also sponsored a small number of monuments during their first decade, including the Mary Washington obelisk, raised in 1894 in Fredericksburg, Virginia; twelve Madonnas of the Trail (placed in 1928–29 in locations from Maryland to California), and others.

The DAR was one of the largest and most influential women's organizations in the country at that time. In Washington State alone, there were sixteen local DAR chapters with nearly two thousand members. A group of Seattle women formed the Rainier Chapter in 1895 and within a few years, they sponsored a statue dedicated to George

Washington. Chapter member Eliza Ferry Leary said that their "constant and loyal love" for the first president had guided their desire to provide for the first statue of Washington west of the Mississippi River.

The Rainier Chapter considered several nationally known sculptors, but coincidentally, the artist Lorado Taft visited Seattle on a lecture tour in November 1905. He offered to create a design and submit it for their review. The chapter had already spoken to Thomas Kane, president of the University of Washington, about placing a statue on campus. Taft's initial concept for the statue was to depict Washington on horseback. He selected a prominent location near the northern side of an oval which was the defining characteristic of an 1898 campus plan by engineering professor Albert H. Fuller. Fuller's oval was incorporated into a John Charles Olmsted plan in 1905 which was updated again in 1909 for the A-Y-P.

Lorado Taft

Lorado Taft was a nationally known, award-winning sculptor whose work was featured in many of the national expositions so popular in the early twentieth century. A graduate of the University of Illinois, Taft continued his studies at the École des Beaux-Arts in Paris. Returning from France in 1883, he became an instructor at both the Art Institute of Chicago and the University of Chicago. His sculptures won numerous awards at the Columbian Exposition in 1893 (Chicago), the Pan-American Exposition in 1901(Buffalo, New York), and the Louisiana Purchase Exposition in 1904 (St. Louis). After these expositions, Taft created many monumental, heroic sculptures, including a fifty-foot-tall statue of the Native American leader, Black Hawk, near Oregon, Illinois. Taft continued working until he passed away in 1936.

The Seattle women sent requests for donations to every DAR chapter in the country. The appeal closed with the statement, "A statue on the shores of Puget Sound will prove a continual reminder that this Republic, from ocean to ocean, loves to honor the chief patriot of the revolution."[1] However, nearly all the chapters replied that they had patriotic projects of their own, and the fundraising drive failed. The local chapter would need to find another source for the money.

One possibility was to raise additional money from schoolchildren. However, a statewide rule stated that no person or organization could collect money in schools, no matter how worthy the project. The DAR petitioned the State Board of Education stating, "We deem it a disgrace to our city and a deprivation to the children if they are not allowed to give their voluntary money to the erection of the statue. We are most anxious to be able to say that the first thousand dollars was given by them."[2] The women presented their fundraising plan and received the endorsement from prominent educators and several leading citizens.

Finally, the State Superintendent of Public Instruction, R. B. Bryan, approved the plan and the Washington Educational Association endorsed it but, as a compromise to the original intent of the donation restriction, said no child would be allowed to contribute more than five cents. In 1907, the DAR designated Washington's Birthday "Monument Day," and facilitated the collection of the children's donations. The fundraising drive gathered $5,500 from schoolchildren and other patriotic societies, but fell short of the required $20,000 to complete the statue.

At the same time, the state legislature was finalizing appropriations to fund the A-Y-P Exposition. The DAR publicized their intent to unveil the statue during the exposition, highlighting that Washington was the only state named after a president. The publicity forced the legislators to provide the remaining funds since they did not want to be blamed for the statue not being completed. All parties agreed that when the statue was finished, it would be unveiled and placed on the grounds of the A-Y-P Exposition.

Lorado Taft prepared models of the statue and regularly sent his ideas to representatives of the DAR. The most significant change to his original proposal was that Washington would no longer appear on horseback, but would rather be a standing, solitary figure. Professor Edmond Meany joined the DAR statue committee as treasurer and visited Taft in Chicago to review his progress. Meany wrote a letter back to Seattle stating that he was entirely satisfied with the design. This statue would be different from the equestrian Washington of early American sculpture, like the 1859 Clark Mills statue in Washington,

DC.[3] These types of statues were done with florid, military airs, and often seemed ill-balanced on their box-like pedestals.[4] Other statues, like Horatio Greenough's 1840 Enthroned Washington, imagined the president as a Caeser-like figure.[5]

As Taft's work on the statue neared completion in Chicago, it attracted the attention of art critics from all over the country. Charles Francis Browne, an influential figure in the art world as a lecturer and writer, published an article in 1908 about the new sculpture. "This [statue] is distinctly original and marks an important step in monumental portrait statues," he wrote. "Washington has come by time and thought to occupy a historical rather than personal position in the national mind. So it was the ideal Washington, the typical historical president, the apotheosized Father of his Country, the Commander of the American forces, rather than a realistic portrait of him as a man and citizen that the sculptor wished to represent." Browne was enthusiastic about Taft's approach and called it a masterly conception carried out in a great way.[6]

The DAR committee unveiled the statue on June 14, 1909, almost simultaneously with the opening of the A-Y-P Exposition, and held an elaborate program of speeches in the auditorium next to the statue. It stood on a temporary pedestal in Puget Plaza near the main entrance to the fair at East 40th Street and Fifteenth Avenue. Edmond Meany was the main speaker and presented a lecture on the life of George Washington. French ambassador Jules Jusserand, attending the A-Y-P as an official guest, spoke about the relationship between Washington and Lafayette and the great friendship between France and the United States. When it came time for Governor Marion Hay to speak, he was nowhere to be found; he mistakenly thought the ceremonies were outside, and had waited alone near the statue for over an hour.

Thomas Kane accepted the statue on behalf of the university, stating that the sculpture would be prized due to the school children's contributions, many of whom would pass by the statue as future students. Three-year-old Eleanor Washington Caldwell was brought on stage by her mother. Born in Seattle, Eleanor was the great-granddaughter of John Augustine Washington, elder brother of the president and the last owner of Washington's home at Mount Vernon before he donated it to the public. The A-Y-P band played "The Star-Spangled Banner," rockets exploded, and thousands cheered as the little girl pulled on one of the ropes, releasing a giant American flag draped over the statue.

The statue shows Washington draped in a long military cloak, falling in ample folds that provide broad, sweeping lines emphasizing solidity and size. His hands rest on a massive sword.[7] Writing in *Pacific Monthly* magazine, art critic O. H. Sample noted, "Mr. Taft's Washington is so vast, monumental and overwhelming in size as to demand a setting of majesty and simplicity that few locations could give, but on the campus of the University of Washington, nature furnished a fitting stage for such a presence."[8] After the end of the exposition, the plan was to move the statue to a permanent location on the campus and mount it on a solid granite base, with the university taking ownership of the monument.

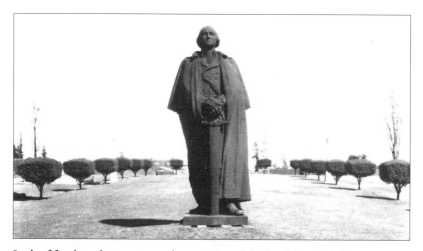

Lack of funds and a permanent home meant that the George Washington statue remained at ground level for a decade. *Courtesy of University of Washington Libraries, Special Collections, UWC0393.*

When the statue was initially cast in bronze, the DAR also planned to build a seventy-five-foot high pedestal. In addition to partially funding the statue, the legislature set aside an appropriation of $5,000 to pay for the stand. However, the permanent base had not been started at the beginning of the exposition, so they placed the statue on a temporary pedestal. When the exposition was over, organizers rapidly cleared the grounds and demolished all but two of the temporary buildings. Distracted by all the closing activity, there was not enough time to build the larger, permanent pedestal before all unspent appropriations reverted to the state treasury. So, Washington remained on his temporary wood and plaster stand.

By 1920, the pedestal of stacks of old railroad ties was unsafe and threatened to topple over. The university lowered the statue and placed in on the ground, where for years, it stood with its feet in the mud at the main entrance to campus. Eliza Ferry Leary, chair of the DAR committee, in an op-ed article in the *Seattle Daily Times* wrote, "Its heroic proportions do not appear to advantage now because it stands on the ground," she wrote. "Someday, when raised to a suitable height, the statue will tower in artistic grandeur as one of the wonders of the Pacific Northwest."[9] An additional letter to the editor complained that "It is allowed to squat on the ground and the effect is absurd and grotesque. It amounts to plain desecration."[10] The legislature repeatedly ignored the issue, pleading that there were more important priorities to fund at the university. They hoped that private citizens or school children would again donate funds to build a pedestal.

Starting in February 1910, the statue became an annual gathering place to celebrate Washington's Birthday. For many years following, patriotic societies, citizens, and school children placed flowers and wreaths by the statue. In 1918, when the First World War was in its final year, the annual ceremony took on an additional patriotic and international flavor. A number of the Allied countries sent representatives including Belgium, Chile, Denmark, France, Great Britain, Greece, Norway, Peru, Russia, Spain, and Sweden.

The university placed the statue on a plain, one-foot-high concrete base in 1930, moving it only slightly off the ground. This half-hearted solution was unsatisfactory and subject to much public criticism. An aging Lorado Taft refused to visit Seattle because the bronze statue he designed for display on a high pedestal was "in the mud."[11] He wrote letters to Meany asking, "Aren't we going to finish the original plan?"[12] The federal government came to the rescue at the end of the Great Depression with a Works Progress Administration (WPA) allotment of $21,182 to build a new base. During a 1934 tour through the Pacific Northwest, Taft finally returned to Seattle and expressed his appreciation when he learned that the Board of Regents approved plans for a new pedestal.

A crew covered the statue with a blanket, loaded it on a truck and moved it one block north to the new pedestal near the Henry Art Gallery. The twenty-four-foot-high sandstone pedestal was on a terrace facing Fifteenth Avenue NE behind Meany Hall. On Washington's Birthday in 1939, the DAR rededicated the statue but neither Taft nor Meany were still alive to see Washington placed on his taller pedestal. Students sadly reflected that the newly elevated statue would be much harder to climb for campus pranks. The morning sun often showed the figure with a paper hat on its head or wearing other playful decorations from a nighttime excursion. Even with the taller height, ingenious students still place masks and other items on the statue.

The statue was moved again in the early 1970s during the construction of the Suzzallo quadrangle. The original plaque from 1909 did not present any information about the statue or who created it. By the state's centennial birthday in 1989, the university and the DAR corrected the omission and affixed an additional plaque to the base:

This statue of George Washington, first president of the United States (1789–1797) and commander in chief of the colonial armies during the American Revolution (1775–1783), was created in 1909 by the eminent American sculptor Lorado Taft (1860–1936) at the request of Professor Edmond S. Meany specifically for the University of Washington campus.

James J. Hill

The George Washington statue was the first statue to be unveiled at the A-Y-P, but the monument demonstrated no real connection to the commercial aspirations of the exposition. The next monument to be celebrated certainly did represent the business and economic underpinnings of the fair.

As planning started for the A-Y-P Exposition, the local Seattle chapter of the Minnesota Club, made up of natives of that state, reflected on how to celebrate the exposition's Minnesota Day. Influential businessmen from St. Paul started the club in 1869 and it had grown into a significant commercial and social force in Minnesota and through local chapters as members relocated across the country. They decided to commission a bronze bust of James J. Hill, the head of the Great Northern Railway, which connected Seattle to the east in 1893. Other Minnesotans donated money and raised funds.

Hill and the Great Northern Railway were important to the economic success of Seattle at the turn of the twentieth century. The announcement of cheap rates for shipping lumber created scores of lumber mills and introduced large-scale logging to western Washington. Hill's Pacific steamships and docks at Smith Cove expanded Asian commerce, and his low passenger fares drew thousands of immigrants to the Seattle area.[13] "Seattle owes a great deal to James J. Hill and the Great Northern, and this idea would be at once an expression of appreciation and a move that would strengthen the ties already existing between the railroad system and this section," said Charles W. Corliss of the Minnesota Club.[14]

Beyond his financial impact, Hill had only a limited personal connection to the Pacific Northwest. His home and the headquarters of the Great Northern were in St. Paul, Minnesota. Lumberman Frederick Weyerhaeuser was a neighbor, and he and Hill had visions of hauling Washington State lumber to markets in the east. Hill also encouraged a Japanese steamship line to make Seattle its West Coast port rather than San Diego. The city was becoming economically successful, and Hill would become known as the "Empire Builder," linking transcontinental rail with transoceanic steamships.

The Minnesota Club commissioned Finn Haakon Frolich to create the statue. Frolich, Norwegian by birth and a graduate of the École des Beaux-Arts in Paris, had only recently arrived in Seattle. While in New York, he worked under celebrated sculptor Daniel Chester French, who later was commissioned to create the statue for the Lincoln Memorial in Washington, DC. A series of troubling events brought Frolich to Seattle; after separating from his wife and drinking too much, he went into New York City's Grand Central Station and asked the ticket agent for the most distant destination available. The agent sold him a ticket to Seattle.

Western Washington was home to a large number of native Minnesotans who streamed through the A-Y-P gates in the early morning hours of August 3, 1909. The occasion was Minnesota

Day, and the state's delegation prepared several activities. Minnesota Governor John A. Johnson delivered a speech in the auditorium; after that, a large crowd including a band, guests, and escorts marched past the George Washington statue to Klondike Circle, where the Swedish building stood with its elaborate turrets, and the draped James J. Hill monument placed in front.

Governor Johnson pulled aside a drapery made from American, Japanese, and Canadian flags to reveal the monument as representatives from those countries spoke about the contributions Hill made to their countries. The pedestal was sixteen feet high and made of granite from a quarry at Index, Washington, except for three blocks: one from the Fox Island quarry in British Columbia, one from Saint Cloud, Minnesota, and one from the Imperial quarry located near Yokohama, Japan.

The statue was six feet tall, one of the largest portrait busts ever made at the time. The sides of the pedestal featured four heavy bronze plates picturing a Great Northern train; the steamship *Minnesota*, which sailed between Asia and Seattle; the seal of the state of Washington; and the coat of arms from the state of Minnesota. Organizers were disappointed that Hill was unable to attend the ceremonies. He sent a letter to demonstrate his appreciation which was read aloud to the crowd. "Seattle has laid the foundations of her future growth and prosperity so broad and deep that nothing will either shake or impair them," he wrote.[15]

Within a year, thieves stole the bronze *Minnesota* plate from the monument. Police believed the plate was removed either as a souvenir or by someone who wished to sell the bronze for its value in metal. After Hill's death in 1916, mourners draped the bronze bust with a floral wreath, and Judge Thomas Burke commented, "It would be impossible to overestimate the value of Mr. Hill's influence in making Seattle the city she is today."[16]

After the conclusion of the A-Y-P, the monument was moved several times, finally to the north end of More Hall, where it stands today overlooking Stevens Way, passed by hundreds of students and staff every day. Shrubbery has grown around the sides and back, making it difficult to view the remaining plaques on the right

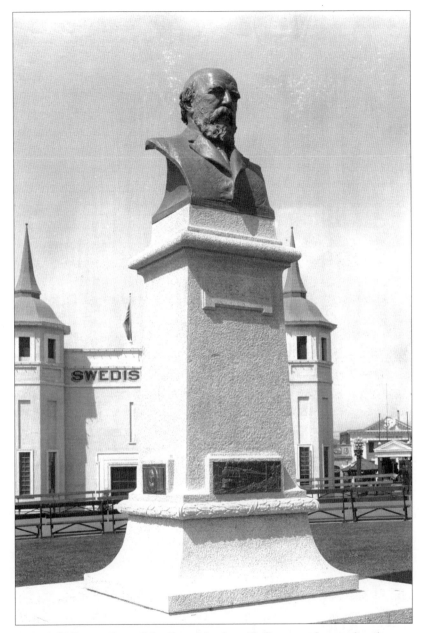

James J. Hill, president of the Great Northern Railway, was honored at the A-Y-P by local businessmen originally from Minnesota. *Courtesy of University of Washington Libraries, Special Collections, Frank H. Nowell, photographer, AYP153.*

side and rear of the pedestal. Hill had once mattered immensely to Seattle, but as time passed both the monument and the man passed into obscurity.

Hill was also instrumental in the creation of two Seattle landmarks granted historical markers as a part of the 1989 Washington State Centennial. The first plaque is at the intersection of South Main Street and Fourth Avenue South and describes the Great Northern Railway Tunnel. Beginning in 1903, an army of 350 workers dug a one-mile-long tunnel by hand under downtown. Seattle City Engineer Reginald H. Thomson directed the construction of the tunnel by both the Northern Pacific and Great Northern railroads to alleviate rail congestion on Railroad Avenue (now Alaskan Way). At the end of 1904, workers completed the tunnel, and it was ready for trains to pass through. The first train would have to wait, however, for the new King Street Station to be completed.

Crews used dirt from excavating the tunnel to fill in the tide flats immediately south of Pioneer Square. This landfill allowed the railroad to build the new station. Hill commissioned the architectural firm of Reed and Stem of Saint Paul, designers of more than a hundred railroad stations, including New York City's Grand Central Station. The scheduled date for the grand opening was June 1906, but Hill moved up the timetable and telegraphed that the first train would steam through the tunnel and arrive on May 10. The construction crews had not entirely finished the station, so it debuted without celebratory speeches or ceremonies.

The station became Seattle's front door for hundreds of arriving passengers each day. Its modest neo-classical style is in dramatic contrast to the 245-feet-tall clock tower modeled after the campanile of the Piazza San Marco in Venice. In the 1960s, the station underwent a full modernization, which included the installation of a suspended ceiling and removed many of the historic finishes. The city of Seattle purchased the building from the Burlington Northern and Santa Fe Railroad in 2008 and began a renovation project to restore the tower clocks, the roof, main entry, and original ceiling. The 1989 Washington Centennial marker is on the wall near the west side entrance to the depot at the end of King Street.

Edvard Grieg

The A-Y-P Exposition was the inspiration for a statue of the Norwegian composer and pianist Edvard Grieg. The Seattle and Puget Sound region was home to a large number of Scandinavian immigrants and their descendants. The exposition specifically celebrated Nordic groups during three special days: Swedish-Finnish Temperance Association of America Day on July 29, Swedish Day on July 31, and Norway Day on August 30, 1909. On Norway Day, a bust of Grieg was unveiled in the Natural Amphitheatre on the exposition grounds. Grieg did for Norway what Chopin did for Poland, Liszt for Hungary, and Dvorak for Bohemia, with his creation of a distinctly Norwegian style of music, which was performed by orchestras around the world.[17]

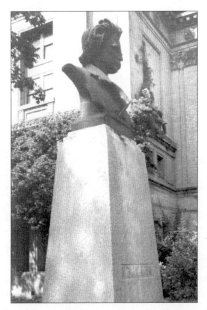

A bust of Edvard Grieg was cast in bronze in 1917 and placed next to Meany Hall on the UW campus. *Courtesy of University of Washington Libraries, Special Collections, UWC1449.*

The statue's artist was Finn Frolich, the same sculptor who created the James J. Hill figure unveiled earlier that month. Norwegians from Seattle commissioned the bust and paid for it by giving Frolich a sixty-three-foot Viking long ship built for the A-Y-P by Sievert Sagstad of Bothell, descendant of a long line of Norwegian boat builders. A crew dressed in traditional Viking garments sailed the vessel from

Kirkland across Lake Washington to dock at the A-Y-P. An audience of 5,000 attendees greeted the ship as it arrived. The afternoon program consisted of speeches, historical reenactments, and the unveiling of the plaster bust which had not yet been cast into bronze.

It took an additional eight years before the Norwegian community would have the bust of Grieg cast in bronze. They officially presented it to the University of Washington on September 3, 1917. President Henry Suzzallo accepted the gift on behalf of the university. He selected the site for the statue, near the music classrooms of Meany Hall, where students could be heard performing the music of the Norwegian composer. The Pacific Coast Norwegian Singers sang a program of songs at the unveiling.

Eventually, Grieg's bust was placed in storage and then moved to Governor's Grove—an area near Suzzallo Library with memorial maple trees planted to honor the governors of the state. After that site was selected for the new Allen Library, the statue was returned to the storeroom again. Negotiations led by the Seattle-Bergen Sister City Association resulted in the bust being placed on an eight-foot pedestal in a large grove of birch trees northwest of Suzzallo Library. In 1990 the university rededicated the statue in its new location on June 15, Grieg's birthday. Dirt from the composer's home and water from the neighboring bay at Troldhaugen, Norway, were ceremoniously placed around the statue.

William H. Seward

William Henry Seward, former governor of New York State, U.S. Senator, and Secretary of State, was the subject of another A-Y-P statue. As a member of President Andrew Johnson's cabinet, he negotiated the purchase of Alaska from Russia in 1867. The acquisition of Alaska eventually provided a significant economic boost to Seattle, which became the principal gateway and outfitting place for commerce between Alaska and the lower forty-eight states. Trade with Alaska, accelerated by the Yukon gold rush, delivered the city out of the severe depression caused by the nationwide economic panic of 1893.

As the city began planning the exposition, Seattle jeweler Gerhard Beninghausen suggested a statue to the man whose negotiation for the purchase of Alaska did so much to improve the city's economy. Former Governor John H. McGraw, president of the Chamber of Commerce, appointed a committee of fifteen men to organize the project. The committee included leading citizens Judge Thomas Burke, Judge Cornelius Hanford, Mayor William H. Moore, Professor Edmond Meany, and Reverend Mark Matthews.[18]

As the committee publicized their project, several people voiced their support. Frederick William Seward, son of the statesman, sent a telegram expressing his appreciation and approval. "Very gratifying to family and friends that William H. Seward is held in such high esteem and remembrance on Pacific Coast. He foresaw the future of Alaska, and said the next generation would find it out," he wrote.[19] Ministers from Seattle's largest churches proclaimed support from their pulpits with Reverend J. E. O'Brien writing, "Seattle owes its present size and prosperity to Alaska's gold mines. Seattle is in much need of monuments, and one such as contemplated would be very appropriate."[20]

Alaskans were divided in their opinion of the best location for the statue. Thomas B. Smith, a prominent miner from Seward, Alaska, wrote that the proposition to erect a statue in Seattle would be received with acclaim by all Alaskans.[21] The governor of the District of Alaska, Wilford B. Hoggatt, expressed his approval, "I think the proposal is timely." He thought the people of Alaska would offer any help needed, but did not think that Seattle would need any financial assistance.[22]

General C. H. Butler, commandant of the U.S. troops at Seward, Alaska, disagreed. He argued, "The monument, I believe, should be erected in the country which he secured to the American people. Juneau is the place in which the monument should be most fittingly erected, or possibly some may say Seward city, the place named after the man who is now to be honored."[23] However, widespread support in Alaska favored Seattle which had already begun planning and did a masterful job of selling the idea in the press. A Seward statue would eventually be erected in Juneau in 2017.

The committee prepared a subscription drive to raise funds and proposed a bronze statue mounted on a granite pedestal. Since they wanted the monument to be a distinctively Seattle project, they decided not to ask for donations from anyone outside the city. They did, however, want to use Alaskan exports such as granite and copper in the construction of the memorial, which would feature a classical, simple statue of Seward without extra ornamentation or adornment. Judge Burke wrote an inquiry to Richard E. Brooks, a noted sculptor from New York City, to ask his opinion regarding the style, size, and cost. The committee planned to unveil the statue on New York Day at the A-Y-P Exposition.

In March 1907, the committee officially selected Brooks as the sculptor. "Mr. Brooks," said Judge Burke "is different from a great many sculptors in that he leaves no part of his work in others' hands. He will have no apprentice help him with any piece as this work is all his own."[24] Three members of the committee, including Edmond Meany, visited Brooks' New York studio to inspect his work and confer with him. Brooks then visited Seattle to examine the proposed site for the statue. Speaking at the Rainier Club, he proposed a budget of $20,000, an amount he indicated would only be possible if Alaskan miners donated the raw materials, which they did.

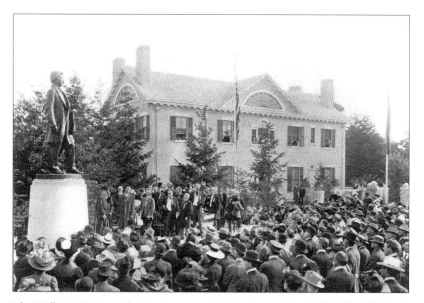

The William H. Seward statue was unveiled in front of the A-Y-P New York State Building, a replica of Seward's family mansion in Auburn, New York. *Courtesy of University of Washington Libraries, Special Collections, AYP1379.*

Brooks returned to New York to begin working on the design. Frederick Seward, son of the secretary of state, furnished the sculptor with all the photos and drawings of his father he possessed. The sculptor then traveled to Paris where he spent two years working on the statue in his studio. Before delivering it to America, he exhibited it in Paris to great acclaim in May 1909.[25] While he finished the sculpture, the committee in Seattle was hard at work raising funds. They distributed placards throughout the city which read, "Seattle honors Seward. As secretary of state, he purchased Alaska. Seattle's prosperity is built largely on the welfare of Alaska. The people of Seattle should, therefore, respond to this call. Subscribe here!" Everyone who donated at least one dollar received a receipt embellished with the picture of Seward.

The committee unveiled the eight-foot, four-inch-tall statue at a ceremony in front of the New York building at the A-Y-P on September 10, 1909. The New York building was a replica of the Seward family mansion in Auburn, New York. Three thousand people cheered and applauded as once again a little girl—this time Harriet May Baxter, granddaughter of former Governor John McGraw—drew aside the American flag and unveiled the monument as the band played "The Star-Spangled Banner."

General William H. Seward Jr., seventy years old, pronounced the statue an excellent likeness of his father. He acknowledged that many people at the time of the purchase of Alaska had denigrated Seward's role in the negotiation. "He intended that his public acts should be such as would stand the test of time and the verdict of posterity. This gathering, nearly forty years after his death, attests that his faith and confidence in the ultimate sound judgment of the American people was not mistaken or misplaced."[26] Brooks was not present at the unveiling, but Judge Burke announced that the artist was on his way to Seattle and would arrive within a few days. Organizers stated the statue would be moved to a more prominent location on campus after the end of the exposition and would become the property of the university.

That announcement was premature as no one agreed on the statue's permanent location. As crews dismantled the exposition buildings, the monument committee, the Park Board, and the Library

Board discussed the possibility of a downtown location. "Negotiations for securing the triangle at Third Avenue and Yesler Way are practically closed. A statue such as that should be centrally located," said Edward Cheasty, president of the Park Board.[27] Erecting the statue at that location was part of a complicated plan to trade the triangle to the Park Board for $20,000 and another lot. This would require a public vote; Burke was uncertain about the outcome of the vote so he recommended placing the Seward statue at Volunteer Park, which Brooks had suggested during an earlier visit.

Brooks noted that the Capitol Hill neighborhood bordering the park was rapidly developing and it would not be long before it would be considered a "close-in" neighborhood. He recommended placing the statue on a high plot of ground in the park with Seward's face looking toward Alaska. In addition, he suggested that Seattle could further recognize Seward's contributions by renaming the park after the statesman.

Renaming the park led to heated discussions at Park Board meetings. Superintendent of Parks John W. Thompson declared that he was opposed to putting statues of dead men in parks; water nymphs or subjects of that sort would be better. Commissioner Ambrose D. Ernst supported the proposal to change the park's name, noting that "the name Volunteer Park is very indefinite. Seattle could very well recognize the services of Seward by renaming the park." But President Edward Cheasty disagreed: "The changing of the name to Seward Park does not command itself to me. We will secure many new parks, and these can be named after Seward."[28] Two years later, in 1911, the city purchased the land for the current Seward Park and named it after the statesman.

On New Year's Day 1910, nearly one hundred people gathered for the second dedication of the statue, this time at its new permanent home in Volunteer Park at the end of a wide boulevard extending from the Fourteenth Avenue entrance. The wind was so severe and bitter that the speakers kept the ceremony as brief as possible. Judge Burke hoped that the memorial marked the start of many impressive statues created for Seattle: "As a great work of art it makes a most auspicious beginning in the movement to beautify and adorn the city of which we are all so proud."[29] Brooks was content; critics admired his work, it was accepted by his patrons, and placed in the location he recommended. Over the years, there were numerous suggestions to relocate the statue from Volunteer Park to Seward Park; however, with the expense and risk of damage from the move, William H. Seward remains on Capitol Hill.

The A-Y-P Exposition closed on October 16, 1909. Thousands of guests had experienced a magical display of lights, elegant buildings, fireworks, and of course, the dedication of statues that are still a part of the landscape today. Businessmen cemented commercial relationships with connections from Alaska and Asia which would continue to grow over the years. The Chamber of Commerce placed a final commemorative bronze tablet at the exposition's conclusion. Originally placed near the University of Washington Forestry Building, the marker was moved and is now located at the bottom of the Rainier Vista, where East and West Stevens Ways meet. The tablet reads:

On these grounds was held between June 1st and October 16th, 1909, the Alaska-Yukon-Pacific Exposition and this tablet is erected by the Seattle Chamber of Commerce as a testimonial to those citizens of Seattle who from a sense of civic loyalty and at great personal sacrifice created and carried to success an exposition of lasting benefit not only to this city but to the entire Northwest. But far more important than all other advantages resulting from such an exhibition is the inspiring example of unselfish and disinterested public service from which these citizens, without material reward or the hope thereof, have given to their city. Such men are the proudest possession of any community and the surest guarantee of its prosperity and its greatness.

Monuments to Japanese Friendship

Significant numbers of Japanese immigrants first came to Seattle in the 1880s to fill construction jobs on the expanding railroad networks and in sawmills, mines, and canneries. Eventually, many of the Japanese developed berry and vegetable farms and a burgeoning business district along Yesler and Jackson Streets. The A-Y-P provided an opportunity for businessmen from other countries to visit and establish connections and relationships with the local Seattle business community; one of these delegations came from Japan. After the exposition had finished, a group of businessmen from Seattle made a reciprocal visit to Japan. One of them, Elbert F. Blaine, a lawyer and former Park Board member, suggested to his hosts that he would like to return home with a traditional stone lantern like those he had seen during the visit.

Kojiro Matsukata, president of Kawasaki Shipbuilding Company, host of the Americans, sent a stone lantern as a gift to Seattle. It resembled a five-story pagoda complete with base and cap.[30] Parks Superintendent John W. Thompson accepted the six-ton granite lantern and placed it on a grassy slope in Mount Baker Park in 1911.[31] The sculpture is located just south of the intersection of Lake Washington Boulevard South and Lake Park Drive South in Mount Baker Park.

A few years later, on September 1, 1923, one of the world's deadliest earthquakes struck Yokohama and Tokyo. The extreme devastation and subsequent firestorms killed 142,800 people.[32] Seattle immediately sent assistance to the residents of Yokohama. As a gesture of gratitude, Japanese consul Kiyoshi Uchiyama presented an eight-ton *Taiko Gata* lantern to the city in 1931. Before a crowd of some one thousand people, including Seattle civic leaders and Japanese dignitaries,

Mayor Frank Edwards accepted the gift at a dedication ceremony in Seward Park. A message from Ichiro Onishi, mayor of Yokohama, explained that the gift was a reproduction of the Momoyama Palace lantern near Kyoto, erected 350 years before by Hotaiko, a general and statesman.[33] As a return gesture of gratitude, the city of Seattle sent the city of Yokohama one thousand rose bushes. Those roses can still be found today in the Yokohama Municipal Children's Botanical Garden.

The Japanese community in Seattle added another Japanese monument to the Seward Park entrance in 1934. Bearing the legend, "Seattle—America's Gateway to the Orient," it was a replica of the most famous *torii* (gateway) in Japan. The original was located on Miyajima, a sacred island in the Japanese Inland Sea.[34] The Parks Department removed it in 1986 due to aging and decay. In 2013, the Friends of Seward Park sought community input to develop a design plan for its replacement, and as of 2016 the fundraising was nearly complete.[35]

A large granite boulder nestled with six smaller rocks and three stone lanterns were added near the entrance to Seward Park in 1976. The symbols carved into the stone are copied from the calligraphy of Japanese Prime Minister Takeo Miki. Roughly translated, the column on the larger figures reads: "Congratulations on the Bicentennial of U.S. Independence." The smaller column to the left is the prime minister's signature. The inscribed boulder and the traditional Japanese rock garden, in addition to 1,000 cherry trees planted along the Lake Washington shoreline, were a gift from Japan to Seattle.[36]

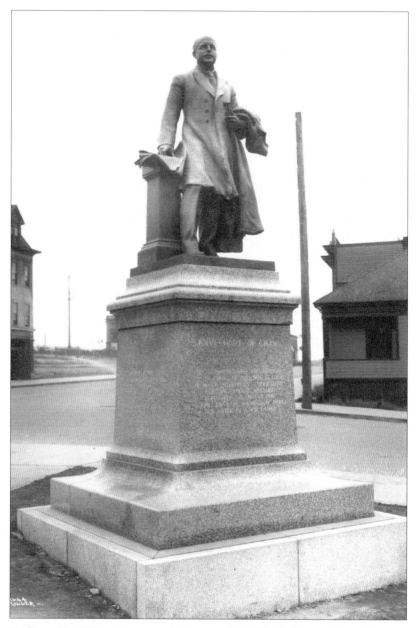

Dedicated in 1913, this statue of Governor John H. McGraw still stands at Westlake Avenue North and Stewart Street. *Courtesy of University of Washington Libraries, Special Collections #CUR1051*

CHAPTER 5

RECOGNIZING SEATTLE'S OWN

The Alaska-Yukon-Pacific Exposition ended on October 16, 1909, having provided thousands of Seattle residents an opportunity to experience a wide variety of statuary and allowed the city to develop relationships with nationally known artists. The statues had been dedicated to men who were not from Seattle, but who had some connection to the state and its people. The next decade would see a shift, as a small number of memorials dedicated to Seattle notables were placed between 1913 and 1916. Richard E. Brooks, the sculptor who created the William H. Seward statue, returned to memorialize John H. McGraw, a leading politician and businessman. The city would also recognize founding father Henry Yesler and businessman Sherwood Gillespy with statues and plaques.

John H. McGraw

John H. McGraw arrived in Seattle in 1876 broke and alone. After working as a clerk at the Occidental Hotel, he joined the Seattle police department. Eventually he was promoted to police chief and then became sheriff of King County in 1886 after he faced down an angry mob who wanted to expel Chinese workers. Next, he studied law and was elected governor in 1892 on a platform supporting the construction of a ship canal between Puget Sound and Lake Washington. McGraw also led the effort to purchase the current site of the University of Washington and to create Harbor Island. Following his term as governor, McGraw joined the gold rush and boarded the famous ship *Portland* as it returned to Alaska. Coming back without having struck it rich, he invested in real estate, served as the head of the Seattle Chamber of Commerce, and as the first president of the Organized Association of Commercial Bodies of Pacific Coast Cities.

McGraw died of typhoid fever in 1910. At the time, the disease was a serious health problem, killing more than one thousand Washington residents between 1909 and 1915. After McGraw's death, his numerous business associates and friends donated money to purchase a small piece of land across the street from the *Seattle Daily Times* (bordered by Stewart Street, Fifth Avenue, and Westlake Avenue.) They named the triangular lot McGraw Place. Based on their recent experience with sculptor Richard Brooks and his William H. Seward statue, a committee commissioned the artist to create a bronze memorial to McGraw.

A crowd filled McGraw Place on July 22, 1913, to watch four of the governor's grandchildren unveil the life-sized statue. For a moment, everyone stood still as they gazed at his likeness, and then a storm of applause broke out over the plaza from the hundreds in attendance. The statue was placed on a marble and granite pedestal and featured the former governor standing beside a table on which he rests his right hand; an overcoat is draped over his left arm. Historian Clarence Bagley wrote that the statue of McGraw was "heroic" and "commemorative of his services as a leader and prominent citizen."[1]

John E. Chilberg, president of the Chamber of Commerce and a close friend of McGraw, presided over the ceremony. Edmond Meany spoke about the governor's bravery and informed the audience that the decision to begin construction of the ship canal (a dream of McGraw's) had been finalized. In accepting the monument for the city, John M. Frink, president of the Park Board, declared that Seattle owed more to McGraw for its advancement and prosperity than any other man. "This statue is a fitting tribute, a proper and deserved recognition of that service," he said. "May it be an incentive to the young men of all future generations to put state and country above personal pleasure and profit."[2]

Currently, the former governor's statue remains in the same small triangle. The city renovated the plaza at the end of the South Lake Union streetcar line in 2011. Its location provides connections from the trolley to the monorail, light rail, and the downtown bus tunnel. McGraw, the astute businessman and Chamber of Commerce president, would surely approve.[3]

Henry Yesler

The Founders' Day celebration in 1905 memorialized the site of Yesler's sawmill with a plaque; ten years later Henry Yesler himself was remembered with a bronze tablet in the county courthouse. Yesler arrived in Seattle in October 1852, just a few months after the Dennys, Bells, and Borens moved across Elliott Bay from Alki. He brought the first steam-powered sawmill to Puget Sound, and, for several years, employed nearly every male settler in Seattle and a considerable number of Natives. Yesler played a part in almost every important event in Seattle's first fifty years and held several public offices.

He was a complicated man who was both a generous benefactor to the community and a businessman whose use of lawsuits and other questionable dealings were less admirable. Yesler contrived a change in state law which allowed him to hold a lottery with much of his property as the grand prize. The state's attorney determined this was unconstitutional and charged Yesler and others with fraud, but the court treated them leniently. He spent much of life in debt, disappointing creditors and partners alike, surrounded by lawsuits and legal entanglements. These traits were largely ignored by fellow businessmen who published the books documenting the city's early history that represented Yesler in a more flattering light.[4]

Yesler built a large forty-room mansion on Third Avenue between James Street and Yesler Street, and when he died in 1892, he bequeathed the building to the city for use as a public library. The mansion was destroyed by fire on New Year's night in 1901 and the county purchased the block from the city in 1906 as the location for the King County courthouse. Construction began in 1914, and Edmond Meany suggested that the county honor Yesler with a plaque placed in the main corridor.

The county commissioners sponsored a competition for local artists and selected Danish sculptor Max P. Nielsen of Seattle to create the marker. After six months of work, Nielsen delivered his creation. The bronze plaque showed a simple, bas-relief portrait of Yesler; local northwest items such as Oregon grapes and a pine cone and sprigs surround his likeness. The county placed the plaque in the lobby of the James Street entrance of the new building. The inscription on the Yesler tablet is as follows:

> *In Memory of Henry L. Yesler*
> *The honored pioneer and former mayor of Seattle, this tablet is*
> *erected by the people of King County, in recognition of his public*
> *spirit and helpful generosity. He died in his beautiful home on the*
> *site of this building in 1892.*

James A. Wehn also crafted a study of Yesler that he entered in the competition. Even though he did not win, his preparatory work was useful. The Leschi Heights Woman's Improvement Club commissioned a medallion of Yesler and awarded the job to Wehn based on his earlier study. The club dedicated the memorial on November 9, 1916, in the entryway of the Seattle Public Library building at the corner of Twenty-third Avenue South and East Yesler Way. The library named the branch after Yesler in recognition of his efforts to begin the city's library. His medallion remains in the entrance of the library which in 1975 was renamed the Douglass-Truth Library to honor Frederick Douglass and Sojourner Truth.[5]

The state centennial program placed a plaque in 1989 at the location of Yesler's Pavilion on Cherry Street east of First Avenue. Yesler built the original building in 1865, and it served as Seattle's first civic and entertainment center. It hosted town meetings, and a few professional music and theater acts each year, along with amateur plays and recitals. It also served as the District Court for King County until 1876. Yesler remodeled the building into offices in 1887, but the Great Fire destroyed it 1889. In 1907, Henry Yesler's nephew James Lowman developed the building still at that location.

Sherwood Gillespy

At the turn of the twentieth century, the game of golf was popular and served as an indicator of a city's prosperity with courses of verdant green grass and manicured fairways. Business leaders established the private Seattle Golf Club in Fremont in 1900 before moving it to the Laurelhurst neighborhood in 1904 and, finally, to its present location in Richmond Beach in 1908.[6] Meanwhile, a group of residents led by Edward C. Cheasty, a member of the Park Board, wanted a public golf course which would allow a greater number of people to play.

Rebuffed by his fellow parks commissioners, Cheasty found an ally in Sherwood Gillespy. Gillespy arrived in Seattle in 1898 and was a prominent businessman who represented the Mutual Life Insurance Company and helped organize Seattle's Independent Telephone Company.[7] Gillespy and Cheasty gathered one thousand signatures to present to the city council with a proposal for a public golf course located in Jefferson Park on Beacon Hill on 137 acres the city had acquired from the state and transferred to the Parks Department in 1909.[8] The city council directed the Park Board to work with the Olmsted Brothers, the nationally renowned designers who had designed the A-Y-P grounds and various Seattle parks and boulevards, to determine the feasibility of a course at the property.

Unfortunately, Gillespy died in 1912, and his friend Cheasty passed away in 1913 before the city completed the project. The Jefferson Park golf course opened to great acclaim and ceremony on May 12, 1915.[9] To honor Gillespy's efforts, Dr. Frank I. Shaw, local golfers, and other admirers commissioned a fountain and statue from sculptor Max P. Nielsen, who was working on the Yesler plaque at the same time. The Parks Department placed the $1,000 statue in front of the course's clubhouse.[10]

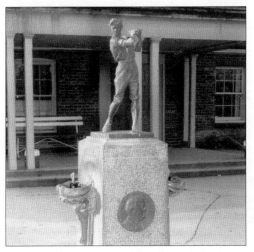

Sherwood Gillespy statue, missing club, Jefferson Park Golf Course Clubhouse, 1950. *Courtesy of the Seattle Municipal Archives #29421.*

In that first year, 1915, over 26,000 players visited Jefferson Park.[11] As they entered the clubhouse, they passed the fountain, statue, and a circular bronze plaque commemorating Gillespy with the inscription: *Erected by friends in honor of Sherwood Gillespy. A kindly, lovable man, an ardent golfer. The father of the idea of a municipal golf course for the city of Seattle.* The weathered, three-foot-high bronze statue, missing its golf club, still stands in front of a new Jefferson Park Golf Course Clubhouse, and continues to inspire the public to play golf.[12] Two additional public golf courses followed, buoyed by the success of Jefferson Park: Jackson Park in north Seattle (1930) and the West Seattle course (1940).

The monuments from this decade were insular, memorializing local men from Seattle. The next decade would look outward and expand the scope for Seattle's monuments. Flights around the world, the importance of local aviation, and a presidential visit would be remembered in the Roaring Twenties.

The Story of Mollie Walsh and Hannah Newman: A Memorial Melodrama

In December 1930, a plaque with a bas-relief portrait of a woman named Hannah Newman was placed on the brick exterior of the Washington Athletic Club, near the corner of Sixth Avenue and Union Street. The origin of this plaque is an intriguing story of gold, infidelity, murder, and unrequited love, and the female protagonist is not even the woman portrayed on the tablet. The story began in 1897 with the Klondike gold rush.

Mollie Walsh was a twenty-four-year-old, unmarried Irish girl who arrived alone in Skagway, Alaska, looking for adventure. She traveled thirty-three miles up the White Pass Trail and opened a temporary restaurant. Mollie caught the eye of several miners who passed through.[13] One who was particularly fond of her was Jack Newman, a packer who made fifty mule-train trips and earned a small fortune.[14] She treated him for frostbite, and he fell in love with her. A rival packer, Mike Bartlett, also declared his love for Mollie. Jealous and angry, Newman demanded she stop seeing Bartlett. Mollie rejected Newman, married Bartlett, and the couple moved to Seattle.

Arriving with a $100,000 fortune, Bartlett and Mollie began to argue and fight. Soon after, Mollie left for Mexico with another man, taking much of their fortune. Within a few weeks, she reappeared, without her new boyfriend or the money. Bartlett was bitter and angry at her dalliance and on the night of October 27, 1902, he chased down Mollie in a rage, shooting his pistol at her. Mollie fell dead at age twenty-nine. Bartlett was tried for first-degree murder and committed to an asylum where he later took his life.

Newman read the story in the newspaper and became heartbroken when he learned his beloved Mollie had died. When the gold rush ended Newman moved to Seattle, where in 1906 he married Hannah Hill Barry, a wealthy widow twenty-three years his senior. A part of her fortune was a large piece of land covering the eastern part of downtown Seattle. The organizers of the Washington Athletic Club purchased their building site at Sixth Avenue and Union Street from her in 1928.[15]

Soon after, in April 1929, survivors of the gold rush worked with a group called the Ladies of the Golden North to erect a monument at White Pass to the pack animals who carried supplies for the miners. The memorial to the 3,000 horses and mules that died on the trail was created by Seattle sculptor James A. Wehn. Newman contributed generously to the project and wrote the inscription on the marker.[16] Pleased with the results, Newman asked Wehn to create a bust of his beloved Mollie, whom he still loved twenty-eight years after her murder. That statue still stands in a park in Skagway.[17]

Newman may have pushed his luck by donating the bust of Mollie in the name of both himself and his wife, Hannah. Speaking at a Sourdough Reunion, Newman admitted that Hannah and he never argued until a few months earlier, "Look here, Jack, are you going to devote your life to putting mules and horses and Mollie Walsh in bronze? Where do I come in?"[18] He commissioned a plaque in honor of Hannah and dedicated it at a ceremony on December 15, 1930. Five months later, Newman died from complications of appendicitis, but Hannah lived a few more years, dying at age ninety-six in 1934. The plaque still is attached to the Washington Athletic Club building on the southwest corner of Sixth Avenue and Union Street, a memorial to a fascinating love story.

• • •

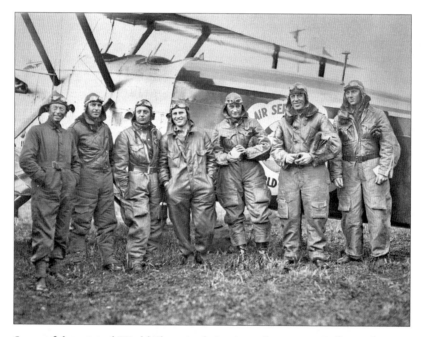

Seven of the original World Flyers in their winter flying suits. Left to right:
Sgt. Arthur Turner, Sgt. Henry Ogden, Lt. Leslie Arnold, Lt. Leigh Wade,
Lt. Lowell Smith, Maj. Frederick Martin, Sgt. Alva Harvey. Not shown:
Lt. Erik Nelson and Lt. John Harding. *Courtesy of the Smithsonian National Air
& Space Museum, NASM 81-8960.*

CHAPTER 6

THE TWENTIES: AVIATION, A PRESIDENT, AND A PRIEST

The conclusion of the First World War in November 1918 led to a period of uncertainty about the impact of peace on local businesses that had mobilized for war production. America's first general labor strike took place in Seattle in February 1919 and lasted five days before Seattle Mayor Ole Hanson used strong tactics to break the strike, which earned him national recognition. The rapid population growth and annexation of nearby communities seen in the years 1890 to 1920 slowed, but air travel increased with the development of airfields at Sand Point, Gorst Field, and Boeing Field. Monuments from the 1920s celebrated aviation, a presidential visit, and one of Seattle's beloved early religious leaders.

World Flyers Column

In the early 1920s, several countries vied to become the first to circumnavigate the globe by air. In 1924 the Americans, British, French, Italians, and Portuguese all launched airplanes in a race around the world. The U.S. Army Air Service selected Seattle as the official starting point for their journey. At 8:30 a.m. on April 6 four American airplanes cast their moorings from a seaplane dock at Sand Point Field and took off from the calm waters of Lake Washington. The army named each of the four Douglas World Cruiser biplanes after an American city: *Boston*, *Chicago*, *New Orleans*, and *Seattle*; newspapers dubbed the eight pilots the World Flyers. The *Seattle* was christened with a bottle of water from Lake Washington rather than champagne since the United States was in the midst of Prohibition imposed by the Eighteenth Amendment.

As the aircraft departed Seattle, they flew westward. Over Alaska one of the planes, the *Seattle*, crashed in dense fog and the two airmen hiked for eleven days until they were rescued by a small motor boat from a nearby cannery. The remaining three airplanes crossed Asia, the Middle East, and Europe. On the North Atlantic leg of the trip, the *Boston* crashed and sank, but the Navy rescued the crew and transferred them to a backup plane, the *Boston II*. The three remaining airplanes reached the east coast of the United States in early September and Seattle began planning a massive celebration for their impending arrival at the finish line.

After crossing the United States, the planes departed San Diego and followed the Pacific coast for the final leg of the long journey, passing through Santa Barbara, San Francisco, and Eugene, Oregon. The increased size of the anticipated crowd forced the organizing committee to select a larger location for the welcome ceremony. They announced that instead of City Hall Park, the larger Volunteer Park would now host the formal greeting and presentation of gifts to the flyers. On Sunday, September 28, thousands of Seattle residents and other visitors witnessed the completion of a journey that lasted 175 days and covered 27,553 miles. The Americans were the first to fly around the world.

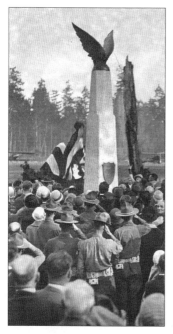

Dedication of the World Flyers monument, 1924. *Courtesy of MOHAI, Seattle Post-Intelligencer Collection, 2000.107.217.07.01.*

The planes approached Seattle from the south, and spectators crowded every vantage point. American flags along with red, white, and blue bunting hung from buildings and homes across the city. The whistle on the *Seattle Daily Times* building blew three blasts to signal every boat horn, factory whistle, and church bell to ring out a greeting. Escort planes flying from Crissy Field in San Francisco and the Vancouver Barracks in Washington arrived overhead first. As the Flyers circled over the airfield at Sand Point they could see the word "Welcome," spelled out in strips of white cloth, twenty feet high and 150 feet long, on the ground. Some 40,000 people crowded the airport as a twenty-one-gun salute boomed across the field when the last plane touched down.

The fliers were first taken by motor launch from Sand Point to Madison Park, where an audience of 5,000 greeted them as they disembarked the boat and boarded cars. They were then driven to Volunteer Park for a formal reception in front of 50,000 cheering spectators. A telegram from President Calvin Coolidge was read to them and they each received a ring made of platinum and gold set with bloodstones from Alaska.

After the day's welcome ceremonies, the Flyers spent the evening at the New Washington Hotel. The next day, they were the guests of honor at a public luncheon in the Hippodrome, a large meeting hall at the corner of Fifth Avenue and University Street. After the luncheon, they returned to Sand Point to dedicate a monument designed by Seattle sculptor Alonzo Victor Lewis. The public had donated $4,000 to a popular subscription initiated by the Seattle Chamber of Commerce. Two thousand people gathered at the airfield's entrance to witness the ceremony. Edmond Meany presided over the ceremony, and U.S. Senator Wesley Jones delivered a speech. Lieutenant Lowell Smith, commander of the flight, made some brief comments and introduced the other World Flyers.

While the Sixth Coast Artillery Band of Fort Worden played the requisite "Star-Spangled Banner," the flyers stood by as Mrs. Francis L. Cole, sister of flyer Leslie Arnold, removed the huge flag covering the monument. It was a polished fifteen-foot tall granite column topped with bronze wings, like a bird alighting from a long voyage.

The inscription on the shield-shaped plaque presented the names of the fliers:

1st Lt. Lowell H. Smith and 1st Lt. Leslie P. Arnold, "Chicago."
1st Lt. Erik H. Nelson and 2nd Lt. John Harding, Jr., "New Orleans."
1st Lt. Leigh Wade and 2nd Lt. Henry H. Ogden, "Boston,"
Maj. Frederick L. Martin and Staff Sergeant Alva L. Harvey, "Seattle."

In a memoir published one year after the flight, the fliers dryly remarked that, "We had certainly never expected to see our names on a monument until we were under it."[1]

After the monument's dedication, the Flyers removed their personal belongings from their planes. For a few minutes, each airman walked around his airplane, touching it as if he was unwilling to say good-bye to the craft which carried them on their long journey. Then, they boarded a train for the trip back to the East Coast, and returned to their regular duties.[2] Today, the monument, which can be difficult to examine carefully due to traffic, still stands at the entrance to Sand Point, now Magnuson Park, part of the Seattle parks system and named for former U.S. Senator Warren G. Magnuson.

Gorst Field

In 1926, just two years after that first around-the-world flight, a small biplane descended through the clouds over the Duwamish River. Grover Tyler peered out of the open cockpit to look down on the strip of land known as Gorst Field before he arrived in a cloud of dust and rolled to a stop. Tyler had flown in from Portland, the last of five legs on a journey stretching north from Los Angeles up the Pacific coast. With a triumphant smile, he handed over Seattle's first airmail delivery to Postmaster Charles M. Perkins.

From 1926 to 1928, Gorst Field was Seattle's only commercial airfield. No one would have dared called it an actual airport; the short 1,800-foot-long runway along the Duwamish River was made from gravel and cinders on a layer of soft sand and sawdust. The field belonged to Vern Gorst, one of the Pacific Northwest's aviation pioneers. Gorst taught himself to fly in 1913 using a Glenn Martin seaplane and soon afterward offered passenger flights. After damaging his plane, he stayed on the ground for a decade before flying the first coastal air mail routes in 1925. King County opened a larger airfield in 1928 less than a mile away, and Gorst Field was no longer needed. Flights from that field stopped when William Boeing bought the land to provide additional space to expand his factory, Boeing Plant 1.

Nearly forty years passed before Seattle would officially remember Gorst Field and its role in early aviation history. The field's location eventually became home to the Ideal Cement Company, which partnered with the Seattle Historical Society for a plaque and fountain. Invitations to the dedication included a 1926 ten-cent blue stamp carried on the first airmail flight to land at the field. Three pioneer aviators were present at the ceremony on September 15, 1966. Clayton Scott and A. Elliott Merrill joined Grover Tyler, the pilot from that first airmail flight. Scott and Tyler were credited with landing the first airplanes at nearby Boeing Field and became test pilots for Boeing. The fountain and plaque can still be found at 5500 West Marginal Way SW at the Lafarge-Holcim Cement plant.

Boeing Field

County and city officials dedicated King County International Airport/Boeing Field on July 26, 1928. William Boeing referred to the day as one of the "happiest days of his life" as the county honored his contribution to aviation by naming the airport after him.[3] The Boeing Company at the time was a leader in airmail service and developed multiple airplanes for the U.S. military. Several different aircraft were displayed in front of the crowd of more than 50,000 people. Airport officials stood on a platform near a plaque and flags as a band played, and guests of honor delivered speeches. "Boeing Field today means more to Seattle and the Northwest than the building of the old Yesler Wharf meant to our pioneer citizens," declared State Senator William W. Conner as he stood before the veiled plaque.[4] Bill Boeing Jr. was just a young boy when he pulled back the banner to reveal the plaque depicting an eagle clutching a propeller blade.

The airport relocated the plaque in 1960, and it became the principal feature of a landscaped area in the main parking lot in front of the terminal. The Boeing Company constructed a new base for the marker. The Chamber of Commerce added a plaque in 1978 to commemorate the fiftieth anniversary of the airport. On the airport's eightieth anniversary, airport officials asked Bill Boeing Jr. to repeat the role he played at the original dedication. He recalled the perch from which he pulled back the banner covering the plaque "seemed awfully high" to him the first time around.[5] The markers remain in front of the main administration building at Boeing Field.

Warren G. Harding

President Warren G. Harding was on a forty-day tour of the western United States when he arrived in Seattle from Alaska on July 27, 1923. During his brief, six-hour visit he stopped by Woodland Park where he recited the Pledge of Allegiance with a crowd of 30,000 boys, many of whom were Boy Scouts. After the event, the twenty-ninth president boarded a train for California, not knowing his speeches in Seattle would be his final public events. He developed pneumonia, complicated by a heart ailment, and died August 2 in San Francisco.[6]

Two years later, members of Elks Lodges from around the state commissioned a memorial at Woodland Park to honor Harding's visit. The crowd at the dedication included many of the boys who had attended the earlier presidential event. They sang "The Star-Spangled Banner," and again recited the Pledge of Allegiance. Congressman John Miller and Mayor Edwin Brown stood on the memorial as the program closed with the singing of "America."[7]

The monument was sculpted by Alice Carr who, after graduating high school in Seattle, studied art in New York and Chicago. After finishing a year at the Art Institute of Chicago, Carr returned to Seattle and completed two monuments. Her first project was a concrete bas relief planter completed in 1924 and located on the north side of the Woodland Park Rose Garden. The following year she created the Harding Memorial, a reinforced concrete structure, both practical and ornamental, that could be used as stage. Two statues of Boy Scouts standing with their hands raised in the pledge flanked the steps on each side of the raised platform. A large plaque placed on the front of the stage described the events behind the memorial. The artist sculptured the figure of President Harding surrounded by a group of boys in bas-relief on the rear wall.

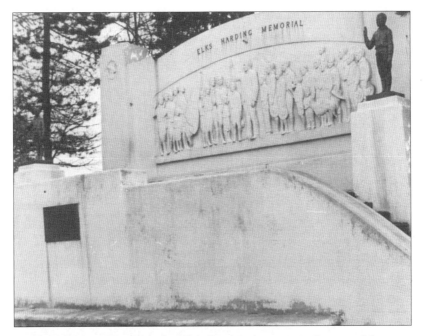

Harding Memorial was placed at Woodland Park in 1925. *Courtesy of the Seattle Public Library #20105.*

For fifty-five years, the concrete monument stood starkly in the middle of Woodland Park Zoo's grassy upper picnic space. In 1980, the zoo developed the area into a large African savannah exhibit. They informed the Seattle Elks Lodge of the plan, but the Elks did not have the desire or ability to salvage the monument. Before the memorial was tipped into a hole dug next to it and unceremoniously buried, the zoo donated the plaque and the two Boy Scout statues from the sculpture to the Chief Seattle Council of the Boy Scouts. They remain in the foyer of their headquarters on 3120 Rainier Avenue South. The remainder of the monument was demolished.[8]

Father Prefontaine

Father Francis Xavier Prefontaine established Seattle's first Catholic Church in 1867. Born in 1838 near Montreal, Quebec, he arrived in Puget Sound immediately after his ordination. Prefontaine entered his religious vocation as a secular priest, meaning he was not required to take vows of poverty and thus allowed to own property. After his death in 1909 at the age of 70, he left an estate worth the impressive sum of $33,173. Included in that sum was a $5,000 bequest for a public fountain, "if possible, in the immediate vicinity of Prefontaine Place," the block of Third Avenue and Yesler Way to Fourth Avenue and Washington Street.[9] The city had named the small street in his honor when the church he founded in 1869, Our Lady of Good Hope, was demolished in 1905 to accommodate the widening of the road.

Henry Yesler donated a small triangular shaped lot bounded by Yesler Way and Third Avenue to the city for a new library. However, the Library Board determined that Yesler Triangle was too small for a library building, so in 1912 they traded the lot to the city. It wasn't until 1925 when Mayor Edwin Brown, the Park Board, and the Yesler estate agreed to build the Prefontaine fountain on the triangle. Carl F. Gould, a prominent Seattle architect and founder of the University of Washington architecture department, designed the fountain. Centered on a terrace is a circular pool with a memorial in its center with the inscription: *Presented by Msgr. F. X. Prefontaine to the City of Seattle, Died March 4, 1909.* There are two sculpted tortoises on the basin's rim, designed to spray streams of water into the pool. The city added the blue tiles in the basin as part of a 1967 restoration of the triangle. The fountain is currently non-operable.

Today, we take for granted the importance of aerospace to Seattle and our area. Boeing is a large, international conglomerate with large factories and facilities in Everett, Renton, and at Boeing Field. However, when the local aviation memorials were erected in the 1920s, no one knew how impactful the industry would be to Seattle. The monuments are not large or grand, and are even a little difficult to find and observe. The President Harding memorial is gone and the Father Prefontaine fountain is forlorn and empty. The historical markers from the decade of the 1920s have lost their sense of importance.

CHAPTER 7

EARLY WAR MEMORIALS: FROM THE BATTLE OF SEATTLE TO THE FIRST WORLD WAR

War memorials can be found all around the world. They may celebrate a war or a victory, but most often they are built to honor those who risked and sacrificed their lives during the battle. The Battle of Seattle was fought in 1856 when settlers and U.S. Marines defended the young settlement against an attack by some Native Americans during the Puget Sound and Yakima Wars. (The 1999 World Trade Organization protests have also been called the Battle of Seattle. No markers appear to have been mounted in memory of that conflict between protesters and police.) Plaques from 1905 mentioned the two blockhouse forts that protected the settlers in the 1856 battle, and a civic group erected a monument to the early skirmish in 1916. Much like other cities across the United States, Seattle erected statues of soldiers from the Spanish-American War of 1898 and World War I to honor local sons who served and died in those conflicts.

Battle of Seattle

The local chapter of the Daughters of the American Revolution had initially discussed the idea of a memorial to the 1856 Battle of Seattle to mark the fiftieth anniversary of the attack in 1906. However, the chapter was preoccupied with planning the George Washington statue unveiled during the A-Y-P Exposition. After the exposition, they were able to turn their attention back to the Battle of Seattle memorial, which they envisioned as a granite boulder with attached plaques. Mayor Hiram Gill and the city council granted permission to place the monument close to the new county courthouse at Third

Avenue between James and Jefferson Streets, in the general area where the Indians had attacked the young settlement. The DAR members used a unique method to acquire the bronze to produce tablets for the monument—they collected discarded copper visiting plates used to receive calling cards.

A large audience crowded City Hall Park and watched from windows of the neighboring buildings for the dedication of the monument on August 15, 1916. A military escort accompanied Governor Ernest Lister, national president of the DAR Daisy Allen Story, and other distinguished guests as they paraded in cars provided by leading citizens from the Hotel New Washington to the park. Four women, costumed in full colonial skirts, bodices, and white wigs, escorted the dignitaries as they mounted the steps to the speakers' platform.

Judge Cornelius H. Hanford delivered a speech in which he described Seattle as it was at the time of the battle. The village then consisted of four business buildings, a church, a sawmill, three hotels, and forty houses scattered among stumps and logs, and the two block-houses. Two white settlers were killed and none wounded that day in 1856, but the small battle had grown in perceived consequence to Seattle as time passed. He said, "The importance of battles is not necessarily to be measured by the number slain."[1] There is a possibility that without the warning of the impending attack from Natives friendly to the settlers, and the presence of the USS *Decatur* with its howitzers and Marines, that the entire settlement may have been wiped out.

The sole remaining eyewitness to the fight, Walter Graham, sat in the front row of the audience. Graham had arrived in Seattle in 1853 and farmed on the shore of Lake Washington, south of Seward Park. His farm was burned during the attack and during a lull in the battle he snuck into a deserted cabin for food.[2] Florence Oliver, leader of the local DAR chapter, presented the monument to Mayor Gill, who accepted it on behalf of the city.

The message of the day's speeches then changed to remember an event which had little to do with Seattle or the battle from sixty years earlier. The Spanish-American War of 1898 became the focus of the ceremony and the memorial boulder. While the DAR was a large and powerful organization, members were mostly prohibited from political activity. As World War I enveloped Europe, however, the DAR strongly advocated for what they called "preparedness." Story, speaking on the subject, stated, "The Daughters of the American Revolution will have unestimated influence in assisting the nation whenever the call comes."[3] By using the Battle of Seattle boulder to also memorialize the most recent American victory over the Spanish, the event supported preparedness for American entry into the First World War (the war had just entered its third year and the stalemate on the western front in Europe had France and Great Britain hoping for American involvement).

Governor Lister gave a long speech about Spanish-American War veterans and the plight of the USS *Maine*. The battleship was at anchor in the harbor at Havana, Cuba, when she was ripped apart and sunk by an unexplained explosion. Americans were goaded on by sensationalist newspaper coverage, and blamed the Spanish government of Cuba for the death of 260 sailors. The U.S. Congress declared Cuba's right to independence and authorized the use of force to secure the withdrawal of Spanish troops from Cuba. Spain declared war on the United States on April 24, followed by a U.S. declaration of war the following day.

The DAR affixed two tablets onto the memorial boulder donated by the Seattle Golf Club. The first plaque was crafted of steel from the USS *Maine* obtained five years earlier when the U.S. Navy raised the sunken ship from the mud of Havana Harbor. On its face is a shield with the words *Patriotism* and *Devotion*. The inscription reads: *In Memoriam, USS Maine, destroyed in Havana Harbor, February 15, 1898*. On the opposite face of the stone is the second tablet made of bronze from the donated visiting plates, entitled *The Battle of Seattle*, bearing the picture of the sloop-of-war *Decatur*. The ship used its howitzer and Marines to repel the attacking Indians in 1856. Also placed in the center of *The Battle of Seattle* plaque is a donated 1856 copper penny.

On one end of the boulder inscribed in deep-cut, gold letters is the state motto of the DAR, "Patriotism, Reverence, Remembrance." The origin of the three small cannonballs mounted on the boulder is under debate. The *Seattle Daily Times* in 1937 published a story which claimed the cannonballs were found on Beacon Hill after being fired from the *Decatur*. Another story stated that the cannonballs were made from metal recovered from the USS *Maine*.

Thieves chiseled off *The Battle in Seattle* bronze plaque in 1966 leaving a gap with four ugly holes at the corners. A *Seattle Daily Times* article in 1972 about vandalized local monuments led to the recovery of the stolen plaque. John Zavaglia, the owner of an antique store, found the plaque in a trunk he purchased from a second-hand store that had gone out of business several years earlier. He did not think much about the plaque until a friend told him about the article in the newspaper. Zavaglia returned it, and the city reattached it to the boulder from which it had been removed.

The Hiker

Two years before the USS *Maine* plaque was placed on the boulder in City Hall Park, the Parks Department set aside the quiet southwest corner of Woodland Park in 1914 as a tribute to the American sailors and soldiers of the Spanish-American War. Within a couple of years, officials placed a plain granite pedestal on the site, but it remained empty for a decade due to lack of money for the statue. Finally, members of the Fortson-Thygesen Camp, a local Spanish-American War veterans group, launched a campaign to raise funds for a memorial. The organizers purchased a replica of "The Hiker," a famous statue sculpted by Allen G. Newman.

The Hiker represented the soldier of the Spanish-American War. Just as the Roughrider was the cavalryman of the war with Spain, the Hiker was the infantryman. The term was used by nineteenth-century infantrymen to casually address each other. The term would become Doughboy in World War I, G.I. in World War II, and Grunt in Vietnam. Newman conceived the statue during the war in 1898 and spent several months interviewing soldiers from the Cuban and Philippine battles before he began his work. Some of these soldiers served as preliminary models for the statue, which depicts a soldier returning from a long march, wearing puttees, a slouch campaign hat, and carrying a Krag rifle. The statue was intended to represent all the fighting men who battled through the campaigns of 1898 and 1899.

Newman copyrighted the work in 1904, and it served as the official monument of the United Spanish War Veterans organization. The original was erected in Tompkinsville Park, in Staten Island, New York,

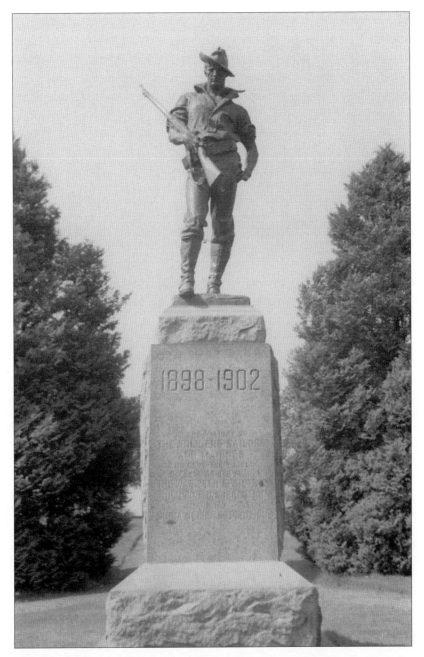

The Hiker in Woodland Park commemorates the infantrymen who fought in the Spanish-American War. *Courtesy of the Seattle Public Library #20103.*

and Newman made more than twenty copies for communities throughout the United States. Lorado Taft, who created Seattle's George Washington statue, called it "the best bronze soldier in America."[4]

Most of the volunteers from the Pacific Northwest fought in the Philippines, many as members of the Third Cavalry, a regiment that camped at Woodland Park before shipping out. On Memorial Day 1926, many of those veterans returned to dedicate the statue to their fallen comrades. After a military parade of some five thousand soldiers and veterans marched through downtown, the veterans' group unveiled the statue at Woodland Park. Mayor Edwin Brown accepted the statue on behalf of the city and two elderly Civil War veterans, one from the Grand Army of the Republic and the other from the United Confederate Veterans, marched forward to lay wreaths at the foot of the pedestal.

The veterans added a copy of the USS *Maine* plaque from the back of the Battle of Seattle boulder in City Hall Park to the granite base of the Hiker. They also placed two large six-inch guns from the USS *Concord* near the statue. The *Concord* was one of the ships in Commodore George Dewey's fleet at the Battle of Manila Bay in the Philippines. Nearby is a boulder with another marker memorializing soldiers, sailors, and marines from Illinois who served in the Spanish-American War. There is no record of why it was placed in the park.

Across town, a smaller Spanish-American War monument stands in Volunteer Park, formerly called City Park. The Park Board renamed the park in 1901 to honor the Washington men who volunteered to join the armed services. Earle K. McNutt, a veteran of that war, donated a pair of plaques crafted from bronze recovered from the battleship USS *Maine*. In 1953, a small group of Spanish-American War veterans, their families, and city and park officials watched a brief dedication ceremony held near the Seattle Asian Art Museum.

The Doughboy

World War I began in August 1914 with Germany, Austria-Hungary, and Turkey fighting against the allies of Great Britain, France, Russia, and Italy. The United States joined the Allies in April 1917, and the fresh American armies turned the tide on the western front and Germany eventually surrendered. As soon as the war ended in November

1918, the United States began to determine how to commemorate the casualties. American Legion posts played a significant role in choosing which type of historical monuments would dominate in the years after "the Great War."[5] Cities debated how to celebrate victory in the face of large numbers of dead and wounded, while organized groups of pacifists wanted to communicate their disillusionment with the cost of war. The national struggle to balance the concept of art versus memorial claimed a victim in local sculptor Alonzo Victor Lewis. He created a piece of work which became the most controversial monument in Seattle's history, a World War I soldier known as "The Doughboy."

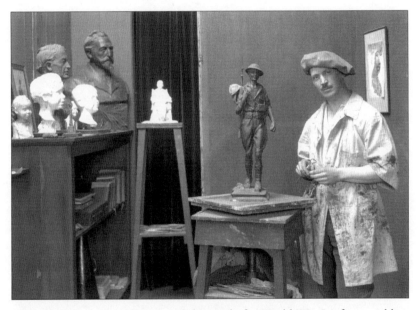

Sculptor Alonzo Victor Lewis with his study for World War I infantry soldier, the Doughboy. *Courtesy of MOHAI, 1974.5923.154.4.*

Born in Logan, Utah, Lewis completed his studies at the Art Institute of Chicago. He worked in New York and Mexico City before arriving in Tacoma in 1914, where he created historical plaques, life-sized historical figures, and exhibited both paintings and sculptures. Lewis was the most well-known sculptor in Washington State when he moved to Seattle in the early 1920s.[6] He proposed massive projects that were never started, including four separate eighteen-foot-high granite busts of George Washington to welcome visitors entering the state at Bellingham, Vancouver, Spokane, and Walla Walla.

The genesis for the Doughboy statue was a study Lewis created for a reunion of the Ninety-First Army Division in 1920. The "Wild West Division" consisted of men representing eight western states who trained at Fort Lewis, near Tacoma. The division shipped to France and fought in the Lorraine, Meuse-Argonne, and Ypres-Lys campaigns. Originally commissioned as a temporary plaster figure, Lewis decided to also use it as a concept for producing a bronze statue.

He spoke to local American Legion posts to determine if they were interested in financing and supporting the project. The original plan for the monument was to erect it on the University of Washington campus, mounted on a large stone surrounded by a field of poppies from a battlefield in Flanders, Belgium. However, as the statue began to take form, the local American Legion post instead suggested placing it at City Hall Park. Mayor Edwin Brown and a small group of representatives of veterans' societies and women's clubs supported the proposal.

Lewis studied the faces, expressions, and thoughts of dozens of Seattle veterans who fought in France. He crafted the fifteen-foot-high statue from three tons of clay and a ton of plaster. When he began to work on it, Lewis called the statue "Bringing Home the Bacon." He based the title and artistic representation of the soldier on an experience common to many of the soldiers. As soldiers shipped out to France, they promised gifts of captured enemy souvenirs to family and girlfriends. After the war was over many downtown stores filled their windows with German helmets, field glasses, mess-kits, Iron Crosses, buttons from the coats of officers, and unexploded shells. Lewis wanted to memorialize the soldiers' satisfaction as they fulfilled their promises by "bringing home the bacon."

The sculpture showed a soldier returning from the enemy's lines, laden with captured German helmets, wearing a smile with his left eye half closed in a wink. "In America, there is a demand for all to forget the war," said the artist. "But I feel that we don't want to forget the war. Rather, we want to forget the horrors of the war. When I started on my American Doughboy, I wanted to portray America's participation in the struggle, America's glorious victory and at the same time, do it with a smile." The torn shirt on the large figure and mud-caked trench shoes demonstrated the victory was not easy. However, the facial expression shows in that brief moment of triumph he has forgotten the suffering he endured.[7]

In the summer of 1928, a full decade after the war's conclusion, Mayor Frank Edwards appointed a citizens' committee to lead a fundraising drive for the statue to serve as a memorial to the First World War. A total of 60,617 Washington men had served in the Army, Navy, Marines, and Coast Guard and 1,642 lost their lives due to action, accidents, and disease. The city initially agreed to pay $50,000 (half from the city, half from private donations) for the statue in 1929 when the economy was good. By 1931, when the memorial was finally ready, the Great Depression had depleted the city's annual budget. The city council offered Lewis only $5,000 in funds that it had already allocated.

Meanwhile, there were a growing number of complaints about both the message and the appearance of the statue.[8] Perspectives of the war had changed, and as time passed, people wanted memorials to focus on the futility of the fighting, not about bringing home enemy souvenirs. Artistic-minded citizens declared the statue might be an appropriate memorial, but it certainly did not qualify as art. Veterans and some civic leaders proclaimed while it might be an excellent work of art, it was not suitable as a war memorial. The Navy lodged complaints that the Doughboy was an Army man and failed to represent the Navy and Marine participation in the war. Veterans and others complained Lewis' soldier carried German helmets over his right shoulder as war trophies.[9] In an attempt to placate the criticism, Lewis renamed the statue "Armistice," while the city proposed a site in the Civic Auditorium Plaza for the memorial.

However, merely changing the name of the statue did not adequately address the protests and concerns from patriotic societies, World War I veterans, and the Park Board. City Councilman Phillip Tindall admitted, "I'm frank to say I don't like the expression of triumph on the Doughboy's face. I don't remember ever seeing a Doughboy come out of the firing line with joy on his face."[10] The smile on the statue represented what critics argued was the expression of a crazed warrior without the vestige of the heroic demeanor of an American soldier.[11] Others suggested he should carry a wreath instead of a rifle. The public furor prevented the city council from finalizing payment to Lewis for the statue.

Eventually, the conflict over the statue ended up in court. Carl Gould, former president of the Art Institute of Seattle and president of the Seattle Fine Arts Society, wrote, "To immortalize this splendid soldier with such a bestial and animal expression is an injustice. While I believe it is most unfortunate that a war memorial has so long been deferred, I cannot subscribe to the theory that something is better than nothing."[12] Lewis filed suit against Gould in Superior Court for $50,000 damages. The complaint stated Lewis' professional standing was damaged, and the failure to sell his statue to the city of Seattle was due to Gould's comments which had inflamed public opinion against him.

The war of words continued in the press. Gould's attorney objected to the complaint on the grounds that Lewis did not provide sufficient facts on which to base the case. The judge agreed and sustained the objection. Knowing his case was almost certainly lost and hoping to regain public support, Lewis dropped the lawsuit. At this point, a decade after beginning to work on the statue, he accepted the initial $5,000 down payment as full compensation for his work. The purchase agreement required that Lewis would remove the German helmets from the sculpture to address criticisms of the statue.

The city made plans to debut the sculpture on May 30, 1932. Crews removed the statue from its storage crate and moved it to the new Civic Center Auditorium (in the current Seattle Center.) The statue's bad luck continued when eleven windows in a nearby apartment building shattered as cannons fired a twenty-one gun salute to celebrate the statue's unveiling. When the organizers removed the draped flags from the statue, the Doughboy still retained the German helmets Lewis had agreed to remove. City Councilman James Scavotto was so enraged he threatened to take off the helmets even if he had to chisel them himself. At the insistence of a couple of council members, a worker removed the German helmets before dedication ceremonies on Armistice Day, November 11, 1932.

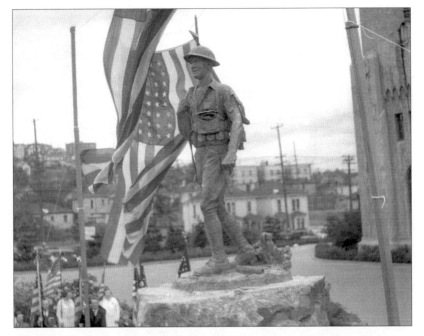

The Doughboy was installed in 1932 in front of the new Civic Auditorium, and now stands in Washelli Cemetery. *Courtesy of MOHAI, Seattle Post-Intelligencer Collection, pi24434.*

Thirty years later in 1961, the much-maligned statue was moved to a new site. The city constructed a new Civic Center/Opera House in preparation for the Century 21 World's Fair and the Doughboy stood in the way. The city relocated it a short distance away to a small landscaped courtyard adjacent to the Veterans' Annex. The statue was not given a raised platform to stand on, so its commanding height was minimized. Surrounded by shrubs, flowers, and trees, it almost disappeared in its remote corner behind the new opera house.

Veterans thought the site was too inconspicuous and argued that the Doughboy was forgotten. In 1970, the statue suffered another indignity when a vandal stole the bayonet from his rifle. The Highline Historical Society proposed in 1983 to move the statue from Seattle Center to near Des Moines, in southern King County. Under the plan, they would relocate the statue to a grove of American elm trees planted in the late 1920s in memory of the 1,200 King County soldiers who died in the First World War. In a mostly symbolic vote, veterans groups vetoed the proposal when they learned the county had allocated $30,000 for the move without notifying anyone; the uproar and bad press stopped the statue from being relocated.

Seattle Center planned to demolish Veterans' Hall in 1998 as part of an expansion plan, after which the Doughboy would no longer be displayed in an appropriate historical or memorial context. Since the city determined there were no other suitable locations on city property for the monument, the statue was declared surplus. This allowed Seattle to enter into an agreement with Washelli Cemetery to provide a new location. Located in the northern part of Seattle on Aurora Avenue, the cemetery is home to the Veterans' Memorial Cemetery, featuring a symmetrical field of simple, marble grave markers. Veterans re-dedicated the Doughboy on November 11, 1998, the eightieth anniversary of the Armistice that ended World War I. The base of the statue is a columbarium, which holds the cremated remains of veterans and their spouses. He still stands there today, overlooking the rows of grave markers and honoring the American infantrymen of the Great War and other conflicts.

The story of the Doughboy illustrates how public perspectives can change over time, and that this can affect how a monument is cared for, maintained, and even where it is located. The initial perception of the smiling soldier frivolously collecting war souvenirs committed the statue to years of conflict and even banishment out of Seattle city limits. Questions of artistic merit and the stylistic choices of the artist enter the public conversation of how the monument represents the subject of the memorial. While intended to become permanent fixtures of the landscape, monuments can be forgotten, like the Hiker, now in a quiet corner of a park; vandalized, like the Battle of Seattle Boulder; relocated, like the Doughboy; or, like the Woodland Zoo's Harding Memorial monument, destroyed.

CHAPTER 8

GREAT DEPRESSION, MODEST MONUMENTS

The Roaring Twenties gave way to the Great Depression soon after the stock market crash of October 1929, when plunging stock prices wiped out millions of investors. Throughout the early years of the 1930s, consumer spending and investment fell, leading to declines in factory production and rising unemployment as failing companies laid off workers. In Seattle, job losses were modest during the first year of the Depression, but soon banks failed, stores closed, and the numbers of unemployed surged with more than one-third of adults in Seattle out of work. Lost jobs quickly turned into lost homes; poverty and homelessness spread across the city. By 1931, a large encampment of shacks called "Hooverville" after President Herbert Hoover, who was in office at the start of the Depression, spread across industrial acreage south of downtown Seattle.

The economic situation halted the funding for large statues like Washington, Seward, McGraw, the Hiker, and the Doughboy. The city was able to dedicate a large granite and bronze monument to Judge Thomas Burke at the beginning of 1930, but only because organizers had raised funds before the start of the Depression. Fewer resources and funds resulted in smaller and less expensive plaques and busts that often honored local civic leaders. In this decade, the people who brought Seattle its water, power, baseball, and religion received their modest recognition at various locations throughout the city.

Judge Thomas Burke

In Volunteer Park, hidden behind some shrubs between the old water tower and the reservoir, is a large monument dedicated to Judge Thomas Burke. Large male and female figures carved in granite flank a bronze relief of Burke with marble inlays representing the West Coast

89

and Asia set into the floor. Created by American sculptor Hermon MacNeil at the cost of $50,000 and dedicated April 5, 1930, it honored a central figure in the political and economic life of Washington State and Seattle.[1] Immediately after Burke's death in 1925, city leaders personally subscribed funds to build a heroic public monument for the man who led the quest for a railroad link to the east and developed friendly trading ties with Asian countries across the Pacific.

Burke arrived in Seattle in 1875 as a young attorney. During the 1880s, logging and coal mining were the primary local industries and Burke saw the need for a major railroad line in Seattle to provide access to eastern markets. In 1885, a group of twelve Seattle investors, led by Burke and Daniel Gilman, began to develop a local railroad, the Seattle, Lake Shore, and Eastern Railway (SLS&E) from Seattle through the Cascade Mountains to Spokane. It was never fully completed, but it did help Seattle become a center of Puget Sound commerce.[2] It also brought Burke to the attention of James J. Hill, the man leading the Great Northern Railway from Minnesota across the northern plains to Washington State.

While the SLS&E went bankrupt in 1896, Hill was impressed with the work and skills of Burke, and hired him as his Seattle attorney. Burke successfully represented the railroad in court and defeated numerous challenges to the waterfront concessions of land and rights-of-way Seattle gave to the Great Northern. Many people felt that Burke supported Hill at the expense of Seattle's interests. As Roger Sale wrote in *Seattle, Past to Present*, "The moment he became Hill's agent, he assumed unblinkingly that what was good for the Great Northern was good for Seattle."[3] Burke seemed unwilling to recognize that Hill needed Seattle's harbor and population as much as Seattle needed Hill's railroad.

Burke retired in 1902 and devoted himself to managing his properties and public affairs. During his fifty years in Seattle, he was constantly in the public eye and vocally supported or opposed nearly every prominent public issue.[4] Andrew Carnegie asked Burke in 1910 to act as a trustee of the Carnegie Endowment for International Peace. This was one of Burke's most important causes during the remaining years of his life.[5]

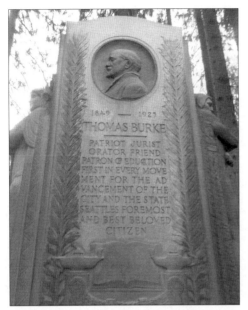

Hidden behind trees in Volunteer Park is a monument to Thomas Burke dedicated in 1930. *Courtesy of the author.*

The sculptor Hermon MacNeil worked two years on the Burke monument in studios both in Germany and America. The first two donations for the memorial came from Theodore Haller, a lawyer who trained as a clerk in Burke's office and donated $1,000, and Naoa Kako, a laborer who gave two dollars. Kako was the first of 215 Japanese and Japanese-Americans living in Washington State who donated a combined $1,100 to the fund with an additional $4,000 contributed from Japan. Burke was a strong supporter of Japan and testified favorably before the U.S. House of Representatives in 1920 regarding immigration from that country.

The memorial's center column, with two figures carved on either side, is a solid, nineteen-ton piece of granite. The artist described his intent: "The gigantic male figure on the right, holding the implements of construction, typifies his [Burke's] power when he came into this young town, saw the things which needed to be done and led the work himself," he wrote. "The calm sturdy female figure on the left typifies the higher, finer things he strove for—peace, culture, and understanding. The dolphin at her feet represents the international relations with the Orient, for which he strove."[6]

Judge Burke participated in the 1905 ceremonies when the first historical plaques were dedicated around Pioneer Square and the Chief Seattle statue in 1909. He also led the fund-raising subscriptions for the James J. Hill bust and William H. Seward figure at the A-Y-P Exposition. As Burke was leading the search for sculptors for those statues, he sat next to the artist at a banquet, and remarked, "Mr. MacNeil, I want you to make a monument for us someday."[7] Little did Burke know then that the monument was to be his own.

Water and Power: Luther B. Youngs and James Delmage (J. D.) Ross

Just a few feet away from the Burke Memorial, attached to the side of the old Volunteer Park water tower by the entrance to the internal stairway, is a plaque dedicated to a superintendent of the Seattle Water Department, **Luther B. Youngs**. In the 1890s the city faced a contest over the future of its water supply; a private company wanted to develop a Cedar River water source, but many citizens favored a publicly-owned utility. Municipal ownership won the day, and supporters quickly followed up on their victory with a new city charter in 1896 that provided the water department with its own superintendent rather than leadership from a member of the Board of Public Works.

Luther Youngs had worked in the department for just over a year when the new charter was signed. Mayor Frank D. Black appointed Youngs to the new superintendent position, and later mayors extended his tenure. Youngs served from 1895 to 1923, longer than anyone else in the history of the water department or its successor, Seattle Public Utilities. During those decades, Youngs developed and expanded both the Cedar River supply system and the system of reservoirs, pumps, and water mains that delivered water throughout the growing city. The plaque is two feet by three feet in size and bears an engraved likeness of Youngs. The Water Department purchased and placed the tablet in Volunteer Park in 1930 with the approval of the city council.

Seattle City Light also commissioned a plaque for a longtime superintendent, **J. D. Ross**, in 1935. Ross arrived in Seattle at the turn of the century after failing to strike gold in the Klondike. He initially worked for private electric utility companies and founded his own electrical business but soon was employed as Seattle's assistant city engineer.

In 1902, Seattle voted to build a municipal hydroelectric power plant on the Cedar River. Ross walked into the city engineer's office with his own blueprints and proposed to design and build the new facility. After the completion of the power plant, he turned it over to the water department for ongoing management. Within a few years, it became apparent the department could not adequately manage both water and power, so a separate utility agency, later called Seattle City Light, was created. After the first superintendent left, the city selected Ross to fill the position, and he stayed with City Light for the rest of his life.

"Monuments and medals are usually for the dead, but we want to honor Mr. Ross while he is alive," said P. C. Trotter, president of the Rainier Heights Commercial Club, in announcing plans for the plaque. "We feel [our club] should sponsor this action because Mr. Ross is a member of our club, a friend, and a neighbor for many years in the Rainier Heights district."[8] James A. Wehn designed the bronze medallion in the likeness of Ross and the club mounted it on its new City Light Building at Third and Madison Avenue in 1935. The building has since been sold, and the medallion's location is unknown.

Will Rogers

While not a local Seattle personality, Will Rogers was recognized with two memorials because of a tragic accident that took his life shortly after a visit to the city. Rogers was one of America's most famous personalities in the 1920s and '30s. He was a performer, humorist, newspaper columnist, social commentator, and actor. In August 1935, he traveled to Seattle and joined Wiley Post, who two years earlier had been the first man to fly solo around the world. They planned to journey to Alaska as a precursor to a long distance flight across the Soviet Union to Europe. The two spent several days making test flights out of the Renton airport.

Large Seattle crowds celebrated Rogers at numerous events and followed him wherever he went. He stayed at the Olympic Hotel and city leaders introduced him to a cheering audience at a banquet held in his honor. Since Rogers also loved to play polo, he drove out to the Olympic Riding and Driving Club north of Seattle near Lake City for a game with local players. The visit to Seattle ended with a crowd cheering Rogers and Post as they departed from Lake Washington by seaplane on their way to Alaska.

As they flew north to Fairbanks, Alaska, Rogers wrote stories about the trip on a typewriter balanced on his knees. On August 15, 1935, they left Fairbanks for Point Barrow, Alaska. Unsure of their location and flying in bad weather, Post landed the plane on an inlet near Wallapi Point, twelve miles short of Point Barrow. They asked a Native who was fishing there for directions to Barrow. He pointed in the correct direction, and Rogers and Post took off. The plane climbed one hundred feet before it tipped and crashed into the water, killing them both.

The entire nation mourned the passing of one of its favorite personalities. Seattle was determined to honor the last mainland departure point of the famed humorist by erecting a memorial at the polo grounds where he played his final game. On July 26, 1936, polo enthusiasts and admirers unveiled a monument and dedicated the Will Rogers Memorial Field at the Olympic Riding and Driving Club. The sculptor, Alonzo Victor Lewis, told the crowd he previously completed two studies of Abraham Lincoln and with the Rogers bronze, he never before had found a face so resembling the spirit of Lincoln in simplicity, kindliness, and humor.[9]

Within two decades, the growing city expanded northward, and developers planned to turn the polo club into housing developments. The monument was in danger of being bulldozed and forgotten. Popular *Post-Intelligencer* sports columnist Royal Brougham wrote an article in 1952 remembering the Rogers visit and telling the story of the impending destruction of the memorial. After reading the article, fans of the humorist formed a committee to find a new location. The trustees of the Lakeside School volunteered a site on campus which was not far from the riding club. The Lake Washington Saddle Club offered to locate the monument at Bridle Trails State Park. Others suggested the University of Washington campus, the Arboretum, or the Museum of History and Industry.

It took a few years, but by 1966 the Parks and Public Grounds Committee of the City Council selected Lake City for the location of the memorial. The president of the Lake City Community Center,

Frank O'Brien, told council members several Lake City civic groups would participate in the removal and permanent care without requiring any city funds. Work crews moved the concrete spire and base, and the monument stands today adjacent to the Lake City Community Center and Library at Twenty-eighth Avenue Northeast near Northeast 125th Street. The plaque on the memorial states:

> *On this field Will Rogers took his last ride—shrines erected by the world will commemorate his passing, but none could be more hallowed than this little patch of ground where the kindly, chuckling, hard-riding cowboy played his last game of polo. Before he went roaring to his last round-up, we still hear his cheery haloo as with broad grin on weathered-lined face he urged his pony into the thick of play. To the spirit of a mighty adventurer, hail and farewell.*

Less than a year after the original dedication at the polo grounds, an additional marker honoring Will Rogers and Wiley Post was dedicated at Boeing Field on March 30, 1937. Alonzo Victor Lewis created the bronze plaque and John C. Stevenson, a former county commissioner, presented it to King County. Stevenson proudly declared that a long list of donors had paid for it with contributions of not more than twenty-five cents each. One of those was eight-year-old Maurice Alvin Mahugh of Oroville, Washington. He wrote a letter to the county treasurer reading, "Here's my bit for the Post-Rogers fund. This is all I have." In the envelope were three pennies.[10] The commissioners placed the plaque in the Boeing Field administration building, but the marker is now missing.

Grandfathers of Seattle Baseball: Daniel E. Dugdale, Emil Sick, and Jack Lelivelt

Three men who ensured that baseball would become a permanent fixture for local sports fans had bas-relief plaques dedicated in their honor. The first was **Daniel E. Dugdale**, who arrived in Seattle in 1898, before baseball was even a sandlot game, and ended up having two baseball fields named after him. In his career, he played for twenty different baseball teams and even purchased a stake in a local team in Peoria, Illinois. After three years there, he gave it all up to travel to Seattle with an eye to joining the crowds heading to the Klondike gold rush. However, he remained in Seattle, invested in real estate, and used those funds to get back into baseball. He founded his own team, which he appropriately named the Klondikers.

Other Seattle teams followed: the Braves, Siwashes, Turks, and Giants. With baseball fever sweeping the city, Dugdale built a stadium in the Rainier Valley neighborhood in 1913 and named it after himself. On July 4, 1932, a serial arsonist set a fire in the stands and burned it to the ground. Two years later, Dugdale died, struck by a Seattle City Light truck as he crossed the street. An estimated 4,500 fans attended his memorial, Dugdale Night, held by the Seattle Indians at Civic Field with music and a parade of the American Legion drum and bugle corps. With Dugdale gone, the team playing in an ill-suited temporary stadium, and the Depression tightening its grip, baseball in Seattle was in danger of disappearing.[11] **Emil Sick**, the owner of the Rainier Brewery, rescued the Indians by purchasing the team in 1937 and immediately built a new stadium on the ashes of the Dugdale stadium site. He changed the name of the team to the Rainiers, and the new facility became known as Sick's Stadium.

Local sports fans applauded the idea of honoring Dugdale with a plaque and consulted with sculptor Alonzo Victor Lewis. With Sick's Stadium complete and the Rainiers in contention for the Pacific Coast League pennant, the time was right, and a location in the new stadium was available. Sports fans also proposed an additional marker for Emil Sick and turned again to Lewis for its design. On September 7, 1939, as a part of the Golden Jubilee celebration of Washington's statehood, the team featured fireworks and speeches at the Rainiers versus San Francisco Seals game. The team unveiled the plaques of Dugdale and Sick in front of the cheering crowd.

One year later, the team added a third plaque crafted by Lewis at Sick's Stadium. **Jack Lelivelt**, who managed the Rainiers in their successful 1938 to 1940 seasons, was one of the great hitters and managers of minor-league baseball. In a career lasting from 1906 to 1940, Lelivelt had a batting average of .328 over 20 seasons, including 347 games in the major leagues. After managing Pacific Coast League rivals the Los Angeles Angels, he accepted an offer from Emil Sick to lead the Rainiers. In 1940 the Rainiers finished in first place with a record of 112–66 and defeated the Angels in the playoffs. The location of all three of the plaques is unknown, but a private collector owns two of the original plaster molds.

21st Century Baseball Icon

The only Seattle baseball player to be honored with a statue, Ken Griffey Jr. was the first Mariner to be inducted into the Baseball Hall of Fame in Cooperstown, New York, and the first player to have his jersey number retired by the team. The seven-foot tall bronze statue at the front entrance to Safeco Field was unveiled in 2017. Artist Lou Cella sculpted the player frozen at the end of a home-run swing, wearing his 1997 uniform, which was the year Griffey was named the American League Most Valuable Player.

Reverend Dr. Mark Matthews

The Reverend Dr. Mark Matthews integrated religion into the social and political life of the city over the first four decades of the twentieth century. Originally from Georgia, he arrived in Seattle at the age of thirty-four, with long, flowing hair and a six-and-one-half-foot frame. Like many of his evangelical peers, Matthews preached an idea of cities as "righteous kingdoms," which religion could cleanse of vice, poverty, and exploitation. Seattle put his beliefs to the test; it was a time of rampant lawlessness, and many social needs went unmet. Matthews led the First Presbyterian Church for 38 years, from 1902 to 1940. He built his congregation into the denomination's largest in the United States, with nearly 10,000 members.

Matthews was often egotistical and irascible and he loved to fight for what he deemed righteous causes. His reputation in Seattle relied as much on that fighting spirit as it did for his evangelical work in the church. Occasionally, criminals threatened him and his family so he purchased pistols and kept them close in his desk. He led many social projects including institutions such as the Seattle Day Nursery, which evolved into Childhaven, and helped to establish Harborview Hospital. He also took controversial positions including supporting prohibition and opposing women's suffrage. His colorful career reflected many of the significant social, political, and religious forces at work in Seattle.[12]

Matthews passed away in 1940, and the search began for an appropriate location for a memorial to the religious leader and his long career. A committee from the First Presbyterian Church suggested a spot in Volunteer Park, but the Park Board had a different idea. They wanted not only to choose a place for Matthews' memorial but also to designate a "Memorial Lane" to provide a location for statues of other civic leaders at Denny Park between downtown and Lake Union. The committee selected Alonzo Victor Lewis to sculpt the life-sized bust, and he declared the site as a "very appropriate, graceful spot."[13] On February 8, 1942, Dr. Matthews' widow unveiled the bronze memorial. The city never implemented the idea for a lane of statuary to other civic leaders, so the Reverend Dr. Matthews bust sits alone facing Denny Avenue.

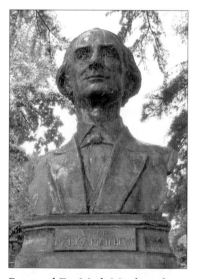

And so, a decade dominated by the Great Depression came to a close. A monument to Judge Thomas Burke was the only large memorial to be dedicated during the 1930s. Smaller, more affordable plaques and busts of local men who brought Seattle water, power, baseball, and religion were dedicated. A nationally-known humorist departed Seattle on his final flight and was remembered in granite and bronze. Soon, however, attention would turn to the sacrifices of local men and women who would fight and die in the Second World War.

Reverend Dr. Mark Matthews bust in the south section of Denny Park. *Courtesy of the author.*

CHAPTER 9

MEMORIALIZING THE SECOND WORLD WAR

The economic carnage of the Great Depression in the 1930s sowed the seeds for the spread of global totalitarianism. Adolf Hitler and the Nazis rose to power in Germany and rearmed while occupying Austria and Czechoslovakia. Benito Mussolini and his Fascist followers in Italy consolidated power and transformed their rule into a dictatorship, occupying Libya and Ethiopia. Japanese militarists invaded Manchuria and China and jealously eyed other possessions in Asia. As China suffered under Japanese occupation and Europe moved closer to war, the U.S. Congress supported an official policy of American neutrality.

America's isolationism ended abruptly after the Japanese attacked U.S. military bases in Pearl Harbor, Hawaii, on December 7, 1941. The next day, America was officially at war with Japan, and on December 11 declared war on Germany. The attack had an immediate effect on Seattle as the West Coast appeared vulnerable to a Japanese invasion. Preparations for war began as men volunteered for the armed services and local shipyards and factories ramped up production of airplanes, ships, and armaments.

Wars require enormous amounts of money to arm and fight. The United States spent nearly $300 billion on the conflict. To finance the war the U.S. Treasury sold Americans a series of war bonds. Posters, radio programs, and a live touring show of movie and radio stars traveled around the country publicizing the bond drives. Within a few months after the start of the war, a group of Seattle's leading citizens— the Victory Square Committee—created a public space downtown to hold rallies for bond drives and to memorialize local casualties.

Victory Square

The patriotically named Victory Square was located on University Street between Fourth and Fifth Avenues in front of the Olympic Hotel and the Metropolitan Theater. The theater has since been demolished, and the space it occupied is now the main entry to the Fairmont Olympic Hotel. The blockaded street had two sections dedicated to fundraising and remembrance. On the west end of the block by Fourth Avenue stood a replica of President Thomas Jefferson's home, Monticello; it functioned as a stage for speakers and dignitaries. On the other end of the block, near Fifth Avenue, stood a seventy-foot-high replica of the Washington Monument, made from plywood, with an eternal flame burning in an urn placed in front of the memorial. The Victory Square committee recorded the growing list of King County war dead on the monument.

An enormous crowd dedicated Victory Square on Saturday, May 2, 1942. The first five months of the war were mostly defeats and reversals for the American and other Allied forces. The successful Doolittle bombing raid on Tokyo two weeks earlier had been the sole piece of good news so far. A U.S. Army band rode on a truck through the downtown streets playing patriotic music to attract crowds to the square. Additional trucks crowded with cheering sailors followed behind. Famous opera singer John Charles Thomas, in town for a concert, sang the national anthem. Speakers urged the audience to buy war bonds to support their soldiers, sailors, marines, and airmen.

A few days later U.S. Navy Secretary Frank Knox visited Seattle and spoke to another large crowd at Victory Square. He praised the local contributors saying: "No city has a greater role to play in the war than Seattle." He was the first of many national dignitaries and celebrities to visit. Bond rallies featured visiting actors Bing Crosby, Betty Grable, and Lana Turner, and comedian Bob Hope appeared numerous times. Nationally known bandleaders and their musicians performed for the crowds. The entertainers attracted audiences who purchased millions of dollars of war bonds each year.[1]

To continue to rally public support, the federal government designated July 17, 1942, as American Heroes Day. As a part of the national holiday, Seattle held a ceremony at Victory Square to honor its first fatalities of the war. The committee mailed invitations to relatives of the first forty casualties listed on the memorial. Later that fall, the Armistice Day rally in November was the largest gathering to date. Active duty service members and local veterans marched into Victory Square carrying banners and flags as patriotic music echoed between the buildings. The mood changed from celebratory to somber as a lone bugler played taps, and names of servicemen who perished in earlier battles were added to the memorial. The towering white monument and the growing list of war dead on its face were a constant reminder of the war.

The tempo of the war increased throughout 1943. Land and naval campaigns rolled across North Africa, Sicily, and Italy. Boeing B-17 Flying Fortress bombers made in Seattle raided German targets in continental Europe. Landings and naval battles took place in Guadalcanal, New Guinea, and other islands in the South Pacific. The committee continued to hold fundraising activities at Victory Square. Movie star Barbara Stanwyck sold bonds and signed autographs on April 28. A group of young women called "Minute Maids" (after the famed Minutemen of the Revolutionary War) sold war bonds on May 23. Youth from farms in rural King County gathered at Victory Square to celebrate Farm Day on June 28 to recognize the agricultural contributions to the war effort. Throughout the year, volunteers continued to add names of the dead to the memorial.

The United States and other Allies prepared to invade Nazi-held France in 1944. Even though the Allies had not yet defeated the enemy, some people began to discuss what type of memorial would be appropriate to commemorate the end of the war. Should it be a building suitable for public use, or a monument set in a public square or park? The *Seattle Daily Times* editorialized: "We want no half-baked architectural or sculptured monstrosity to express our community's gratitude to its heroes, living and dead. It must have dignity, beauty, and permanence, to record our gratitude in enduring and visible form. It is a job to be performed by a public-spirited committee of unquestioned good taste and judgment, and that committee should be put to work without delay."[2]

While this request for thoughtful planning and community input led to initial discussions, the war continued to drag on, and the sides of the memorial continued to fill with the names of those who would not return home.

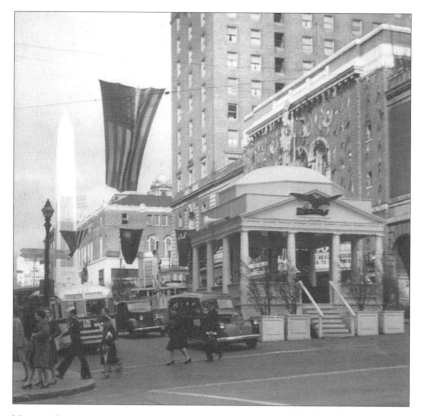

Victory Square, University Street between Fourth and Fifth Avenues. *Courtesy of the Seattle Public Library #20039.*

Bond sales continued into May 1944 with two different events held at Victory Square. At the beginning of the month, the American Legion Auxiliary and the Women's War Savings League sponsored a "Buy a Bond for Baby" campaign and launched a new organization called "The Cradle Roll of Honor" for children under fourteen years of age. Parents and grandparents were encouraged to purchase war bonds in the names of their young family members. Two weeks later on Mothers' Day, state, civic, and patriotic groups paid respect to the mothers of men and women in uniform. Officers of the women's branches of the armed services escorted Gold Star mothers to the portico of Victory Square, where they could look up at the names of their sons and daughters inscribed on the white memorial.

When the shaft had first been placed in Victory Square, a passing police officer reprimanded a boy named William Westlake for scribbling on the monument. As he erased his name from the memorial, he declared to the officer, "Someday I'll be a hero, and my name will be up there." He was so eager to join the war effort that within a year he lied about his age and enlisted in the Marine Corps. After serving nine months, PFC William Westlake died in action in the South Pacific. His mother was informed of his death, at the age of fifteen, on a remote island thousands of miles from Seattle in late 1944, and his name was added to the memorial.[3]

Westlake's name would not be the last to be placed on the memorial. In September 1944, 225 more names were added to the pylon, increasing the total to 525. There were delays in receiving up-to-date casualty lists from the armed forces, so the list grew longer as the dead from battles in Western Europe, Italy, the Philippines, and Pacific battlefields were added. Winter 1944–45 slowly passed, and the hope that the Allies would defeat the Nazis by Christmas evaporated as the Germans counterattacked in December during the Battle of the Bulge. January and February saw the Allies slowly push through cold and icy battlefields toward the German border. Through the winter months, Victory Square looked sad and run-down. Flowers left by mourners soon withered and gave the memorial a "forlorn appearance" according to a *Seattle Times* columnist.[4]

The German armies finally collapsed under the weight of the Allied troops, and the war in Europe ended on May 7, 1945, V-E (Victory in Europe) Day. Later that month, an additional 465 names were added to the pylon. Germany was defeated, but the fight against Japan continued, and the U.S. suffered enormous losses during the battle for the island of Okinawa. The Memorial Day observance was solely dedicated to the men carrying on the fight in the Pacific; six children placed memorial wreaths at the foot of the monument that now bore their fathers' names.

American soldiers of Norwegian descent were recognized at a Victory Square program in late June. Ingre Stang, seven-year-old daughter of the Norwegian consul, dressed in a brightly embroidered peasant costume, placed a wreath of flowers as a color guard escorted her forward. Bond sales totaled nearly $1.5 million, making it one of the biggest fundraising days of the year. The following month, thousands of spectators lined Second and Third Avenues in Seattle to watch the Independence Day parade. Admiral Marc Mitscher, the commander of a Pacific naval fleet, led 7,500 service members in the parade, their units interspersed with floats and military equipment. Afterward, a memorial program attracted hundreds of spectators to Victory Square.

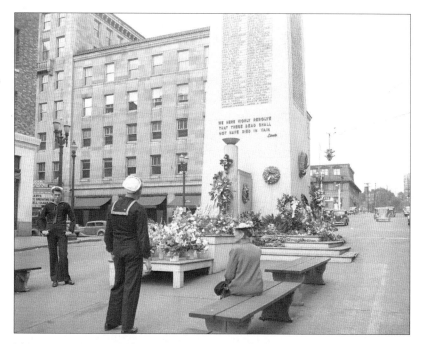

The Victory Square obelisk, where more than 1,000 names would be added before World War II ended. *Courtesy of MOHAI, Seattle Post-Intelligencer Collection, pi23390.*

A little over one month later, the United States dropped two atomic bombs on the Japanese cities of Hiroshima and Nagasaki. Japan surrendered on August 14, 1945, V-J (Victory over Japan) Day, and the long struggle of the Second World War was finally over. Victory Square, which for three years and three months had hosted fundraising drives and served as a memorial, was the focus of an immense Victory Day celebration. The District Coast Guard Band and the Jive Bombers jazz band from the Naval Air Station at Sand Point played to the crowd.

The people surrounding the memorial that day radiated a mixture of joy, sorrow, and compassion. The crowd parted as an older couple approached the monument to lay a wreath at the base for their son, killed in 1944. Lieutenant Douglas Lemmel was twenty-five years old when he perished in a plane crash on the last day of training as an Army Air Force pilot. His father, Laurence, smiled with hopefulness as he faced the crowd and spoke, "We're so doubly happy today. The mothers next door will not have to go through what we had." As the ceremony wound down, William Devin, then Seattle's mayor, laid the last wreath of the war at the foot of the memorial. "There are still 80 names to be added," Jerry Ross, master of ceremonies, said of the pylon's 1,041 names of Seattle war dead. "We hope they will be the last."[5]

Celebration soon turned to concern for the future of the temporary memorial and how Seattle would remember its war fatalities. The *Seattle Daily Times* editorial board suggested keeping the monument in the current location, "Victory Square seems a logical place for such a memorial. A civic committee should be named without too much delay to consider this question, to decide upon the nature of the memorial and to make plans for its construction."[6]

Within a week, the Seattle Civic Arts Committee submitted a proposal. They suggested a new, permanent Victory Square, one block east of the temporary memorial, occupying University Street from Sixth Avenue to Eighth Avenue (now Freeway Park with Interstate 5 running underneath). With a $400,000 budget, the monument would occupy eight city lots of prime downtown real estate and feature another seventy-five-foot-tall column with a memorial chamber at its base. Inside would be tablets bearing the names of King County members of the armed services who lost their lives. George Stoddard, Seattle architect and a member of the Victory Square committee, presented the downtown plan: "Such a memorial should be located where the public can rub elbows with it." The committee estimated 75 percent of Seattle would want to keep the memorial where it was and make it permanent.[7]

The following day, favorable reactions to the plan appeared in the newspapers. Many supported the central location of the memorial where it would be visible to downtown visitors. PFC Ross Steele of the Army Air Forces said, "It would stand there for years and years as a constant reminder of the cost of war." Anthon Videtto, a Navy sailor from the Puget Sound Navy Yard in Bremerton, agreed, "There should be such a monument, right in the city where everyone could see it plainly so we will remember." Ruby Gilbert of Seattle said, "I am in favor of a Victory Square monument. I think it should be beautiful, and a place where people would want to go. It would be a constant reminder that we paid very dearly for the freedom we enjoy."[8]

Others were not so sure of the plans. Some doubted the estimated cost of $400,000 and believed it would be at least a half-million dollars plus ongoing maintenance costs. After years of rationing, deprivation, and purchasing war bonds, the thought of paying for a vast and grandiose memorial was troubling. Some citizens thought if money were spent on a monument maybe it should be for something that the public could use. Mrs. L. E. Pealer, whose husband served in Europe, said, "Something to help the living. It should be something that will always make us remember what they died for. It might be a park, or it might be something else, but whatever it is it should be useful."[9]

For some, especially those whose loved ones were listed on the memorial, Victory Square was sacred ground. Some families never had the opportunity to bury their deceased who were never recovered or interred overseas. They wondered if a new memorial elsewhere would have the same sentimental appeal.[10] Mrs. Nora Burton of Seattle wrote a letter to the editor of the *Seattle Daily Times*:

> I lost two beloved sons in this last war, and I think the new Pylon should be erected right there in Victory Square. That piece of ground is sacred with the blood of our sons and should be kept a very sacred spot in the heart of our city. The Pylon is the only grave that many of our boys will ever have. One of my sons went to his death in a flaming plane into the Baltic Sea. We who are left to remember need some place to go. I keep flowers beside my sons' pictures all the time, but on special days, I, and others like me, need a special place to take our flowers, just as anyone would want to visit the grave of a loved one. Let us have the Pylon right there at Victory Square where our sons pledged their lives.[11]

Even as the memorial remained a focal point for grief and loss, two names on the memorial returned from the war very much alive. Carefully holding back their emotions, Cratie and Ethel McGuire watched as their son, William, removed his name from the pylon. McGuire was a sailor aboard the battleship USS *California* when the Japanese attacked Pearl Harbor on December 7, 1941. When the order was given to abandon ship, an officer ordered McGuire to transfer to the tug *Vireo* and help care for the wounded. Due to a misunderstanding, the Navy listed him as missing in action. Therefore, he ended up on several casualty lists, and the committee added his name to the memorial.

Hazel Bailey received word her husband, Marine Technical Sergeant Vincent Bailey, whom she believed was dead, was still alive. Bailey, a former Ballard High School student, removed his name from the memorial with assistance from his daughter. "It's too bad that more boys can't return and remove their names from the pylon," said Russell Young, chair of the Victory Square committee as he supervised the removal of McGuire's and Bailey's names.[12]

Even though there was strong public support for making Victory Square permanent, many people objected to keeping the memorial in its original location. They thought the street was too narrow to accommodate a larger monument with an attached structure where the names could be listed. A suggested smaller replica of the pylon mounted on an arch over the street with the names inscribed on the pillars of the arch gained little public support.[13] Another objection came from businesses located in the block. During the war, they had endured traffic jams that choked off the entrance to their places of business three or four times a week. They were worried a permanent memorial would become a rallying point for every civic affair all year long and thus reduce their income.[14]

However, the largest obstacle was that the memorial was located on state-owned land belonging to the University of Washington. They, in turn, had leased the property to the Metropolitan Building Company until 1954. The UW Board of Regents regretfully refused to allow the placement of a permanent war memorial. Quoted in the *Seattle Daily Times*, the regents stated "that compliance with your request would constitute a deviation from the terms of the lease and thus require legislative action."[15] The Victory Square committee rejected this argument and considered seeking the approval from the state legislature. Unfortunately, the legislature would not meet for several months, and there was no guarantee they would vote to reduce the valuable land holdings, which provided significant financial support for the university.

In the meantime, individuals, veterans' groups, the media, and representatives of the newly formed War Memorial Committee suggested various alternate locations. The Bon Marché department store offered $1,000 in prizes for the best suggestion. Among the many proposals were: a memorial Olympic Boulevard near the Civic Auditorium (the current McCaw Hall in Seattle Center); a tower and beacon similar to San Francisco's Coit Tower on the cliff at Duwamish Head in West Seattle; and a memorial hall in the rotunda of the proposed Seattle Historical Museum.

As the committee continued to meet, and newspapers published editorials and letters, the wet and soggy weather exerted a toll on the plywood construction of the Victory Square memorial. By spring 1946, the paint was peeling and the "everlasting flame" had been extinguished. Dust and pollution from passing cars, buses, and trucks soiled the flags on the memorial. In a letter to the editor of the *Seattle Daily Times*, Patrick O'Reardon noted, "A nameplate of one of our honored dead has fallen from the south face of the pylon." He enclosed ten dollars to start "a fund for the painting and repair of the pylon and for the placing of flowers at Christmas-time."[16]

Public outcry about the memorial's declining condition led to small improvements. In February 1948, officials of the Veterans of Foreign Wars donated six new flags. In May, the Junior Chamber of Commerce sponsored a "Cleanup-Fixup-Paintup Week." The next month saw the addition of a niche on the west face of the column, a few feet above the ground, to shelter flowers left by relatives and friends, and crews removed the urn for the flame. The Metropolitan Building Company donated the work to soften public perception of their decision to not allow the permanent memorial to remain on their property.

The wooden pylon was so rotten it was in danger of collapsing, and it needed repairs to survive the winter of 1948–49. The city spent $2,000 for new plywood to shore it up. Just three months later, Mayor Devin's War Memorial Committee had the structure torn down. Where inspiring music and speeches had mingled with tearful prayers and sacred memories, hammers and wrecking bars now dismantled the memorial.

There were no ceremonies to mark the end of the Victory Square memorial. The nameplates from the pylon were stored in the official city vault. A remembrance plaque was placed in 1949 on the White-Henry-Stuart Building at Fourth Avenue and University Street. When a developer demolished the building in 1974, it took workers ninety minutes to pry the bronze plaque from the corner where it had been attached for thirty years. The plaque was moved to the Rainier Square underground concourse between Fourth Avenue and Two Union Square where it remains today.

The stirring scenes staged at Victory Square to support the war effort and remember the men and women of Seattle who made the ultimate sacrifice faded into memory.[17] Plans for three competing memorials precipitated Victory Square's demise: High School Memorial Stadium in Seattle Center, a memorial in the Veterans' Cemetery at Washelli, and a plaza in the new Seattle Public Safety Building.

High School Memorial Stadium

Not quite a year after the war was over, a group of eighteen civic and business leaders met with Mayor Devin to plan a permanent war memorial. One possible site was the new High School Memorial Stadium under construction at Civic Field (the current Seattle Center.) The city deeded the nine-acre site to the school district for one dollar with a restriction that the district would return the property to the city when it no longer needed it for athletics. When school district and city officials dedicated the new stadium in November 1947, Superintendent Samuel Fleming announced that it would be a living memorial, "dedicated to the memory of boys who have made the supreme sacrifice for their country in World War II."[18] Everyone in the crowd knew someone who had fought in the war, and many communities around the country constructed war memorials to provide solemn locations for citizens to process their feelings of loss and grief.[19]

The initial plans for the memorial called for a large concrete pylon at the east entrance to the stadium. Names of the war dead that had been at Victory Square would be cast in bronze and placed on the permanent memorial. The idea of a solemn memorial at a noisy stadium where schools played local football games was controversial. The mayor's committee was divided over the appropriateness of the stadium memorial, but in the end, committed themselves to the project.[20]

The memorial project moved ahead with a design contest open to Seattle students. The winner was Marianne Hansen, from Garfield High School; judges selected her submission from sixty entries. Her design replaced the initial pylon idea with twenty-four limestone slabs and fountains featuring an inscription across the top of the wall: "Youth hold high your torch of truth, justice and tolerance lest their sacrifice be forgotten." In 1951, the city and school district dedicated the memorial as an addition to the east end of the stadium; Hansen stood in front of the crowd and cut the ribbon to unveil the shrine. Etched into slabs are the names of 762 young men from Seattle who never returned. Listed on this memorial are the war's dead who had graduated from Seattle high schools; other King County names from the Victory Square memorial were not included.

By the late 1980s, the stadium and memorial were falling into disrepair. An overgrown hedge covered some of the names. The lights were broken, and the approach became an empty parking lot. Garbage filled the dry fountains and planter boxes stretching the length of the memorial. Transients sometimes slept behind the hedge, hidden from view. Over the years, the city discussed plans to transform the space into an entrance for the Seattle Center with an underground parking garage.

World War II veterans stood firm against plans to remove the stadium, calling the stadium and memorial wall a sacred place. In 1989, veteran and activist Guy Gallipeau led a march on City Hall to successfully protest the demolition. However, the stadium and memorial continued to deteriorate, and the World War II veterans who cared most about the monument began to pass away as the "greatest generation" aged. "No one remembers anything about it anymore," a frustrated Gallipeau said in 2006. "That part of our history will be lost, and that is too bad. I would hate to see it torn down, but if it is just going to deteriorate, then maybe we should just let it go."[21] Today, the stadium hosts high school football games, women's professional soccer, and adult recreational leagues. The memorial wall remains unkempt and continues its long, slow decline.

Veterans' Memorial Cemetery at Washelli

As the High School Memorial Stadium plans were under way, the directors of the Veterans' Memorial Cemetery called a meeting in late 1947 to approve a proposal to reproduce the Victory Square pylon, possibly with a memorial chapel, on a knoll overlooking the graves of veterans on the sloping south side of Washelli Cemetery. They did not think their proposal interfered with the hopes of Mayor Devin's committee to perpetuate Victory Square in a central Seattle location, but rather would complement any downtown Seattle plan. After the UW Board of Regents failed to commit to a permanent shrine in Victory Square, the cemetery's board of trustees quickly approved the plans for a Washelli Memorial. The veterans group appealed for community donations to fund their memorial. Work on a memorial chimes tower began in October 1950.

The project started with a budget of approximately $40,000. At sixty-five-feet, the tower was intended to be visible from Aurora Avenue. A lighted cross was placed on the unfinished tower in 1953, but work on the structure stopped the next year when the foundation ran out of money. In 1957, they raised an additional $25,000 to complete the six-story concrete framework and install the chimes. The memorial provided a place for burial services in inclement weather and for Gold Star mothers or other relatives to pay their respects. The tower's carillon bells still ring out the hours and Memorial Day services are held there each year.

Memorial Plaza at the Public Safety Building

Another opportunity for a memorial presented itself in a new downtown building the city was building for the Seattle Police Department. Plans for the new Public Safety Building included a plaza for statuary on the Fourth Avenue side. This space provided an ideal location for a World War II monument.[22] It was on a block already owned by the city, in a central downtown location, and the cost would be minimal since the city council had already approved funds in the budget. An appropriation of $63,468 for the additional work seemed a bargain since the city council had already agreed to allocate $150,000 for a permanent war memorial. On January 17, 1949, Mayor Devin announced the approval of the memorial plan by the building committee in charge of the new structure.

The first step was to produce an accurate list of casualties from the war. The list from the temporary memorial was a start, but it had relied on casualty lists that were sometimes inaccurate due to the speed of the war and its widespread battlefields. Ethyl Fulton, a Gold Star mother and a member of the War Memorial Committee, volunteered for the enormous task of checking the names of all King County personnel who died in service.

The job was important to her because her foster son, Staff Sergeant Edward Ronan, had been killed in Italy. "Because I lost my boy," Fulton said, "I want to make sure no one is forgotten on the new memorial." She bought a typewriter and card index and started with the list of names from the temporary memorial. All the high schools in King County provided lists of graduates who had been killed. Fulton obtained Army and Navy lists of the dead and gathered newspaper clippings mentioning others who died in service. Her efforts resulted in the original list of some 1,200 casualties expanding to more than 2,000 names. Newspapers published a list to provide the public a final opportunity to examine the names before the monument was completed.[23]

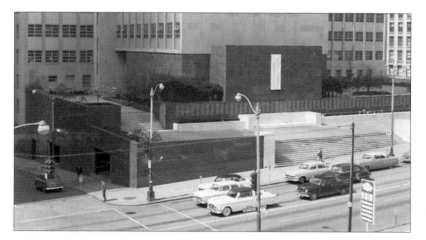

The new Public Safety Building included a War Memorial Plaza on the Fourth Avenue side of the building. *Courtesy of the Seattle Municipal Archives #52585.*

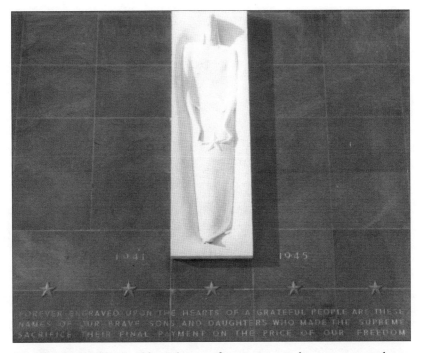

A 14-feet high white marble sculpture of a grieving mother was mounted over the wall of the names of the fallen. *Courtesy of the Seattle Public Library #19320.*

Along the memorial plaza, workers inscribed 2,488 names in gold leaf on a nine-foot-high, red granite wall. Additional granite formed a retaining wall along Fourth Avenue; a broad flight of stairs separated the wall into two sections. These steps led to a block-long, stone-paved plaza. A bench of white marble ran the length of the space, beneath the carved names. Mounted on the wall above the engraved names was a figure of a symbolic Gold Star mother, designed by Dudley Pratt, a Seattle sculptor. He carved the four by fourteen feet figure from a seven-ton slab of Carrara white marble.

The city dedicated the Memorial Plaza at the new Public Safety Building on the afternoon of January 7, 1951. The program began with patriotic music performed by a military band. Mayor Devin unveiled the carved figure, which symbolized the spirit of peace, mercy, and benediction. Gold Star mothers, religious leaders, and representatives of veterans' organizations placed wreaths at the memorial.

Some of the most heartfelt moments occurred after the officials delivered their speeches. Five-year-old Thomas Lee III stepped forward and placed flowers at the base. His father, Thomas J. Lee Jr., had been a paratrooper and his was among the names carved in granite.

The plaza became Seattle's primary war memorial and was the scene of many observances, parades, and festivities. In 1951, former commander of the U.S. Army in Korea, General Douglas MacArthur, came to town and placed a wreath at the memorial, saying "I have placed this wreath with a degree of reverence and emotion I find hard to put into words. Many of these men were mine. I do not know the dignity of their birth, but I do know the glory of their death."[24] In 1963, Jimmy Doolittle, the famed former airman who led the first bombing raid over Tokyo in 1942, visited the memorial while in Seattle for a reunion of his flyers and he, too, placed a wreath there.

An additional plaque was added in 1966 to honor the memory of ten U.S. airmen who died when their B-17 Flying Fortress bomber was shot down over Warsaw, Poland, in 1944. The bomber was one of 107 airplanes that flew from England to Warsaw to drop supplies to Polish freedom fighters battling the German army. The Polish Home Association of Seattle presented the plaque to the city and Ian Hutchinson, a crew member on one of the aircraft flying the mission, helped unveil it.

World War II would not be the final conflict for the city to memorialize. In 1976, the city added 1,518 names of Washington State service members killed in Korea and Vietnam to the red granite panels of the War Memorial. At the same time, the names of World War II casualties that were inadvertently left off the memorial were added to the wall, bringing the list to a total of 2,640 fallen men and women.

Garden of Remembrance at Benaroya Hall

By the 1990s, the Public Safety Building had become obsolete, and the city decided to demolish it and construct a new building for the police department; therefore a new location for the memorial was required. The city officially decommissioned the war memorial, and the red granite panels with the names of the fallen were crushed to prevent them from being reused in a disrespectful way. The Gold

Star Mother sculpture hanging above the memorial was loaned to the Evergreen-Washelli Veterans Memorial Cemetery.

In 1998, in anticipation of the demolition of the memorial, developers built a Garden of Remembrance as part of the new Benaroya Symphony Hall. It is an L-shaped memorial that runs along Second Avenue and then up the hill facing University Street. The tree-lined space features reflecting pools of water running down the grade with granite tablets bearing the names of nearly 8,000 Washington State residents who have died in wars since 1941. What had been a King County monument was now a statewide memorial to all military servicemen and women who lost their lives in World War II and the conflicts since then: Korea, Vietnam, Grenada, Iraq, and Afghanistan. Individual contributions and corporate donations primarily funded the $3 million project.

Other War Memorials

In addition to the large monuments, there were other, smaller, more specialized war memorials dedicated around the city. After the Second World War, Seattle's Japanese-Americans erected a memorial in 1949 to their war dead, lost in battle fighting for the United States. The community raised $10,000 within a few days. The fifteen-ton granite shaft located in a quiet corner of Lake View Cemetery near Volunteer Park commemorates the gallantry of 56 Nisei—Americans of Japanese descent—who gave their lives in World War II. Near the top of the twenty-foot-tall spire are the names of the battles they fought in: Naples-Foggia, Rome-Arno, Rhineland, North Apennines, Po Valley, Aleutians, Guadalcanal, India-Burma, Leyte, and Ryukyus. A simple inscription reads: *Americanism is a matter of the mind and heart; Americanism is not, and never was, a matter of race or ancestry.—Franklin Delano Roosevelt.* The men on the memorial died fighting for their country in order to prove the loyalty of their families. Most of them had volunteered for active duty from behind the barbed wire of relocation camps where their country imprisoned them as a security precaution after the Japanese attack on Pearl Harbor.

Colonel James Hanley, an officer from one of the primarily Nisei regiments that fought in Italy and France, was the principal speaker at the dedication. "Each man, no matter how young," he said, "considered himself a personal representative of his people in the battle against prejudice." After a bugler played taps, the crowd of more than a thousand lingered even though the ceremony was over. Fumi Hashimoto of Fife, whose husband, John, was killed in France, took Jonathon, their six-year-old son, to see his father's name on the memorial. "It doesn't mean much to Jon now, but when he grows up, I believe he'll understand that this monument symbolizes our loyalty and that because of what his father and the others did we live in dignity today."[25]

Chinese-American soldiers also have a memorial dedicated to their service in World War II. Cathay Post 186 of the American Legion conceived the idea for a memorial in 1950. Seattle native David "Gobby" Woo established this post in 1945. Shot down while serving as a gunner on a bomber, he survived twenty-seven months of imprisonment in German prisoner-of-war camps. Woo and the post members coordinated a fund drive which was enthusiastically supported by Seattle's Chinese community.

The monument is a six-foot block of polished rose granite etched with the names of ten local casualties, and was originally placed on a playfield located on Weller Street between Seventh and Eighth Avenues behind the Chong Wa Benevolent Association in Seattle's International District. A child-sized drinking fountain was set in front of the memorial so that children would be mindful of those who died in the war. The monument was eventually moved to Hing Hay Park to provide more visibility to the public. The community holds an annual service in the park featuring the Seattle Chinese American Girls Drill Team, a twenty-one gun salute, prayers, and the presentation of wreaths at the base of the memorial.

The Second World War was the most widespread and deadliest conflict in human history, and Seattle was profoundly affected by the war. As citizens of the city feared a potential Japanese attack, they produced warships, bombers, and other war supplies. Thousands volunteered to serve in the armed forces, and more than six thousand Washingtonians paid with their lives. Thousands of other American cities and towns saved tanks, planes, and cannons from the scrap heap to display in city halls and parks. Seattle differed and followed what the U.S. Commission on Fine Arts advocated in 1946, when it advised communities to avoid standing-soldier statues and piles of cannon balls and instead, "provide an effective setting for an annual meeting or act or remembrance, such as the placing of a wreath on Memorial or other commemorative days."[26] It is with gratitude that Seattle remembers its war dead with memorials.

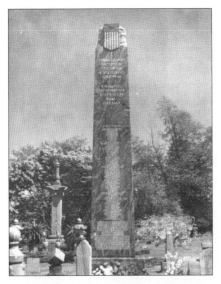

This 15-ton granite monument in Lake View Cemetery lists the names of fifty-five Americans of Japanese descent who died in WWII. *Courtesy of the Seattle Public Library #20002.*

Remembering Exclusion

In April 1942, two thousand Americans of Japanese descent, including U.S. citizens, were removed from their homes in Seattle and sent to an Assembly Center at the Western Washington Fairgrounds in Puyallup. Executive Order 9066 was signed by President Franklin Roosevelt with the expressed purpose to prevent espionage and protect the Japanese Americans from harm. Later that year, 7,500 people were transferred from the center at Puyallup to the Minidoka internment camp in Idaho and the Manzanar camp in California. A memorial plaque remembering the forced displacement was placed in 2002 on Bainbridge Island, across Puget Sound from Seattle. A more extensive Japanese American Exclusion Memorial with a story wall was dedicated there in 2011.[27]

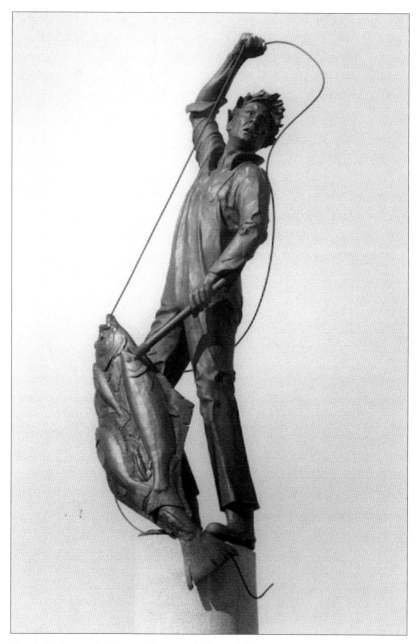

Seattle Fishermen's Memorial statue dedicated in 1988 at Fishermen's Terminal.
Courtesy of the Seattle Municipal Archives #57718.

CHAPTER 10

MARITIME MEMORIES AND MEMORIALS TO FISHERMEN

It's hard to be in Seattle and not sense how important the waterfront is to the city. Water surrounds Seattle, with saltwater Puget Sound to the west and freshwater Lake Washington to the east. Rugged mountain ranges encircle the area, making water routes the preferred means of travel and commerce. It was no mistake the Denny Party arrived from Portland in 1851 by ship instead of by land. Ships and waterways were a necessary and integral part of Seattle's development as over the years hundreds of small steamers and ships transported people and goods around Puget Sound.

While lumber and coal were the primary local businesses in the late nineteenth century, industries such as fishing, shipbuilding, and shipping increasingly contributed to Seattle's economic expansion and population growth. Gold strikes in the Yukon and Alaska led to a rapid increase in the number of ships sailing the waters to the north. In 1911, King County voters approved the creation of the Port of Seattle to improve the planning and coordination of the waterfront and harbor facilities. By the 1920s, Seattle's waterfront was teeming with activity on the large piers and warehouses. Alaskan commerce and trade across the Pacific developed and continued unabated throughout the twentieth century. Fishermen from Seattle's fishing fleet sail forth each season and face dangerous and often deadly conditions in the northern Pacific.

Annual Maritime Plaques

To help celebrate Seattle's centennial in 1952, the Board of Public Works gave the Yukon Club, a civic group working in conjunction with the Port of Seattle, permission to erect fifteen temporary signs to mark important sites from Seattle's maritime history. The plywood markers were three feet square and each featured a drawing of a ship and the words "Historical Point of Interest." The markers were stored at the end of the summer of 1952, then repainted and remounted along the waterfront the following summer.

After the Yukon Club had displayed the temporary markers for four years, city and maritime leaders decided to replace them with permanent bronze tablets at a rate of one per year. The Yukon Club partnered with the Propeller Club and the Puget Sound Maritime Historical Society to determine the locations.[1]

From 1957 to 1986, the city celebrated Maritime Day each year with dinners, tugboat races, wreaths placed in Elliott Bay for missing seamen, and the dedication of a new maritime historical marker. Each was a thirteen-by-twenty-inch bronze plaque attached to an anchor. Usually the plaque would be unveiled by "Miss Maritime," a young woman working in the marine industry chosen from a group of finalists by the Propeller Club. The markers primarily line the central waterfront, but some were placed in other locations like Duwamish Head, Harbor Island, Chittenden Locks in Ballard, Smith Cove, and Lake Washington. A few have disappeared; those that remain provide a fascinating reminder of a maritime history that was the foundation of modern day Seattle. The inscriptions from each of the plaques, noted in bold, are listed in Appendix I.

The majority of the maritime historical markers were placed around Elliott Bay. The Duwamish people lived around the bay for thousands of years, and established at least seventeen settlements in the area.[2] The bay was noted by Captain George Vancouver of the Royal Navy in 1792, and was first surveyed by Midshipman Sam Elliott of the U.S. Navy Wilkes Expedition in May 1841. A maritime marker for **Elliott Bay Harbor** was placed in May 1982, by Pier 56.

The first permanent maritime marker celebrated the arrival of the famous **Ton of Gold**, which launched the Klondike gold rush. It was attached to a concrete guardrail at Pier 58 on Alaska Way at Union Street in 1957. This was location of the old Schwabacher Wharf where the steamship *Portland* docked in 1897 and disgorged its treasure.[3]

Seattle's Founding

Henry Yesler's sawmill was Seattle's first significant industry, his wharf was the first waterfront facility, and, beginning in 1853, his cookhouse was the center of village life for many years.[4] The site of the sawmill was first recognized with a plaque in 1905, but the marker disappeared, only to resurface in 1972, when it was placed into the collection at the Museum of History and Industry. Another plaque dedicated to Yesler himself in 1915 was placed on the King County courthouse. The **Yesler Sawmill, Wharf, and Cookhouse** maritime marker was unveiled on May 20, 1964, by Seattle Mayor James Braman at the site of the sawmill on Alaska Way at the foot of Yesler Street.

The Battle of Seattle was previously commemorated by a marker placed on a boulder at the City-County Building in 1916. The role of the U.S. Navy in the skirmish was also commemorated by the placement of a maritime marker specifically honoring the sloop-of-war **USS Decatur**. Anchored in Elliott Bay on January 26, 1856, the *Decatur* provided cannon and howitzer fire, sailors, and Marines to defend the settlement against the Indian attack. A bronze plaque at the foot of Yesler Way, south of Pier 51, was unveiled on May 21, 1959. Victor Denny, a grandson of David Denny, participated in the ceremony.

Reshaping the Waterfront

Four of the maritime plaques represent places where people have dramatically altered the original waterfront and the waterway connection between Lake Washington and Puget Sound. Through the use of locks, dredging, and sluicing of hillside dirt into the tidelands of Elliott Bay, the boundaries between land and water have changed from the days when the first settlers arrived. In 1951, historian Murray Morgan described the waterfront as, "not as busy as New York's, not as self-consciously colorful as San Francisco's, not as exotic as New Orleans', but a good, honest working waterfront with big gray warehouses and trim fishing boats and docks that smell of creosote."[5]

The **Hiram M. Chittenden Locks**, known locally as the Ballard Locks, connect saltwater Puget Sound with the freshwater Lake Union and Lake Washington. The U.S. Army Corps of Engineers completed the construction of the Lake Washington Ship Canal and Locks in 1917, and eventually named the locks to honor Major Hiram Martin Chittenden, the Seattle District Engineer for the Corps from 1906 to 1908. Today spectators watch sailboats, motorboats, tugs, barges, and yachts traverse the locks as the staff adjusts the water levels to allow for safe passage between the bodies of water. There are multiple historical plaques on the premises.

The old stone administration building stands north of the locks. On the east side of the building is a large bronze plaque from 1916. At the top is an eagle, grasping a banner in its beak, proclaiming "Essayons!," which is the Corps' motto, meaning "Let Us Try." The plaque states the Puget Sound Lake Washington Waterway was approved June 25, 1910. The Yukon and Propeller Clubs dedicated the annual maritime marker on May 22, 1967, the fiftieth anniversary of the locks. The marker is located on the north side of the locks.

Nearby are the Carl S. English Gardens. English worked for the Corps of Engineers as a horticulturist for forty-three years and transformed the barren space resulting from the locks' construction into a beautiful garden. The Corps honored his work with a bronze plaque on December 10, 1974. An additional plaque remembers Michael E. Fleming, a horticulturist who spent three decades maintaining the garden from 1974 until his retirement in 2004.

Ballast Island was created by sailing ships in the late 1800s when they dumped their ballast of boulders and other materials at the southern end of the waterfront before loading cargo and goods destined for California and other ports. The Duwamish and other Native people traveled by canoe to the Seattle waterfront and camped in cattail mat shelters on the "island" made from the debris. By 1885, some Duwamish made Ballast Island a permanent, year-round residence, living in canvas tents. By the start of World War I, even this parcel of land became valuable, and the Duwamish were pushed out again.[6] The maritime plaque was placed in May 1983, on Alaska Way, just south of the Washington Street Boat Landing.

Harbor Island was created in 1909 when four million cubic yards of soil from Beacon Hill was sluiced into Elliott Bay at the mouth of the Duwamish River. The area had been a marshy tideland with mud flats extending from Pioneer Square around the southern boundary of Elliott Bay to West Seattle but the river channel was straightened and dredged and the fill created an artificial island in the harbor. A maritime historical marker was placed May 24, 1972, at the entrance to Harbor Island, in a small grassy industrial park north of the intersection at Southwest Spokane Street and Eleventh Avenue Southwest. The expansion of Terminal 18 in 1999–2001 necessitated the relocation of the marker to the center of a nearby shoreline park built and maintained by the Port of Seattle.[7]

Smith Cove was honored with a maritime marker on May 19, 1978. The cove was named after Dr. Henry A. Smith, a pioneer who settled there in 1853, only a year after Seattle was founded. The Northern Pacific Railway completed a coal bunker pier there in 1891 and the Asiatic Dock at the turn of the century. In 1912, the Port of Seattle purchased the area now known as Piers 90 and 91 and built massive 2,580 foot-long piers in 1921. During World War II the U.S. Navy took control of the docks and used them until 1976, when the Port of Seattle repurchased them. The maritime marker is currently located at Smith Cove Park at Twenty-third Avenue West and West Marina Place.

Remembering Ferries and Steamers

As the area's population grew, so did the use of ferries and steamers to transport commuters and travelers across Puget Sound and Lake Washington. In the early twentieth century residents referred to these ships as the Mosquito Fleet because they appeared to flit back and forth across the water. Several maritime plaques honor the boats and docks that made getting around the area possible.

The **Colman Ferry Terminal** was just north of the original location of Yesler's Wharf. It was named for James M. Colman, who arrived in Puget Sound in 1861 and spent his first decade building, repairing, and owning multiple sawmills. He then moved to Seattle to lease and manage Henry Yesler's sawmill. He built the ferry terminal in 1882 for the passenger steamers that served the Seattle waterfront. Washington State Ferries, operator of the nation's largest ferry system, replaced the old dock in 1966 with a new Seattle Ferry Terminal at the foot of Marion Street. The maritime marker was unveiled at the terminal's dedication ceremony.

Also located at the Seattle Ferry Terminal is a 1971 maritime marker commemorating the famous mosquito fleet steamer *Flyer*. Built in 1891 for the Seattle-Tacoma passenger route, the *Flyer* was one of the most popular boats on Puget Sound; everyone wanted to "Fly on the Flyer." She steamed between the two cities at sixteen knots and made four runs each day. A one-way ticket cost thirty-five cents. Competitors introduced newer steel-hulled ships to the route, and the *Flyer* met her demise at Richmond Beach in 1929 when salvagers dismantled her for the metal fittings.[8]

Nearby, at the foot of Madison Street, a 1958 plaque commemorates the early days of the Puget Sound ferry system. The first ferry to provide regular service was the ***City of Seattle***, which ran between downtown Seattle and West Seattle. Her first trip across Elliott Bay took place on Christmas Eve 1888 and cost fifteen cents. Once streetcars provided easier access to West Seattle, ferry ridership declined, and the old boat was sold to a group of investors in California. The side-wheel ferry's final route was during the Second World War as she transported shipyard workers around San Francisco Bay.

The ferry ***San Mateo*** was launched in 1922 in San Francisco Bay. She later moved north to Puget Sound and made her final run in 1969 as the last steam ferry on the West Coast. Her interior was furnished with elegant stained-glass windows, wooden benches, and carved posts, so in 1971 Washington State purchased the ferry to turn it into a museum. Organizers placed the annual maritime plaque onboard in 1974. Unfortunately, there were not enough funds to restore the ferry and she seemed destined for the scrap yard. Plans to refurbish the boat and locate it either on Lake Washington or the Duwamish River in Tukwila fell through. In 1994, a Canadian investor purchased the ferry and planned to convert it into a dance studio or a museum. Nothing ever came of this, and the ferry remains half sunk and decaying in the mud of the Fraser River in British Columbia. The location of the maritime marker plaque is unknown.

Another ferry maritime marker, dedicated in 1979, is located near the Leschi Moorage on Lake Washington Boulevard. Steamships began operating on **Lake Washington** beginning in the 1880s and carried passengers from Seattle to Mercer Island and other communities on the east side of the lake. The last ferry tied up at the Leschi dock when service was discontinued after the floating bridge was completed in 1940 and commuters could easily drive their cars across the lake.

A Maritime Disaster

One maritime marker tells the tragic story of the worst maritime disaster on Puget Sound, the **Sinking of the Steamer *Dix*.** One of the mosquito fleet ships was the passenger steamer *Dix*, built in 1904 in Tacoma. The ship was 102 feet long and 20.5 feet on the beam; her slim design left her unstable in the water and caused her to roll uncomfortably in the waves. The shipyard added thirty tons of ballast to her hold for stability, but, even then, the ship wallowed in rough weather and pilots considered her hard to handle.[9]

The Port Blakely Mill Company chartered the *Dix* to ferry passengers between Seattle and Port Blakely on the southern tip of Bainbridge Island. On Sunday night, November 18, 1906, the weather was calm and clear, and the moon had risen. Mill workers and their families finished their weekend of shopping and visiting in Seattle and boarded the ship at Colman Dock for the voyage home. As the *Dix* began the routine forty-minute trip across Puget Sound, the captain turned the helm over to the first officer and disappeared into the passenger cabin to collect fares. At the same time, across Elliott Bay, a large freighter, the 1,071-ton *Jeanie*, pulled out of the piers at Smith Cove for its trip southward to Tacoma.

Marcus Otnes, a twenty-nine-year-old passenger, stood on the deck of the *Dix* when he saw the massive shape of the *Jeanie* closing in on the right side of the smaller ferry. He yelled a warning to the wheelhouse. The *Dix's* first officer didn't see the freighter and inexplicably spun the wheel to the right and turned the steamer directly into the path of the larger ship, which reversed its engines in an attempt to avoid striking the *Dix*. The forward bowsprit of the *Jeanie* caught on the superstructure of the *Dix*, pushing the small steamship over. Seawater poured in, the *Dix* rolled over, split in two, and sank within five quick minutes.

Passengers who were on the upper decks escaped, but those below decks were trapped by the flooding water and went down with the ship. Otnes survived by clinging to the *Jeanie's* floating bowsprit chain, along with another passenger, thirteen-year-old Alice Simpson.

She made it to the upper deck before being tossed overboard; only her head remained above the water when a line was thrown down to them, and they were saved. The ship carried seventy-seven passengers, and as many as forty-five are thought to have died in Puget Sound's worst maritime disaster. Port Blakely grieved as word of the tragedy reached the mill. Everyone knew someone who died that night; the mill halted all operations and schools closed so the town could mourn their dead.

In 1973 Otnes, age 96, and Simpson, 80, sat together on Duwamish Head in West Seattle, as organizers unveiled a historical marker by the shoreline to memorialize the victims of the sinking. In early 2011, researchers thought they had finally located the sunken ship with surface sonar, and completed a visual survey of the wreckage using a submersible vehicle. In a later excursion divers used equipment to create a three-dimensional scan of the wreck, which they compared against actual plans and photographs. Unfortunately, the two images did not match, and the researchers doubted whether the wreckage was the long-lost *Dix*. While the shipwreck remains undiscovered, the historical marker remains on the Duwamish Head waterfront.

Shipbuilding

By the late 1880s shipbuilding was one of the major industries contributing to Seattle's economic expansion and population growth. Several shipyards, including the Moran Brothers Company, profited from the gold rush by refitting old boats and building new steamers to provide miners with transportation to the gold fields. During World War I, over 40,000 workers were building wooden and steel ships in Seattle's twenty shipyards.[10]

On the south side of the Chittenden Locks stands a maritime marker erected on May 21, 1976. It commemorates pioneer shipbuilder **Thomas Petersen**. Near this site, before the construction of the locks, Peterson built two separate schooners in 1891 and 1900. He was a native of Denmark who immigrated to San Francisco in 1857 and constructed twenty-eight ships in northern California. By 1907, Petersen moved to Puget Sound and built several ships at Port Ludlow, Port Townsend, Port Madison, and, finally, where the marker stands today.

The Moran Brothers Shipyard laid the keel for the **USS *Nebraska***, the first and only battleship built on Puget Sound, in 1902. Financed partly by contributions from local citizens, she was delivered to the U.S. Navy five years later. A maritime marker was placed by Pier 42 on May 19, 1965. Malcolm and John Moran, sons of shipbuilder Robert Moran, were at the dedication.[11] The plaque is still in its original location on the Elliott Bay Trail, south of King Street and roughly opposite Century Link Field.

Next to the USS *Nebraska* plaque is a maritime marker for the **Skinner & Eddy Shipyards**, owned by David E. Skinner and John W. Eddy. They began constructing ships in 1916 and during World War I their shipyard built seventy-five vessels and became the largest shipyard in Seattle. At the war's conclusion, the need for new ships decreased, and the owners sold the shipyard in 1923.[12] The maritime marker was placed on May 22, 1969, at Pier 42; present at the ceremony were Ned Skinner, president of the Alaska Steamship Company and grandson of David E. Skinner, and J. Franklin Eddy and Garrett Eddy, sons of John W. Eddy.[13]

Military and Other Vessels

The ***Idaho***, a side-wheel steamship built on the Columbia River, arrived on Puget Sound in 1882. After serving several cargo routes on the sound, including delivering contraband goods from Canada, its machinery was removed and the remains were sold to Dr. Alexander de Soto. The doctor purchased the ship using proceeds from his surgical practice and turned the *Idaho* into the Wayside Mission, a hospital for the poor and struggling people of Pioneer Square and the waterfront. Placed above the high-tide on wooden pilings, she served her patients faithfully from 1898 to 1907, until that section of the waterfront was developed for piers. The *Idaho* was added to the fill at the foot of Jackson Street where the ship remains buried under the street. The maritime marker was unveiled May 26, 1960, at Alaska Way and Washington Street, where it remains today.

Organizers commemorated the visit of the **Great White Fleet** to Seattle on May 24, 1961, with the placement of a maritime marker north of Piers 62 and 63 overlooking the Bell Street Marina. The plaque was mounted by Pier 64 near the location where the crews from the ships came ashore for liberty visits. After becoming president in 1901, Theodore Roosevelt upgraded and expanded the U.S. fleet to protect American global interests. To demonstrate that the Navy's ships could quickly shift from the Atlantic Ocean to the Pacific, Roosevelt ordered the Great White Fleet to sail around the world. Sixteen battleships painted gleaming white and manned by 14,000 sailors and marines left Hampton Roads, Virginia, on a cloudy morning on December 16, 1907.

The 43,000 mile, fourteen-month circumnavigation of the globe would be the first around-the-world cruise by steam-powered steel battleships. The fleet sailed around the tip of South America to the West Coast and several ships visited ports in Washington State including Seattle, Bellingham, and Tacoma. They then weighed anchor and continued their journey across the Pacific. The fleet arrived at Hampton Roads on a rainy February 22, 1909, completing its record-setting voyage.[14]

A maritime marker honoring the **U.S. Coast Guard Cutter *Bear*** was placed in 1963. The *Bear* was acquired by the U.S. Navy for northern exploration missions. In 1885, the Navy transferred her to the Treasury Department as a revenue cutter. That was the beginning of forty-one years of service on the Alaskan Patrol where the *Bear* patrolled the Bering Sea with frequent visits to Seattle. The ship carried mail, supplies, and government officials north to Alaska and brought back news to Seattle. Her crews improved maps and charts, performed search and rescue missions, administered justice, and provided medical assistance to the Alaska natives. She left the Alaska patrol and Seattle in 1929. In 1963, the *Bear* foundered under tow in the Atlantic Ocean and sank. The maritime plaque stands at Alaska Way and Seneca Street in front of the Argosy ticket booth.

The fireboat ***Duwamish*** was honored with a maritime marker in 1984. Crowded with wooden docks, piers, and warehouses, Seattle's waterfront always struggled with the possibility of large fires. The need to fight fires from the water, as well as from shore, was evident. The *Duwamish* joined the waterfront fire service in 1909 when she was delivered to Fire Station Number Five at the foot of Madison Street. The 120-feet long fireboat had a ram bow to sink burning wooden vessels, a shallow draft to allow access to fires on the tide flats, and the ability to pump 22,800 gallons per minute. The ship was retired from service in 1985 and now is docked on Lake Union near the Museum of History and Industry as a part of the Northwest Seaport Maritime Heritage Center.

Maritime Commerce

Lumber and coal provided the first cargoes from the Seattle waterfront. Both cargo and passengers on steamers increased during the gold rush. A group of investors formed a company to transport passengers and fishing products between Seattle and Alaska. The steamer *Willapa* was the first ship to sail under the flag of the Alaska Steamship Company when it departed for Alaska on March 3, 1895. The maritime marker from 1962 that honored the ship was located at the foot of Pike Street at Pier 58 but is now missing.

The year 1896 witnessed the first regular freight service to Japan as the steamship *Miike Maru* departed Seattle for the cities of Yokohama, Kobe, and Nagasaki. This voyage was the beginning of regularly scheduled service between Asia and Seattle. The Yukon and Propeller Clubs placed the 1968 maritime marker between Piers 57 and 58, but it disappeared within a few years, and was thought to have been stolen. However, scuba divers discovered the marker in the bay; it may have been accidentally knocked off of the seawall by an errant truck driver. The marker was hauled out of the water, reinstalled, and remains there today.

In 1900, Great Northern Railway president James J. Hill wanted to capitalize on the ability of his trains to travel quickly from Seattle to the East Coast carrying Asian goods. He commissioned two steamships named the *Minnesota* and the *Dakota* and developed Pier 88 on Smith Cove. The company transferred large shipments of valuable, raw silk from the ships to specialized trains for a quick run to the fashion houses on the East Coast. The **Silk Train** maritime marker from 1970, now missing, was placed at Pier 88 by the north entrance to Elliott Bay Park.

Another large dock and warehouse, the **Ainsworth & Dunn Dock** at Pier 70 was built in 1902 by local businessmen in the fishing and shipping industries. Fire destroyed a section of the pier in 1916, but the structure was repaired, and it served at various times as a warehouse for the Washington State Liquor Board and as the Seattle base for the U.S. Coast Guard. The marker from 1981 has disappeared.

Pier 66 was the **headquarters of Washington State's first public port**, which was established in 1911. The Port of Seattle was created when the Washington State Legislature passed the Port District Act. This law allowed municipalities to create public port districts, which could acquire, construct, and operate waterways, docks, wharves, and other harbor improvements. King County voters approved a proposal to create the Port of Seattle which would transform a large number of privately-owned and competing companies into a publicly owned organization that could organize the Seattle waterfront and turn it into a major trading center. A plaque honoring the port was placed in 1986 on the corner of the building facing Alaska Way.

In 1925, the Pacific Steamship Company built the **first modern freight and passenger terminal** in Seattle. During the Second World War, the terminal served as the Port of Embarkation for the U.S. Army and saw thousands of soldiers depart for battlefields in the Pacific. The 1980 plaque is located there under a covered archway on Pier 36.

Joshua Green was a local legend in the shipping community and was present at several maritime marker dedications. Green's family moved to Seattle from Mississippi in 1886 when he was seventeen years old. He began his career working on a sternwheeler before purchasing a ship with three other officers. From this beginning, Green expanded their fleet and served as captain on several ships. The business profited from the Alaska gold rush, and in 1903, Green merged with a competitor and became a leader in Puget Sound shipping over the next three decades. After his retirement, he remained dedicated to his beloved waterfront and Seattle's maritime industry. On May 23, 1975, the clubs honored his commitment to Seattle's maritime community with a marker dedicated to him at Seattle's Waterfront Park at Pier 58.

The home port of the Seattle fishing fleet was honored with a maritime marker placed on May 20, 1985, with a dedication at the **Fishermen's Terminal** at Salmon Bay. The Salmon Bay terminal was designed and built by the Port of Seattle Commission in 1913 to serve as headquarters for the Puget Sound fishing fleet. This was one of the first projects completed by the Port Commission, which recognized the importance of the commercial fishing fleet that called Seattle their home port. Port Commissioner Hiram Chittenden declared the terminal's purpose was "to organize and solidify the scattered fishing industry, to give such aid in protecting the fisherman in marketing his hard-earned products."[15] The marker is located at the southeast corner of the Fishermen's Terminal building.

Remembering Fishermen and Those Who Go to Sea

Native people and early settlers depended upon the area's abundant supply of local fish, especially salmon, for food and trade. Later, local companies processed Alaskan fish in canneries that lined Seattle's waterfront. Commercial fishing boats and crews sailed north every year to haul in their catch of fish, crabs, and other seafood. The weather was often dangerous, and ships and crews were sometimes lost. Survivors, friends, and family members wanted memorials to those who went to sea and did not return.

The **Seattle Fishermen's Memorial** is the largest memorial to missing fishermen and is located at Fishermen's Terminal on Salmon Bay. Members of the fishing industry desired a suitable monument at a central location to display a list of the names of those lost at sea. Often, those victims simply disappear, leaving their families without any remains to bury. In the 1980s, a group of fishing industry men and women formed the Seattle Fishermen's Memorial Committee and set out to compile a list of names for the memorial, raise $100,000, and create a suitable place of remembrance. Their first choice was the Chittenden Locks, but the U.S. Army Corps of Engineers was hesitant. Instead the monument was placed at Fishermen's Terminal, on property donated by the Port of Seattle.

Organizers initially thought the Coast Guard maintained a centralized list of missing sailors, but this was not the case. So, they took a model of the memorial and an initial list of 120 names to commercial fishing trade shows and asked people to identify missing friends and family members to include. Newspaper accounts of fishing accidents also provided additional information, and by 1987, the count of missing fishermen increased to some five hundred names. "There's lots of stories on that list, but no happy ones," said Tink Mosness, who helped collect the names for the memorial. Organizers worried they would unintentionally leave out some names.[16]

In addition to gathering names, the committee needed to select an artist. They organized an open design competition, stating the winning concept should be "a representation that reflects positively upon fishermen, the fishing industry and the community at large. Provision must be made to allow placing up to 1,000 permanent names on or near the piece of art." They allocated a budget of $50,000 for the conception, execution, and installation of the memorial.[17] Ninety-two artists responded and submitted their ideas, with the selection committee selecting four finalists.

The winner was Seattle artist Ron Petty, whose submission depicted a life-size fisherman on top of a marble pedestal. The figure hauls in a mythical fish in the shape of a halibut but also representing features of salmon, cod, and other local fish. The fisherman looks back over his left shoulder as if to watch boats depart toward Puget Sound and the open sea. Native fish surround the bottom of the pedestal. Bronze tablets are attached to stone walls next to the statue with twenty-five names placed on each tablet. A fishermen friend offered to model, but Petty learned about a superstition regarding using a real fisherman as a model for a memorial, so he based the figure on himself.

The Seattle Fishermen's Memorial was dedicated in 1988 in front of a large crowd. It provides a mourning place for commercial fishing families who have lost relatives at sea. The names of 675 local commercial fishermen and women who lost their lives pursuing their livelihood since 1900 are listed on the monument. Over the years, as ships continue to be lost, the committee adds names to the tablets, and the memorial is the site of an annual blessing of the fishing fleet. Dan Pugh, chairman of the memorial committee, explained the lure of fishing the dangerous waters between Seattle and Alaska: "There is a special feeling, almost of arrogance in saying 'I'm a commercial fisherman,' an independence of spirit and not choosing a safer way. Unfortunately, that choice has a price."[18] That price can be seen in the names placed on the waterfront side of the Fishermen's Terminal.

The Seattle Fishermen's Memorial is particular to the missing fishermen from the area, while the **Shipmates Light** is a memorial dedicated to all sailors who perish at sea. In 1969 twenty-six sailors drowned when the freighter *Badger State* sank en route from Puget Sound to Vietnam. After the disaster, family members and industry representatives considered a memorial. Some wanted an impressive waterfront monument listing the names of lost sailors. Others wanted something simpler, like a statue to honor those who did not return with their ships. The city was developing the new Waterfront Park between Pier 57 and Pier 59, and organizers asked Mayor Wes Uhlman to include the memorial. However, the mayor's office did not submit the request to the project manager in charge of the park's construction.

The idea for a memorial was kept alive by Captain Frank Huxtable, representative for the Maritime Administration, and Captain Gunnar Olsborg, a waterfront skipper. The parks department suggested the memorial be located in the city, but the organizers held out for a waterfront location. At first, the Port of Seattle suggested a small space near Pier 48. A California sculptor sketched an idea for a $10,000 statue of a lost seaman's father, wife, and son. However, the proposal did not gain any support, and the design was shelved.

In early 1977, the Port of Seattle provided a site on the Elliott Bay Parkway between Pier 70 and Pier 88 for the memorial. The resulting structure resembles a small lighthouse with a light shining from the top. On Maritime Day, May 22, 1977, organizers dedicated the memorial as two buglers played "Echo Taps." The reigning Miss Maritime laid a wreath at the base of the monument as a fireboat offshore sprayed a salute and the steamer *Virginia V* sounded her whistle. Shipmates Light also provided Seattle maritime unions a new place to set the wreath they previously floated on Elliott Bay for Maritime Day. The memorial is still on the Elliott Bay Trail in Myrtle Edwards Park.

In a narrow strip of Sunset Hill Park, overlooking Shilshole Bay and Puget Sound, stands the **Fishermen Lost at Sea** memorial, a granite boulder five feet wide and weighing 11,900 pounds. The sinking of the fishing boat *Jane* off Cape Flattery in September 1959 was the impetus to create the memorial. On March 12, 1961, the fishermen and their relatives dedicated the first memorial to Seattle's missing fishermen.

The Halibut Fishermen's Wives Association sponsored the memorial. This group of women, married to captains and crewmen, originally sponsored social events but soon became a powerful force for promoting the halibut fishing industry.[19] For years afterward on Memorial Day, families placed wreaths at the boulder. After the annual ceremony, the wives and children took the wreaths onto a boat and laid them on the waters of Puget Sound. The memorial remains in the 7500 block of Thirty-fourth Avenue Northwest.

The placement of the annual maritime plaques between 1957 and 1986 is the city's longest running program to place heritage markers. While four of the markers have disappeared the remaining tablets share stories about Seattle's maritime past and remember a time when the waterfront was the most important facet of the young city's life. Small bouquets of flowers left by grieving family members at the Fishermen's Memorial remind us that despite modern technology and safety regulations, the sea remains a dangerous place and exacts a toll on those who fish it.

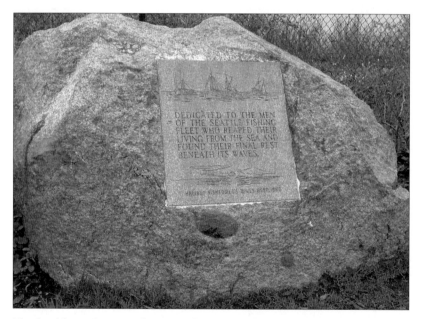

This boulder and engraved memorial to Seattle's lost fishermen rests in Sunset Hill Park. *Courtesy of the author.*

CHAPTER 11

HEROES, LEADERS, AND LEGENDS

Seattle's community groups have dedicated several memorials to honor a disparate list of heroes, leaders, and legends. Two statues honored sea-going explorers: Scandinavian-Americans backed a memorial to Leif Erikson in 1962 and Italian-Americans supported a monument to Christopher Columbus in 1978. In the 1980s and 1990s, statues were placed to honor Seattle's quirkiest restaurateur, Ivar Haglund; musician Jimi Hendrix; Dr. Martin Luther King Jr.; and fallen firefighters. These memorials share the past of people who, in their own ways, inspired and helped define Seattle.

Leif Erikson

Seattle is home to many people of Nordic descent thanks to waves of Danish, Finnish, Icelandic, Norwegian, and Swedish immigrants, many of whom arrived in the late 1800s. In 1956, citizens of Scandinavian descent formed a social club, the Leif Erikson League of Seattle, with one of its stated goals to establish a memorial to their namesake.

The group approached Seattle Mayor Gordon Clinton in early 1959 to ask if a statue of Erikson could be placed in a public park, preferably at the Civic Center (the present Seattle Center.) The Parks Department opposed the proposal, fearing every immigrant and civic group in the city would want a statue in a park. The City Art Commission agreed and did not think the suggested location was appropriate, so while withholding support for the idea, they did recommend the Shilshole-Golden Gardens breakwater area, which was closer to the water. City Councilman Charles Carroll asked to keep the Erikson statue out of the Rainier Valley, an area called "Little Italy," for fear of conflict between the immigrant Italians and the Scandinavians.[1]

The group began to raise $40,000 in funds and held a contest to select a sculptor. Even though he did not submit a design, August

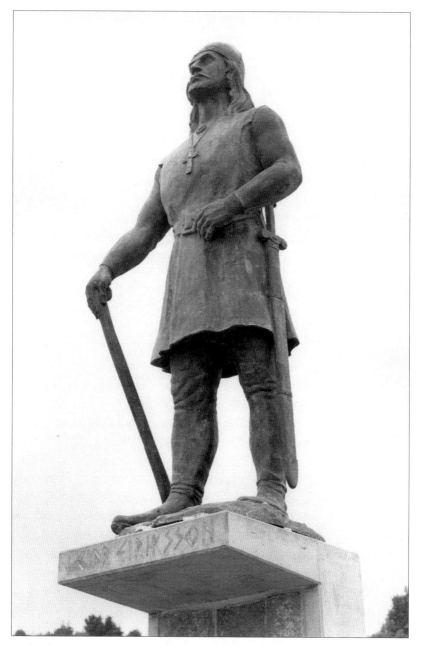

Leif Erikson Memorial, unveiled at the Shilshole Bay Marina to coordinate with Norway Day at the Century 21 World's Fair in 1962. *UW SOC1674.*

Werner, a longtime member of the University of Washington faculty and a prominent member of the Scandinavian community, was selected as the sculptor due to his influence with the Erikson league. Nearly two years later, Werner put the finishing touches on a clay model of the statue. The four-foot model still exists and is the property of the Nordic Heritage Museum in Ballard. Werner disagreed with the proposal to place the statue next to a parking lot at the Shilshole Bay Marina, stating, "It is idiotic to put it up among a bunch of automobiles."[2] However, the Port of Seattle Commissioners stuck to their original plan and voted to place the statue at the marina.

On the afternoon of June 17, 1962, the Leif Erikson Memorial was dedicated to coordinate with Norway Day at the Century 21 World's Fair. The sixteen-foot statue on a fourteen-foot base of imported Norwegian blue granite was surrounded by a small landscaped pool, set off with low benches and a wall made of the same blue granite. Icelandic poet Jacobina Johnson unveiled the statue in front of a crowd of 3,000 spectators. The Norwegian ambassador to the United States listened to Reverend Burton W. Smith, pastor of Ballard's First Lutheran Church, dedicate the statue, "in the memory of one who was willing to risk his life for the unknown and unseen."[3]

Within a year, Coast Guard officials placed the statue on the official nautical charts of the area and passing Norwegian ships gave three long whistle blasts and dipped their flags as they sailed by on their way to Seattle and other Puget Sound ports. Thousands attended annual Nordic Festivals at the memorial as bands played and children performed traditional Norwegian dances near the statue. The statue became a royal destination in May 1968, as a crowd gathered to sing, dance, and cheer for King Olav V of Norway. Three additional copies of the statue were made from a mold created in 1996 and installed in Trondheim, Norway (1997); Brattahlid, Greenland (2000); and L'Anse aux Meadows, Newfoundland, Canada (2013).

The Leif Erikson International Foundation updated the statue's setting on a rainy day in 2007 when they unveiled a new base that included a list of 850 Scandinavian immigrants' names. They added more names in both 2010 and 2014 for a total of 2,351 names as people submitted their information to the foundation. The new base is a large granite stone approximately six feet high, in the middle of a plaza circled by standing stones, featuring Viking carvings and plaques with the names of immigrants, along with their hometowns and the year they immigrated to the United States.

Christopher Columbus

In the late 1970s, the Italian-American community planned a statue for their countryman, Christopher Columbus. The Italian Community Hall, a group of nine organizations from King County, agreed to raise funds and proposed either the waterfront or Seattle Center as a location. The Seattle Center declined since their grounds were supposed to be inclusive, and they did not want to favor any particular ethnic group. The fundraising committee suggested the new Waterfront Park under construction at Pier 57, but the Seattle Arts Commission needed to unanimously approve the proposal.

The community raised $75,000, and the Parks and Recreation department approved their initial plan, even though nearly two decades earlier they had objected to the Erikson statue being placed on park grounds. The committee selected Seattle sculptor Douglas Bennett for the project. Bennett graduated from the University of Washington with a degree in art and served in the Navy as a pilot during World War II. He studied at the Art Center of Los Angeles and exhibited a sculpture at the Metropolitan Museum of Art in New York. The Columbus statue was his first major sculpture after spending twenty-five years as an industrial designer.

Bennett submitted a clay model, which the Italian-American committee accepted. Final approval of the project had to come from the Art in Public Places Committee of the Seattle Arts Commission before the Italian Community Hall placed any artwork on city-owned property. The committee visited Bennett's studio overlooking Lake Union. After seeing the model, they voiced their disapproval of his version of Columbus, whom he portrayed in a modernist, industrial style as a gaunt, almost anguished figure leaning on a sword. "The proposed work does not meet minimum artistic standards, either in concept or in realization, and therefore it cannot be expected to function effectively within the scale or the context of the proposed site."[4]

Hoping for a more heroic representation of Columbus, the commission rejected the proposal in a split vote with the discussion about the statue described as "prolonged and agonized."[5]

The commission recommended that Mayor Wes Uhlman turn down the Italian-American's gift to the city on its artistic merit. The mayor overruled the commissioners and asked the city council to accept the statue. Within a few weeks, the Parks and Public Grounds Committee and then the full city council approved the placement of the statue of Christopher Columbus in Waterfront Park at Pier 57. With approval in hand, Bennett began to work on the full-scale sculpture in the garage studio at his house. He hammered and shaped twenty-five bronze sections which he pieced together with metal fittings. The artist often opened the door of his garage studio and rolled the statue outside to observe it in the natural daylight and see how the sunlight would play across the pieces. People stopped and watched him at work, as the seven-foot-high bronze figure with a terrazzo and marble base began to take shape.

The city dedicated the statue on October 8, 1978, as the finale of a ten-day Italian Heritage Celebration. Bennett described his artistic goal: "No one really knows what Columbus looked like aside from a few salient characteristics mentioned down through history. But I wanted to synthesize in an appropriate art form what makes him one of the ten great men of the world; the qualities of courage, persistence, never say die."[6]

The debate over the artistic merit of the Columbus statue continued after its dedication.[7] The depiction of the explorer is undoubtedly different from the more realistic portrayals of Columbus.[8] Bennett defended his work against the critics: "I was trying to reflect a Columbus whose crew had mutinied, some gone mad, looking out for land and dangerous reefs in a howling storm the night they landed after 33 days at sea. I chose to depict tenacity and courage." The criticism of his Columbus ended his career as an artist. After the dedication, Bennett and his wife retired to Jefferson County.[9]

Christopher Columbus and the celebration of his arrival in the New World increasingly fell out of favor as scholars and historians researched and documented his interactions with indigenous tribes

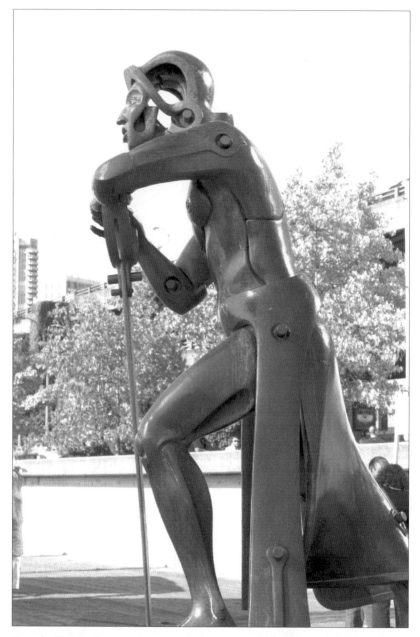

Douglas Bennett's representation of Christopher Columbus was removed from Waterfront Park to avoid being the target of vandals. *Courtesy of Brenda Kean © 123RF.com.*

in the Caribbean. The use of violence and slavery, the forced conversion of Natives to Christianity, and the introduction of new diseases had cast a different perspective on Columbus. The statue on Seattle's waterfront was not immune to these perspectives; Columbus Day protesters often doused the statue in red paint. In 2009, the city placed a crate around the statue to protect it, but within a couple of years, protesters broke through and defaced the statue again.

To prevent further damage, the city removed the statue before Columbus Day 2012. While in storage they restored it by removing the paint and repairing the patina to return the statue to its original color. Calandra Childers, a spokesperson for the Seattle Office of Arts & Culture, said the city would work with the community to prevent vandalism in the future when the Columbus statue is relocated.[10]

The statues of Leif Erikson and Christopher Columbus in Seattle followed an established, nation-wide pattern of statues initiated by local ethnic groups seeking to valorize their explorers. Erikson statues were erected in Milwaukee, Boston, Chicago, St. Paul, and Duluth, Minnesota. Columbus was the subject of hundreds of monuments during events to remember the four hundredth anniversary of his landing in America in 1992. Even though the two men had no connection to Seattle, the stories behind their monuments demonstrate the impact of their ethnic communities on Seattle.

Ivar Haglund

Located along the waterfront at Pier 54 is a Seattle dining institution, Ivar's Acres of Clams and Fish Bar. The restaurants were founded by Ivar Haglund, an eccentric Seattle character. A famous representative of a working class, older Seattle, Haglund established Seattle's first aquarium at Pier 54 in 1938, and then a fish-and-chips stand which led to his restaurant business. Beginning in 1965, he provided a fireworks show over Elliott Bay every "Fourth of Jul-Ivar." He was a radio personality, reluctant port commissioner, philanthropist, and real estate investor who in 1976 purchased Seattle's iconic Smith Tower.[11]

After Haglund's death in January 1985, a group of longtime friends commissioned a bronze, life-size statue created by artist Richard Beyer. They asked the public for $50,000 to fund the project. Those who donated ten dollars were rewarded with a songbook; a gift of twenty dollars received an audio cassette of Haglund singing. The statue is a cast bronze and aluminum sculpture of Ivar feeding french fries to oversized seagulls with the names of the donors engraved on the back of the statue. The welcoming chair and broad backs of the large gulls invite people to sit and interact with the piece. Underneath this statue is a time capsule filled with Ivar's artifacts and predictions of the future to be opened on the restaurant's hundredth anniversary in 2038.[12]

Martin Luther King Jr. Memorial

The Reverend Dr. Martin Luther King Jr. visited Seattle only once— in 1961—but his legacy is well represented in Seattle. In 1974, Harrison Elementary School was renamed Martin Luther King Jr. Elementary School. A major north-south thoroughfare originally named Empire Way was renamed Martin Luther King Jr. Way. In 1986, the King County Council passed a motion to rename King County to commemorate Dr. King rather than William Rufus de Vane King, the vice president-elect for whom the county was originally named in 1852.[13]

In the summer of 1983, community activist Charlie James approached sculptor Bob Kelly, who taught art and design at the University of Washington and Shoreline Community College.[14] Inspired by King's "I've Been to the Mountaintop" speech delivered in Memphis the day before his assassination in 1968, Kelly envisioned a sculptured mountain of granite symbolizing King's strength and his life. He estimated the project would cost $50,000; the funds would be raised from the community.[15]

The organizers initially proposed to place the sculpture in the northwest corner of Powell Barnett Park, in the heart of the Central District at the corner of Jefferson Street and Martin Luther King Jr. Way. Concerned the space was not large enough to accommodate such a large statue, the Parks Board proposed a space a mile and a half south at South Walker Street and Martin Luther King Jr. Way.[16] A groundbreaking ceremony in 1984 drew a group of political dignitaries and community leaders. However, the project stalled as the organizers struggled to raise the money.

By 1988, the only progress made was a peeling, graffiti-covered sign featuring drawings of the park and monument. The plans were impressive: a symbolic mountain would be formed by large slabs of polished black granite in shapes inspired by African art forms. The sculpture would sit in an elliptical pool, surrounded by a small wall and walkway. Around its edge, bronze plaques would recall events in King's life. It was fortuitous Kelly created such detailed plans; sadly, he drowned in Hawaii in the spring of 1988, at the same time the project seemed to be languishing.[17]

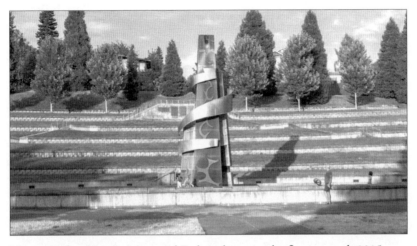

Martin Luther King Jr. Memorial Park sculpture and reflecting pool, 2015. *Courtesy of the Seattle Municipal Archives #178174.*

That summer the fundraising drive received a boost as several prominent minority leaders joined the effort. Finally, the black granite blocks quarried in Zimbabwe and polished in Spain were unloaded on the waterfront in the fall of 1990.[18] Groundbreaking began in May 1991, despite objections from citizens concerned that the location, across from a bottling plant and facing the rear of several warehouses, was unsuitable for the monument. They preferred a location six blocks north over the Interstate 90 tunnel. City officials disagreed, stating that while the idea was admirable, it came too late in the process.[19]

Costs had ballooned to $450,000, but in 1991, the dream was finally realized.[20] On Saturday morning, November 16, a crowd gathered in the wind and rain on a muddy hillside to honor Dr. Martin Luther King Jr.'s memory and ideas. Speakers stressed the park was not intended to be a playground, but a memorial where people can think about solutions to problems and remember King's speech that inspired the statue.[21]

Jimi Hendrix Bust and Statue

Jimi Hendrix was a Seattleite who made a large impact on the world of popular music. The first memorial to Hendrix was a bronze bust of the alumnus of Garfield High School, placed in the school library. Sculpted by Whidbey Island resident Jeff Day in 1982, the Hendrix family donated it in the mid-1980s. The school was hesitant to accept the gift. At the statue's dedication ceremony, when reporters asked the artist about the propriety of Hendrix being honored in a school because of his association with drugs, Day replied, "The sculpture would be inspirational to kids at the school because it shows what he [Hendrix] overcame." The statue is now enjoyed by the students who play pranks and often use it as a destination for scavenger hunts.

A life-sized bronze statue of Hendrix entitled "The Electric Lady Studio Guitar" by Seattle artist Daryl Smith was dedicated in 1997. It is on the east side of Broadway, north of the intersection with Pike Street. Unveiled in a veil of colored smoke, a reference to the song "Purple Haze," the figure of Jimi shredding his Stratocaster was based on a photo taken during the Monterey Pop Festival in 1967. Mike Malone, a real-estate developer and music fan whose guitar collection includes Hendrix's last guitar, commissioned the statue. It was nearly moved to the Jimi Hendrix Park, but, for now, it remains a destination on Capitol Hill for music fans and graffiti taggers.[22] Hendrix is also memorialized with a 1983 "living memorial" of plants, a mosaic path, and small brass star next to the African Savannah exhibit at the Woodland Park Zoo.

Seattle's Fallen Firefighters

Occidental Park in Pioneer Square is home to a memorial to Seattle's fallen firefighters. Four bronze figures representing four firemen who died while fighting a warehouse fire in Seattle's Chinatown International District on January 5, 1995, are surrounded by slabs of granite which depict a collapsed building. Their names, Walter D. Kilgore, Randall Terlicker, Gregory Allen Shoemaker, and James T. Brown, are etched in granite near the figures. The firefighters responded to a five-alarm blaze at the Mary Pang Frozen Chinese Food plant at South Dearborn Street and Seventh Avenue South and died after the first floor collapsed dropping them twenty feet into the burning basement.[23]

While the memorial names the four lost firefighters, the faces of the sculpted figures are covered with air masks. Hai Ying Wu, an internationally recognized artist who studied at the University of Washington, said he wanted the anonymity of each figure to represent "any of the thousands of firefighters who have donned the uniform of the Seattle Fire Department." The memorial is a tribute to all Seattle firefighters who have died in the line of duty since the department was created, and lists each of their names. The first name on the memorial is Herman Larson, who served aboard the fireboat *Snoqualmie* and died March 3, 1891.[24] Additional names continue to be added as fatalities occur.

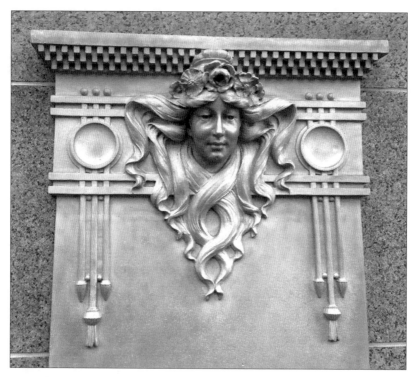

A metal casting made from an original plaster decorative element from the restaurant of the Savoy Hotel. Built in 1906, the Savoy was advertised as "12 stories of solid comfort." *Courtesy of the author.*

CHAPTER 12

REMEMBERING PLACES

Pioneer Square Was Rough and Ready

Heritage markers tell the stories of many historical places in Pioneer Square. Reborn and rebuilt after the Great Fire, the brick and stone buildings constructed in the two decades after the disaster offer one of the nation's best collections of Romanesque Revival architecture. Thanks to the buildings' owners and developers, community organizations, and the Washington State Centennial historical marker program, pedestrians walking around the neighborhood can see the plaques and discover a little piece of history about where they are standing.

For years, Pioneer Square was the heart of Seattle. It was originally the site of a Native village and later, pioneer cabins and clapboard buildings. By the late 1800s, the area south of Yesler Avenue had turned into a crowded accumulation of saloons, pawn shops, cheap hotels, tenements crowded with itinerant workers, and crib houses where prostitutes served their customers.

The White Chapel District

The White Chapel District is marked by a square silver plaque on the Norton Building at 206 Third Avenue South, which tells the story of the surrounding blocks and Seattle's first Chinatown. This area has been referred to by many names. First, it was called Maynardtown, after Doc Maynard, who arrived early in 1852 and was Seattle's first physician. The neighborhood's seedy character took shape during the 1870s when entrepreneurs took advantage of Seattle's bachelor problem (men outnumbered women three to one) and opened numerous establishments that provided liquor, gambling, and female companionship. It was also called the Lava Beds, the Tenderloin, and the Great Restricted District.[1] The original Whitechapel, located in the East End of London, was notorious for overcrowding, prostitution, crime, and squalid living conditions.

Seattle's White Chapel was next to another decrepit area called Black Chapel. They each housed one to two hundred crib houses—buildings of small, sparsely furnished rooms where the most destitute prostitutes lived and worked. White Chapel was populated by white women, while the women of Black Chapel were other races, including Indians. Newly elected Mayor James T. Ronald was a former district attorney who in 1892 was supported by a coalition of progressives and moralists. He fired the police chief on his first day and enforced state-wide anti-gambling laws for the first time. These actions forced the closure of the two infamous enclaves; in his words, they were a "stench in the nostrils of decency and a disgrace upon the good name of Seattle." In 1895, Great Northern crews tore down the bleak rows of crib houses and filled in the tide flats to make room for railroad facilities.[2]

The White Chapel plaque also presents information on Seattle's original Chinatown, located on Washington Street, between Second and Third Avenues. Hundreds of male Chinese immigrants were drawn to the West Coast to dig in mines and work in salmon canneries. Two-thirds of the men who laid track for the Western Division of the Northern Pacific Railway were Chinese. Anti-Chinese sentiment peaked when an armed mob drove 350 Chinese settlers from Seattle in 1886.

Madame Lou Graham's Sporting House

An early Seattle business run by Madame Lou Graham is marked by a plaque at the intersection of South Washington Street and Third Avenue South on the north exterior of the Washington Court Building, present home to the Union Gospel Mission. Lou Graham arrived in Seattle on the steamer *Pacific Pride* in February 1888. Following other earlier prostitution operations, she established her "house of ill repute" opposite Father Prefontaine's church in Pioneer Square. Graham created the most elegant, lavish bordello in the city. She advertised her house's services by parading her new girls around town in horse-drawn carriages. Patrons, including city officials and men from Seattle's finest families, were invited to the house to dine, drink, and be entertained by what were advertised as Seattle's most beautiful women.

It all unraveled in December 1902, when Seattle's police chief issued an order closing all "disreputable" houses. Recognizing the new environment would adversely affect her business, Graham moved to San Francisco to open a new house in the West Coast's other Sin City. Within a month, and before she could open her new business, Graham died of syphilis. At the time of her death, she owned many properties, which some sources say she bequeathed to the public schools of King County.[3]

The Seattle Fire

By the turn of the twentieth century, industrial and commercial interests occupied Pioneer Square's blocks. A fire on June 6, 1889, destroyed most of the neighborhood's older structures after a worker named John Back accidentally started a fire in the basement of a building located at the southwest corner of Madison Street and Front Street (now First Avenue). By the next day, twenty-nine city blocks, nearly the entire business district including most of its wharves and railroad terminals, were a smoldering ruin. Referred to as the Great Fire, this conflagration spurred the construction of the brick and stone buildings that make up current-day Pioneer Square.[4]

Sometime after the blaze, volunteer firefighters commissioned a Seattle Fire plaque to mark the location where the fire began and placed it on the Rainier-Grand Hotel, which was built after the fire. In 1931, developers demolished the hotel and replaced with a new Federal Office Building. The fire department salvaged the plaque from the debris. In 1952, Robert B. Rogers, assistant fire chief, used the sixty-third anniversary of the catastrophe as an occasion to reattach the marker to a wall at the site of the fire's origin. As a four-year-old boy, Rogers had watched the fire from his house on Fifth Avenue.[5] The original plaque and a registered state historical plaque remain on the corner of the federal building at First Avenue and Madison Street.

Pioneer Square Pergola and Occidental Park Information Booth

An elegant iron pergola stands in Pioneer Square Park. Erected in 1909 as a stop for the Yesler & James Cable Car, it provided shelter and a large, underground, public restroom. Seattle architect Julian Everett designed the structure of delicate intersecting barrel vaults of glass, which have a cast-iron framework supported by ornate columns.

A 1972 restoration returned the pergola to its former elegance and sealed off the restrooms. The pergola's proximity to a busy intersection proved to be problematic when on January 15, 2001, a truck ran into it while turning the corner. Seidelhuber Iron & Bronze Works completed the repairs and restoration by referring to old drawings and plans.[6] They also supplied a plaque which was placed next to the pergola. It reopened on August 17, 2002, and the structure continues to shade visitors who come to the park.

Located nearby on the south side of Occidental Park is an Information Booth made from an ornate 1897 elevator car from the Maynard Building. The owner of the building, Alan Black, donated the elevator car and refurbished it into an information booth in 1977. A plaque is on the exterior of the stall.

Marking the Founding of the United Parcel Service

Many people have no idea the international delivery service, United Parcel Service (UPS) was founded in Seattle. Messenger boys, among them James E. Casey, started the business in August 1907 in a small office at the corner of Second Avenue South and South Main Street. While the modern corporation is now headquartered in Atlanta, Georgia, the company never forgot its Seattle roots. In January 1967, with the cooperation of the Seattle Historical Society, employees placed a plaque on the sidewalk at the corner.[7] In 1977, a Waterfall Garden dedicated to UPS employees was created by the Annie E. Casey Foundation, which was established by James and his siblings in honor of their mother. In 2007, to celebrate the centennial anniversary of the company, employees gathered at its birthplace and placed an additional plaque.

Downtown Hotels

The start of the 1900s brought about the construction of some residential hotels to provide housing for laborers, immigrants, and others who lived and worked in the downtown area. One example is the **Panama Hotel** (1910) located in the International District and designed by Sabro Ozasa, one of the earliest Japanese architects in the country and the first to practice in Seattle. The hotel served as a home for generations of Japanese immigrants, Alaskan fisherman, and travelers. Jan Johnson purchased the hotel in 1985 and discovered a unique collection in the basement. When Japanese American residents were deported to internment camps in 1942, some stored their personal belongings in the basement of the hotel. More than forty years later, Johnson found these possessions, returned what she could to the owners, and preserved the remaining items as part of the hotel's history. In 2006, the property was designated a National Historic Landmark, and a bronze plaque was installed in the building's tea and coffee house.[8]

Other hotels sought a wealthy clientele and offered a higher level of service along with accompanying elegance and architectural details. The **Brooklyn Building** (1890) at 1212 Second Avenue and the **Colonial Hotel** (1901) at 1119 First Avenue both have plaques describing their history. The **Savoy Hotel** (1905) was demolished in 1986 to make way for a skyscraper, but a plaque and casting from one of the decorative sculptures from the hotel's restaurant are present on the south side of University Street between Second and Third Avenues.

The **Olympic Hotel** was the most prestigious and luxurious hotel in Seattle when it opened in December 1924. Financed by a public bond subscription campaign, it was considered one of the finest hotels in America. While Seattle had grown into a prominent city, it lacked a luxurious hotel that might appeal to VIP visitors and guests. A joke around town was "if the president came to visit Seattle, where could he possibly stay?"

Two thousand people attended the grand opening of the Olympic Hotel as searchlights lit the downtown skies. One of the numerous events celebrating the grand opening was the placement of a plaque, sponsored by the Daughters of the Pioneers of Washington State, embedded in the pillar of the vestibule at the main entrance on Seneca Street. The marker commemorated the original location of the University of Washington, land on which the hotel was built.[9]

Doris Lamping, a granddaughter of Rolland Denny, unveiled the tablet in front of a crowd that included members of the first class who attended the university in 1861. Edmond Meany provided a historical overview of how Washington Territory selected the site for the school, the legislative appropriation, and the role of Reverend Daniel Bagley in the 1861 selection of a location. Arthur Denny offered a nearly ten-acre section from his original claim on a hillside overlooking Elliott

Bay. From 1861 to 1895, the university's first building, featuring a portico and four graceful columns, overlooked Puget Sound and the Olympic Mountains from this site.

Albert Sperry Kerry led the effort to finance and build the Olympic Hotel. Originally a lumberman regarded for his business savvy and strong sense of public service, Kerry was vice president of the A-Y-P Exposition in 1909 and served as president of the Chamber of Commerce in 1923. He was selected to lead the Community Hotel Corporation and completed the construction of the Olympic. In 1927, Kerry donated land to the city for the eponymous Kerry Park on Queen Anne Hill which provides a viewpoint to look across the city and Elliott Bay. A plaque in the park reads, *Kerry Park was given to the city of Seattle in 1927 by Mr. & Mrs. Albert Sperry Kerry Sr. so that all who stop here may enjoy this view.* A few months after his death in 1939, a bronze bas-relief by Alonzo Victor Lewis was placed between the main doors of the entrance to the Olympic Hotel as a tribute: *In memory of Albert Sperry Kerry, past president Community Hotel Corporation—Patriotic, Unselfish, an Outstanding Citizen.*

The hotel underwent a significant renovation in the early 1980s, and the owners relocated the existing plaques and added a new marker. The UW Board of Regents, representatives from the Olympic Hotel, and several descendants of Seattle's first families unveiled a new plaque to honor Daniel Bagley and Arthur Denny for their roles in constructing the first University of Washington building on the site. The Bagley/Denny plaque is under a flagpole by the sidewalk on the University Street entrance. The other markers, displayed in different locations before the renovation, were moved to the University Street entrance to the right of the front doors.

These and many other historical markers were placed after 1940 in various locations around Seattle. While the majority of these recognized specific buildings, some mark the locations of events, businesses, neighborhoods, and even a railroad tunnel. The buildings' owners and developers commissioned some of the markers; the Assistance League of Seattle, a local chapter of a national philanthropic organization, dedicated some of them. The state created another series of plaques as a part of the Washington State Centennial celebration in 1989.

CHAPTER 13

WHAT MIGHT HAVE BEEN

Through the years a number of monuments were proposed that never came to be. Many were small; a few were grandiose ideas offered as little more than flights of fancy and imagination. The reasons they were never finished varied. In some cases, interest in the subject matter waned. For others, the Great Depression and the Second World War distracted attention away from the projects. A few were simply too large and too complex for a city the size of Seattle. All represent interesting stories of what might have been.

Pioneer Place

Just two years after the Seattle Chamber of Commerce erected the Pioneer Place totem pole in 1899, local citizens submitted a proposal to add a nearby fountain. Initially, it was to be a memorial to the Washington State volunteers who died fighting in the Philippines during the Spanish-American War. Local citizens would need to raise $50,000 for the monument, which they would dedicate to Captain George F. Fortson. A former Seattle City Attorney and a volunteer with the First Washington Volunteer Regiment, Fortson died in 1898 from wounds received in battle.

The city council and Chamber of Commerce questioned the viability of a memorial to Fortson as a representative casualty of the Spanish-American War. Some suggested it would be more suitable to have a monument dedicated to Seattle's pioneers in the historical center of Seattle where the Yesler, Maynard, and Boren claims all intersected. While the city council shelved the plans for a monument to Captain Fortson in Pioneer Place, they did memorialize him in 1901 with the dedication of a small public park, Fortson Square, at the southeast corner of Yesler Way and Second Avenue. The First Washington Volunteer Association suggested building a memorial in that location to the state's soldiers who died in the Philippines. The city never seriously considered their suggestion, but a similar statue, "The Hiker," was placed in Woodland Park in 1926.

The idea for a pioneer monument was raised again in 1906. In preparation for the Alaska-Yukon-Pacific Exposition and the completion of several trolley lines with a terminus in Pioneer Place, the city planned to develop an underground comfort station with public restrooms there. However, an anonymous citizen wanted to privately finance up to $75,000 for a pioneer monument instead. In the end, the city constructed the pergola with underground restrooms, and the Birthplace of Seattle shaft placed on Alki Beach in West Seattle in 1905 remained the only large memorial to the original settlers of Seattle.

Governor Ferry

Elisha P. Ferry was elected as Washington State's first governor and served until 1893, when Governor John H. McGraw was elected. A statue of McGraw was erected in 1913 and Ferry's friends thought the city should also honor the first governor. Joseph W. Robinson, a well-known Seattle attorney, offered to contribute $1,000 to start a fundraising drive but wanted a civic group or pioneer association to assist in raising additional funds.

By this time, however, the influence of the pioneer generation was beginning to wane, and the new generation of business leaders was not interested in statues of old pioneers and politicians. Robinson was not able to raise funds or interest in a memorial to Governor Ferry. In 1926, sculptor James A. Wehn tried to reignite interest in a public monument honoring Ferry. While Wehn never completed a statue, he eventually created a small bronze plaque of Ferry's portrait for the state capitol building in Olympia. The location of that marker is unknown.

The Peace Memorial

At the end of the First World War in 1918, the Seattle post of the veterans' group, Grand Army of the Republic (GAR), proposed a large marble monument to honor Union veterans of the Civil War. The Parks Board provided space at Yesler Triangle at Third Avenue and Yesler Way and local architect Charles L. Thompson was selected to

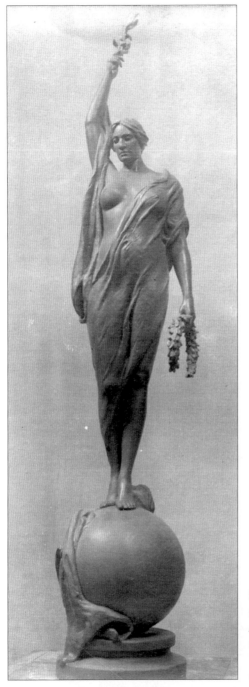

Statue by James A. Wehn, a
study for proposed Grand
Army of the Republic veterans
memorial, 1922. *University of
Washington Libraries, Special
Collections #SOC9045.*

design the memorial. With a budget of $150,000, it was to be one of the most massive and impressive monuments in the West.

Thompson designed a thirty-foot-high column topped by a four-foot globe upon which stood a statue of the goddess of peace. He chose Washington granite for the base of the monument, which would be twenty-eight feet square with a nine foot ceiling, and would serve as a hall of records for Civil War veterans. Included were restrooms and a small shop for souvenirs. Outside were six life-sized statues. On the pedestal facing east stood a life-sized statue of George Washington, the west side featured a statue of Abraham Lincoln. On the north and south sides were two soldiers and two sailors in Civil War uniforms. The overall height of the monument was seventy-six feet.

The female figure perched on the top of the column gave the monument its name—the Peace Memorial. Even with the city's donation of the Yesler Triangle, private fundraising went slowly. The dwindling number of GAR posts around the state raised only a few thousand dollars. In the winter of 1921, James A. Wehn joined the project and created a model of the female figure. The four-foot-high plaster model was based on the original Thompson sketch but was now semi-nude with her toga falling off of her raised arm. Wehn also wanted to design Washington, Lincoln, and other soldier statues. The GAR publicized the fundraising effort, but by 1928, support for the monument evaporated. Many issues contributed to the failure of the project; the decade-long timeline, along with no detailed plans for financing and construction, sapped energy from the public.[1] There was no precedent for a local memorial of this size. At the time, there were a limited number of statues in Seattle, and only a handful of these were larger than life (George Washington, William H. Seward, and John McGraw.) Even these were smaller than the proposed Peace Memorial. Thompson's classical Greek-style design did not appeal to the local audience either, and the Civil War faded from public consciousness. The land would soon be the location of the Father Prefontaine Fountain.

A "Statue of Liberty" for the Pacific

Extending north into Elliott Bay, Duwamish Head at the northernmost tip of West Seattle provides a natural point, either on the beach or above on a plateau, to watch vessels entering the harbor from Puget Sound.

The first proposal for a monument on Duwamish Head appeared in the 1911 Bogue Plan. Virgil Bogue was a civil engineer hired by Seattle to create an overall plan for the future development of Seattle. His plan was ambitious and demonstrated his goal to grow the city in an organized arrangement rather than in a random, scattered way. Part of his plan was the creation of a large concourse overlooking Elliott Bay with a park at the north end of California Avenue. This site would feature a great civic monument on the promontory, which would be to Seattle what the Statue of Liberty was to New York Harbor. His architectural drawing featured a giant obelisk on a large, much adorned square base with columns and accompanying statues.[2] Ordinary citizens were daunted by the size and cost of the entire plan. On March 5, 1912, voters rejected the plan and Bogue's vision was never fulfilled.

The next idea for Duwamish Head came during the Great Depression. Captain Clayton J. Hutchinson, a Seattle mining engineer, proposed a large, gray sandstone statue to honor the pioneer mothers of America. Hutchinson selected sculptor Aatto Annala and presented his plans for a 235-foot, $500,000 monument to the Seattle Port Commission and the federal Works Progress Administration, a Depression-era federal jobs program. They referred to the statue as the "The Statue of Liberty of the West."

The 135-foot tall shaft of the memorial would be topped by a 100-foot figure of a pioneer woman, a baby in her left arm, and her right arm curved protectively around her son who stands beside her, his face upturned. Illuminated by powerful floodlights, the monument would be visible for miles, and an airplane beacon would shine from the top. At its base would be a frieze including a series of figures depicting the roles women played in the development of the United States. The inside of the shaft at the base would be decorated with a similar frieze of figures donated by each state plus Alaska and Hawaii.[3] Neither this monument, nor a similar one proposed in 1945, were constructed.

Other massive projects were put forth in the 1940s and 1950s as well. The Tacoma Public Forum on September 28, 1941, proposed a "mammoth statue of George Washington as the western counterpart to the Statue of Liberty" to be placed at the entrance to the Strait of Juan de Fuca. In 1944, Joseph Guldner of Seattle proposed a "monster replica of a torch on a long handle, guarded by a huge statue of George

Washington." It was to be placed on Whidbey Island facing the Strait of Juan de Fuca and was to be financed by contributions of students.[4]

As World War II came to a close, James A. Gibbs, president of the Park Board, shared plans for a towering monument at Duwamish Head to honor Seattle's first settlers. While no public funds were available, Gibbs said the Parks Board hopes "some generous hearted citizen will bequeath to the city the $300,000 we expect will be necessary." The plans called for a monument to Seattle's founders similar to the Coit Memorial Tower in San Francisco.

The idea for a large monument somewhere on Puget Sound continued to be advanced in the 1950s. A citizens committee met in November of 1951 with the goal to create a giant national monument, a "sister to the Statue of Liberty," facing toward Asia as an enduring symbol of peace and democracy. U.S. Senator Harry P. Cain praised the project as "so big that it merits the support of all citizens."[5] The project never got off the ground.

Yet another proposal for Duwamish Head came from John S. Detlie, a Seattle architect and chair of the Seattle Art Commission. In 1957, he proposed a tower which he also compared to the Statue of Liberty. Detlie's modernist proposal was a three-to-four-hundred-foot stainless steel shaft supported by exposed braces so the main shaft would seem to float above a large pool and fountain. The "Tower of Hope" monument would stand not on the plateau, but rather on the old Luna Park site on the shoreline. The shiny tower would be visible for miles up and down Puget Sound. Detlie suggested the symbol could be gifted to Seattle by a country, possibly Japan, since Seattle was the gateway to Asia. If not Japan, he thought perhaps a group of nations or Americans would finance it as a "joint venture in international understanding."[6]

In the end, none of the ideas for Duwamish Head survived the design phase. There would be no massive monument, western mother, George Washington, or modernist shaft. Apparently, Seattle would not have its "West Coast Statue of Liberty." Instead, it would retain open park space and viewpoint at the north end of California Avenue. While the city purchased the property in 1914, it would not become a public park until 1954. The Park Board named it after Rupert Lehn

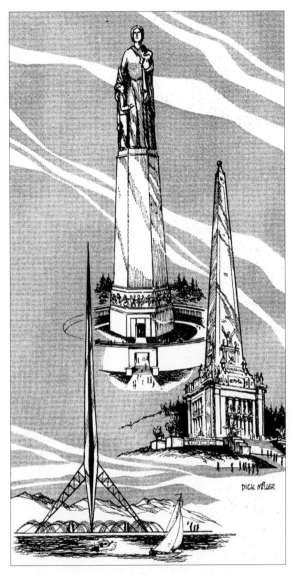

Duwamish Head, the northernmost tip of West
Seattle, has been the location for multiple monument
proposals. Top: a 235-foot tall statue to honor western
mothers proposed during the Great Depression. Right:
Virgil Bogue's 1911 proposal for a massive obelisk with
columns and statues. Bottom: a 1957 modernist
"Tower of Hope." *Courtesy of the Seattle Times.*

Hamilton in recognition of his efforts to promote parks and view-points in West Seattle and his work to develop the community while editor and publisher of the *West Seattle Herald*.

A Carillon and Fountains

Toward the end of the Second World War, a Seattle resident made an anonymous bequest of $250,000 to be spent on a carillon tower to be placed in Volunteer Park. Park Board president James A. Gibbs stated the tower was inspired by and would rival the beauty of the 205-foot-tall Bok Tower in Lake Wales, Florida. The bell tower for Seattle was never built.

The Allied Arts of Seattle and the Municipal Arts Commission discussed the possibility of a spectacular international fountain in 1958. Originally proposed for Volunteer Park, it was instead built in Seattle Center in 1961 for the Century 21 World's Fair. The excitement about this fountain aroused interest in adding additional fountains around the city. The *Seattle Daily Times* art critic Louis Guzzo encouraged the design and financing of other fountains by various local communities. The Japanese and Italian communities expressed interest in contributing fountains to the city. The newspaper suggested that other groups, such as the Swedish, Norwegian, Chinese, German, French, and British might be interested in taking up the challenge. While each one would be responsible for the financing, the designs required approval by the Art Commission.[7] None of these fountains were completed.

The Sourdough–The Prospector

Seattle and Alaska were economically linked after the famous Ton of Gold arrived from the Klondike. During the gold rush, miners formed a fraternal organization called the Yukon Order of Pioneers to maintain law and order and settle disagreements among prospectors and settlers. Many of the Alaskan miners settled in Seattle and in 1912 formed a local lodge. The name of the Seattle lodge changed to the Alaska Yukon Pioneers in 1921. Within a few years, Captain Albert J. Goddard, the head of the Seattle lodge, proposed a statue of "heroic proportions" as a memorial to the prospectors who departed from Seattle to Alaska and the Yukon.[8]

The twelve-foot tall bronze statue, depicting a prospector on his hunt for northern gold, was estimated to cost $25,000 and suggested for Alaskan Way, City Hall Park, or Denny Park. The lodge selected Alonzo Victor Lewis as the sculptor, and in 1927, he completed a three-foot study using several different prospectors as models. The organizers used this small statue for fundraising, but after a decade, they had raised only $7,000. Despite the lack of funds, Lewis over the next decade crafted a clay statue from which to cast the bronze monument.

At first, members of the Alaska Yukon Pioneers wanted the face of the statue to be that of George Washington Carmack, the prospector credited with the discovery that set off the Klondike gold rush. Carmack had passed away in 1922, so Lewis based his sculpture on photographs provided by the prospector's widow. The lack of a live model was problematic and no one liked how the statue's face turned out. The pioneers suggested Lewis use "Skagway Bill" Fonda, who arrived in Seattle in 1888 and headed north to the gold fields in 1897. Lewis sliced Carmack's head from the massive clay sculpture and replaced it with one of Fonda's likeness.

Even with the improved likeness, fundraising proceeded slowly. In 1938, the Reverend Dr. Mark Matthews suggested the city purchase the statue; a city council committee deferred the issue to Mayor Arthur Langlie who took no action. In 1940, the Alaska Yukon Pioneers again asked the city to assist with funds. The statue, made from three tons of clay, was ready to be cast in bronze if the city council would provide the remaining funds. The Great Depression and then the Second World War intervened, and Goddard resigned from the monument committee in 1942. The completed clay figure, a plaster cast ready to be bronzed, and the small model, were left in Lewis' studio. Lewis considered "The Sourdough" his masterpiece.[9]

Alonzo Victor Lewis died without a will at the age of sixty in November 1946. His daughter Charmain married into a prominent Alaska family. Her father-in-law, William Gross, was a well-known Juneau businessman and theater owner. He proposed that the statue be completed, but for Alaska, not Seattle. Charmain bid for her father's estate items at auction and took possession of the model. Gross and his friends lobbied and convinced two members of Alaska's Territorial Legislature to submit a bill in 1947 for the state to pay for a foundry to cast the statue. Charmain donated the plaster cast, and the Alaskans raised enough money to cast the statue in bronze and ship it to Sitka. Two years later, on Alaska Day, October 18, 1949, the completed monument was erected in front of the Pioneers Home, and its name changed from "The Sourdough" to "The Prospector." The statue remains there.

Charmain donated the small original model from 1927 to the Alaska Yukon Pioneers in Seattle as a reward for years of support for the project. They displayed this smaller statue during their reunion celebrations but otherwise kept it out of public view. At one time, they loaned it to the Museum of History and Industry. When the Pioneers wanted it back for another reunion, the museum refused; they believed the statue was their property. After a thorough search through the acquisition documentation, the museum determined the statue was owned by the Pioneer group and returned the statue to one of the group's officers. In 1981, the Pioneers loaned it out again, with a more substantial paper trail, to the Klondike Gold Rush National Historical Park in Seattle. It remains there today on display at the small museum in Pioneer Square, not only as a reminder of the Alaska gold rush but also as a remembrance of a grand monument which might have been located in Seattle.

This selected list of proposed monuments that were never completed demonstrates that it is not merely enough to have an idea for a statue. Detailed planning, financial and political backing, and public support are all key factors in the success of a large public artwork. Even with all of those items lined up, timing is everything and war or economic depression can interfere with the best-made plans. It is only in our imagination that we now can envision what a grand "Statue of Liberty" of the Pacific might look like on Duwamish Head, or how Seattle might have become a "city of fountains."

AFTERWORD

There are many ways to encounter Seattle's monuments, memorials, and historical markers. It might be by chance while walking to lunch or relaxing in a park, or it could be a more purposeful tracking down of a particular monument or story. It might be only a fleeting glance or a careful reading of information on a plaque. The types of monuments, the content, and the recurrence of themes communicate messages to residents and visitors. They provide a framework for understanding the character and history of Seattle and how leading businessmen, politicians, sculptors, activists, and ordinary people endeavored to present and preserve our history.

Whether the goal was to cement commercial ties to Alaska and Asia, honor a long forgotten governor, or commemorate the first around-the-world flight, these places mark Seattle's social and political interests and represent particular historical narratives. The stories of their creation are often stories of conflict about whom and what is being honored and how decisions were made to best represent that person, place, or event. After an organization or group unveils a memorial, the public often discovers and claims ownership of the monument as it becomes popular, and original issues of artistic merit, historical accuracy, vision, and ownership are forgotten. The monument is appreciated simply because it is there, even as it may continue to prompt debate and disagreement.

It is interesting to reflect on those who did not receive memorials. Two small plaques commemorate Arthur Denny's first cabin and home site, but there is no statue of the person himself, who arguably did the most to shape Seattle's founding and character. What about Erastus Brainerd, whose publicity and prose brought the riches of the Alaska gold rush to Seattle? What about Reginald H. Thomson, the turn-of-the-century city engineer responsible for much of the city's current layout? Perhaps monuments should be dedicated to labor leaders and the 1919 Seattle General Strike, or to Bertha Knight Landes, who in 1926 became the first female mayor of a major American city. Perhaps recognition should be given to the Reverend Samuel B. McKinney, who lead Mt. Zion Baptist Church for over forty years and was intricately involved in the struggle for civil rights; or to John Charles Olmsted, the landscape and parks architect who provided Seattle a plan for green spaces which largely survives to the present day in our parks and boulevards, the University of Washington campus, and the Arboretum.

Monuments are a product of their time and place in history. Sometimes that history can be unpalatable to our current perspectives of culture, race, and ethnicity. Typically, monuments and memorials of the past did not go through the same type of public review process they might today. Members of the public who might have objected to early statues did not have an opportunity to influence what was being memorialized. Often private groups like the Chamber of Commerce and civic clubs used public spaces like city parks for their monuments.

Today, it is difficult to get approval for a new statue or memorial. Park space is limited, so the placement of monuments is tightly controlled and limited given their permanent nature. Multiple, competing stakeholder groups, whose voices are often amplified by social media, may make the creation of a "memory place" to any person, event, or idea extremely challenging.

Perhaps the future lies in pop-up memorials that temporarily mark the anniversary of a historical event, such as attaching wreaths to a fence to remember the centennial of the Everett Massacre; or informal memorials that are created spontaneously, like the Kurt Cobain park bench in Viretta Park; or statues paid for by private individuals, like the Jimi Hendrix statue on Capitol Hill.

Indeed, it is difficult to envision another great leader of Seattle's past, present, or future having a permanent public statue or monument dedicated in their honor. From the Pioneer Square totem pole up through the Ken Griffey Jr. statue at Safeco Field, the first century of statues in Seattle may end up providing the city with its greatest number of public monuments, memorials, and markers. It is my hope that, even as Seattle constantly changes over the generations, this book will provide future residents a snapshot of how our community chose to remember itself from our founding to the early twenty-first century.

ANNUAL MARITIME PLAQUE INSCRIPTIONS (1957–1986)

These annual historical markers discussed in Chapter 10 are listed in the chronological order in which they were dedicated.

Ton of Gold from steamer *Portland*

The famous 'Ton of Gold' that started the Alaska gold rush was unloaded here in 1897. The S. S. Portland landed the valuable cargo at this pier then known as Schwabacher Dock.
Erected National Maritime Day 1957

Seattle's First Ferry Boat, *City of Seattle*

Here at the turn of the century the Puget Sound Navigation Co., under the leadership of Joshua Green, pioneered our vast ferry system and so contributed materially to the growth of Seattle. Here also in 1888 the 'City of Seattle' began regular ferry service to West Seattle.
Erected National Maritime Day 1958

Sloop-of-war, USS *Decatur*

Indians attack Seattle! Jan. 26, 1856. The settlement would have been destroyed but for the presence of the U. S. Sloop of War "Decatur". Anchored off this point, she fired a volley at the attackers, frightening them into a hasty retreat.
Erected National Maritime Day 1959

Hospital Ship *Idaho*

Beneath your feet lies the wreckage of the pioneer side-wheel steamer 'Idaho', which served from 1900 until 1909 as Dr. Alexander de Soto's famous wayside mission hospital. Here Dr. de Soto ministered to the needs of Seafarers and the destitute, donating his time and funds to their care.
Erected National Maritime Day 1960

The Great White Fleet

The U.S. Navy's "Great White Fleet" arrived Seattle May 23 and departed May 27, 1908 to continue their famous 46,000 mile round the world cruise. Part of the fleet anchored in Elliott Bay near this site and the crews disembarked here at the foot of

Lenora and Virginia streets – then known as Piers 9 and 10.
Erected National Maritime Day 1961

Steamship *Willapa*

Plaque is missing. Erected National Maritime Day 1962.

U.S. Coast Guard Cutter *Bear*

In memory of the Coast Guard Cutter "Bear." Seattle, the summer base of the Bear for 41 years, 1885 – 1926. Launched 1874, Greenoch, Scotland, veteran of the Arctic & Antarctic. Rescuer of many seafaring men & explorers. Beloved by all who served on her. Lost at sea, the North Atlantic, March 19, 1963.
Erected National Maritime Day–May 22, 1963

Yesler's Sawmill, Wharf, and Cookhouse

Seattle's first pier lies buried beneath your feet. The famous Yesler sawmill and wharf, constructed in 1853, marked the birth of Seattle's great lumber and shipping industries. For many years it was the center of Seattle's business district.
Erected National Maritime Week 1964

Battleship U.S.S. *Nebraska*

The U.S.S. Nebraska, first battleship constructed in the Pacific Northwest for the United States Navy was launched from this site on October 7, 1904 by the Moran Brothers Company. The Nebraska was financed in part by contributions from citizens of Seattle.
National Maritime Week 1965

Early Ferry Terminal, Colman Dock

Colman Dock was built on this site by J.M. Colman in 1909. This dock was center of ferry boat activity on Puget Sound. Seattle Ferry Terminal dedicated May 18, 1966.
National Maritime Day 1966

Chittenden Locks

Commemorating the 50th Anniversary of the Hiram M. Chittenden Locks. Dedicated in 1917, the locks have served both pleasure and commercial craft to the enhancement of the Seattle area.
National Maritime Day 1967

Miike Maru, first regular freight service to Japan

At this site on August 31, 1896, the Nippon Yusen Kaisha steamer 'Miike Maru' arrived with her cargo of tea. This was the first regularly scheduled steamer service between the Orient and Seattle, and marked the birth of Seattle as an international port.
Erected Maritime Day 1968

Skinner & Eddy Shipyards

Site of Skinner and Eddy Shipyard, 1916-1920, which built 75 ocean going vessels. Famous during World War I for delivering ten per cent of steel ships built in the United States, with a record of 42 days from keel laying to launching.
Erected National Maritime Day 1969

Silk Trains and Ships *Dakota and Minnesota*

Plaque is missing. Erected National Maritime Day 1970.

Mosquito Fleet Steamer *Flyer*

Located near this site was the home dock of the Flyer, one of Puget Sound's best known steamers. Operating primarily on the Seattle-Tacoma route during the early 1900s, the Flyer held numerous records for speed, total miles traveled, and number of passengers carried.
National Maritime Day 1971

Harbor Island

Harbor Island, world's largest man-made island, created by dredging 1895-1912, comprises 445 acres. Plays a major role in the economic growth of the City and Port of Seattle. Sailing ships started it unknowingly by dumping ballast at anchor. Home of state's largest shipyards, a flour mill, petroleum storage, deep sea terminals, and major industrial/commercial enterprises.
Erected National Maritime Week 1972

Sinking of the Steamer *Dix*

On the evening of November 18, 1906, approximately two miles due west of this site, the steamer Dix, while traversing from Seattle to Port Blakely, collided with the Alaska Steamer, Jeanie. Forty-two persons were carried to an early watery grave. That tragic collision culminated grief unsurpassed to date, within Puget Sound residents and seamen alike.
Erected Maritime Week 1973

Ferryboat *San Mateo*

Plaque is missing. Erected Maritime Week 1974.

Joshua Green

Joshua Green began his waterfront career on Puget Sound in 1888 when steamshipping was in its infancy. He founded the LaConner Trading and Transportation Co., operated freight and passenger steamers and eventually became president of the Puget Sound Navigation Co. His ownership of vessels ranged from early paddle-wheelers to swift passenger vessels including shares in the unique six-masted barkentine Everett

G. Griggs. His legacy to the Northwest maritime industry is the modern Washington State Ferry system.
Erected Maritime Week May 1975

Thomas Petersen

Thomas Heinrich Petersen, 1836–1915, Shipbuilder
Near this site, when Salmon Bay was still a tidal creek before the locks were built, Thomas Petersen built the two four masted schooners Transit, in 1891, and Stimson in 1900. A native of Denmark, Petersen immigrated to San Francisco in 1857 and built twenty-eight vessels there and in northern California, including the first two three-masted schooners ever built on the Pacific coast. Two vessels followed in Oregon and by 1907, Petersen was established in Puget Sound contracting for and building six sailing vessels and steamers at Port Ludlow, Port Townsend, Port Madison and finally in Salmon Bay. His design work also contributed toward the building of other vessels at the Moran Yard in Seattle at the turn of the century.
Erected Maritime Week May 1976

Shipmates Light

In honor and in memory of the seamen who have given their lives in service to mankind, this memorial beacon is erected and dedicated this 22nd day of May 1977 A.D.   Let the rays of this light serve as a symbolic link between us ashore and our fellows who have gone down to the sea in ships for the last time.
Erected Maritime Week May 1977

Smith Cove

The cove is named after Dr. Henry A. Smith, pioneer who settled here in 1853. Early shipping began here in 1891 when the Northern Pacific Coal Bunker Pier was completed. At that time it was not uncommon to see steamers and sailing vessels berthed on either side of this 2500 foot trestle loading coal from railroad cars. That came to an end in 1899 when the adjacent Great Northern Piers, Piers 88 and 89, were completed linking the Transcontinental Railroad to the Orient. In 1912, the Port of Seattle purchased tide flats presently known as Piers 90 and 91 for $150,000. At a cost of $3,500,000 the 2580 foot piers were completed in 1921, at which time they were recognized as the longest earth-filled piers in the world. The Port of Seattle operated these piers as a public facility until 1942 when they were sold to the U.S. Navy. They remained under Navy control until 1976 when they were repurchased by the Port.
Erected Maritime Week May 1978

Lake Washington Ferries

Steam ferries began operating near this site during the 1880's carrying passengers to Mercer Island and communities on the east side of Lake Washington. The largest and

most elaborate ferry, the Issaquah carried 600 passengers. Service on the lake came to an end with the completion of the floating bridge in 1940.
Erected National Maritime Week–1979

First Modern Freight and Passenger Terminal

The first of the modern freight and passenger terminals, built in 1925 on the Seattle waterfront, was the headquarters building for Pacific Steamship Company whose vessels served California, Alaska and the Orient. During World War II it was the Port of Embarkation for the U.S. Army, then acquired by the U.S. Coast Guard in 1976 to serve as the Regional Support Center.
Erected National Maritime Week 1980

Ainsworth and Dunn Dock at Pier 70

Plaque is missing. Erected National Maritime Week 1981.

Elliott Bay Harbor

One of the world's best harbors. Noted by Captain George Vancouver in 1792 and first surveyed by Midshipman, Sam Elliott of the Wilkes Expedition in May 1841. With its depths to 100 fathoms the bay can accommodate the biggest ships. Through the portals of Elliott Bay, Seattle is the gateway to Alaska, the Orient, and all the worlds' ports.
Erected National Maritime Week 1982

Ballast Island

In this area, once part of the bay, vessels from ports all over the world dumped their ballast. Untold thousands of tons were unloaded into the water by ships crews, including 40,000 tons from San Francisco's Telegraph Hill. The island, long a gathering place for Indians on their annual migrations, was covered in the 1890's by construction of Railroad Avenue (now called Alaskan Way).
Erected National Maritime Week 1983

Fireboat *Duwamish*

Built 1909 at Richmond Beach, WA, as a steam powered vessel with pumping capacity of 9,000 gallons per minute and a "ram" bow designed to sink burning wooden ships. Refitted after 40 years of service with diesel electric motors to become the world's most powerful fireboat delivering 22,800 gallons per minute. Official welcomer and protector of Seattle's waterfront.
Length 122'8" Beam 28' Draft 9' 332 gross tons
Dedicated National Maritime Week 1984

Salmon Bay Terminal

Designed and built by the Seattle Port Commission in 1913 as a 'Snug Harbor' and headquarters for the Puget Sound fishing fleet. This was among the first projects

completed by the commission recognizing the importance and needs of the commercial fisherman in Seattle.
Dedicated National Maritime Week 1985

First Headquarters for Port of Seattle

The site of the Indian camping place called Muck-Muck-Wum. In 1911 the headquarters of Washington's first public port was established here by commissioners H.M. Chittenden, C.E. Remsberg and Robert Bridges. This tablet dedicated May 19, during National Maritime Week 1986 to the honor of the 75th anniversary of the Port of Seattle.
Dedicated National Maritime Week 1986

APPENDIX II

MONUMENTS AND STATUES

Seattle's monuments and statues are listed in the order in which they were dedicated. Not every historical marker made it into the book. Those the author did not discuss are marked *. See maps (M1, M2, M3) on pages 180–182 for locations. (For example, M1-1 indicates Map 1, location 1.)

Name	Year	Type	Location	Artist
Pioneer Square Totem Pole (Ch. 1)	1899	Sculpture	Pioneer Place Park, M2-15	Original by Tlingit people; duplicate carved 1940 under direction of Charles Brown; 1972 restoration by John C. Hudson Jr.
Birthplace of Seattle (Ch. 2)	1905	Obelisk	Alki Point, West Seattle, M1-2	Unknown
William Seward (Ch. 4)	1909	Statue	Volunteer Park, M1-31	Richard E. Brooks
James J. Hill (Ch. 4)	1909	Statue	University of Washington, M1-14	Finn H. Frolich
George Washington (Ch. 4)	1909	Statue	University of Washington, M1-9	Lorado Taft
Chief Seattle (Ch. 3)	1910	Statues (3 busts produced, 1 missing)	• Tilikum Place Park, M2-15 • Renton History Museum	James A. Wehn
Japanese Stone Lantern (Ch. 4)	1911	Sculpture	Mount Baker Park, M1-15	Gift from Kojiro Matsukata
Chief Seattle (Ch. 3)	1912	Statue	Fifth Ave. and Denny Way, M3-2	James A. Wehn
John Hart McGraw (Ch. 5)	1913	Statue	Fifth Ave. and Stewart St., M3-9	Richard E. Brooks
Henry Yesler (Ch. 5)	1915	Bas-Relief Plaque	516 Third Ave., M2-12	Max P. Nielsen
Sherwood Gillespy (Ch. 5)	1915	Statue	Jefferson Park Golf Course, M1-24	Max P. Nielson
Henry Yesler (Ch. 5)	1916	Medallion	Douglass-Truth Library, M1-12	James A. Wehn

Name	Year	Type	Location	Artist
Edvard Grieg (Ch. 4)	1917	Statue	University of Washington	H. Finn Frolich
Warren Harding memorial (Ch. 6)	1923	Monument (destroyed)	Woodland Park; plaques and statues are at Seattle Boy Scouts headquarters	Alice Carr
World Flyers Shaft (Ch. 6)	1924	Obelisk	Sand Point Way NE/ NE 74th St., M1-32	Alonzo Victor Lewis
Father Prefontaine (Ch. 6)	1925	Fountain	Third Ave. and Yesler Way, M2-6	Carl F. Gould
The Hiker (Ch. 7)	1926	Statue	Woodland Park, M1-13	Allen G. Newman
Plymouth Rock (Ch. 2)	1926	Rock	Birthplace of Seattle monument, M1-2	Unknown
Thomas Burke (Ch. 8)	1930	Statue	Volunteer Park, M1-16	Hermon MacNeil
Luther B. Youngs (Ch. 8)	1930	Bas-Relief Plaque	Volunteer Park, M1-16	Vasileos Theta Goumas
Hannah Newman (Ch. 5)	1930	Bas-Relief Plaque	Washington Athletic Club; Sixth Ave. and Union St., M3-8	James A. Wehn
Japanese Lantern (Ch. 4)	1931	Statue	Seward Park, M1-29	Gift from Ichiro Onishi
The Doughboy (Ch. 7)	1932	Statue	Washelli Cemetery	Alonzo Victor Lewis
Japanese Arch (Ch. 4)	1934	Arch (removed)	Seward Park	Unknown
James D. Ross (Ch. 8)	1935	Bas-Relief Plaque (missing)	Seattle City Light Office	James A. Wehn
Edmund Meany (Ch. 2)	1935	Pool and Bas-Relief Plaque	Washelli Cemetery	Richard E. Brooks
Will Rogers (Ch. 8)	1936	Monument and Bas-Relief Plaque	28th Ave. NE and NE 125th St.	Alonzo Victor Lewis
Daniel E. Dugdale (Ch. 8)	1939	Bas-Relief Plaque (missing)	Sick's Stadium	Alonzo Victor Lewis
Emil Sick (Ch. 8)	1939	Bas-Relief Plaque (missing)	Sick's Stadium	Alonzo Victor Lewis
Albert Kerry (Ch. 12)	1939	Bas-Relief Plaque	Olympic Hotel, M3-14	Alonzo Victor Lewis
Jack Lelivelt (Ch. 8)	1940	Bas-Relief Plaque (missing)	Sick's Stadium	Alonzo Victor Lewis

Name	Year	Type	Location	Artist
Reverend Dr. Mark Matthews (Ch. 8)	1942	Statue	Denny Park, M3-12	Alonzo Victor Lewis
Victory Square pylon (Ch. 9)	1942	Obelisk (destroyed)	University St. between Fourth and Fifth	Unknown
*Hiram Gale, Civil War veteran	1948	Medallion and plaque	Veterans Memorial Cemetery at Washelli	James A. Wehn
Japanese American Soldiers (Ch. 9)	1949	Column	Lake View Cemetery, M1-21	Unknown
*Judson Toll Jennings, Director of Seattle public library, 1907–1942	1950	Medallion and plaque	Central Library Administration Offices	James A. Wehn
Memorial Plaza (Ch. 9)	1950	Structure (destroyed); statue lent to Washelli Cemetery	Fourth Ave. between Cherry and James Sts.	Dudley Pratt
High School Memorial Stadium (Ch. 9)	1951	Structure	Seattle Center, M1-20	Marianne Hansen
Statue of Liberty replica (Ch. 2)	1952	Statue	Alki Ave. SW and 61st Ave. SW, M1-28	Unknown
Veterans' Memorial Chimes Tower (Ch. 9)	1957	Structure	Washelli Cemetery	Unknown
Chief Seattle Bust (Ch. 3)	1958	Statue	Seattle University, M3-1	James A. Wehn
Leif Erikson (Ch. 11)	1962	Statue	Shilshole Marina, M1-18	August Werner
Gorst Field (Ch. 6)	1966	Fountain and plaque	5500 West Marginal Way SW, M1-10	Unknown
*George Alfred Caldwell Rochester, chairman of Seattle library commission, 1907–1912	1967	Medallion and plaque	Central Library first floor	Everett de Pen
Japanese Rock of Friendship (Ch. 4)	1976	Boulder	Seward Park, M1-29	Unknown
Shipmates Light (Ch. 10)	1977	Structure and plaque	Myrtle Edwards Park, M1-25	Unknown
Christopher Columbus (Ch. 11)	1978	Statue (in storage)	Waterfront Park at Pier 57	Douglas Bennett

Name	Year	Type	Location	Artist
Jimi Hendrix (Ch. 11)	1982	Bust	Garfield High School	Jeff Day
Ivar Haglund (Ch. 11)	1985	Statue	Pier 54	Richard Beyer
Fishermen's Memorial (Ch. 10)	1988	Statue	Fishermen's Terminal, M1-23	Ron Petty
*Sadako Sasaki, famous survivor of the Atomic bombing of Hiroshima, Japan	1990	Statue	NE 40th St. and Ninth Ave. NE	Daryl Smith
Reverend Dr. Martin Luther King Jr. (Ch. 11)	1991	Sculpture	2200 Martin Luther King Jr. Way S	Bob Kelly
Jimi Hendrix (Ch. 11)	1997	Statue	1604 Broadway	Daryl Smith
Garden of Remembrance (Ch. 9)	1998	Sculpture	Second Ave. and University St., M3-6	Robert Murase
Seattle Fallen Firefighters (Ch. 11)	1998	Statue	Occidental Park	Hai Ying Wu
Bernie Whitebear Memorial Leschi Dream Catcher (Ch. 1)	2003	Sculpture	32nd Ave. and E Yesler Way	Lawney Reyes
*Jim Owens, UW football coach, 1957–1974	2003	Statue	walkway between Alaska Airlines Arena and Husky Stadium	Ken Bjorge
*J. P. Patches the clown, star of a local children's TV show, 1958–1981	2008	Statue	N 34th St., east of Fremont Ave N	Kevin Pettelle
*Medal of Honor memorial, dedicated to eight UW alumni awardees	2009	Sculpture	University of Washington campus	Heidi Wastweet and Mike Magrath
Ken Griffey, Jr. (Ch. 8)	2017	Sculpture	Safeco Field entrance	Lou Cella

APPENDIX III

HISTORICAL MARKERS AND PLAQUES

Seattle's markers and plaques are listed in the order in which they were dedicated. Not every historical marker made it into the book. Those the author did not discuss are marked *. Plaques commissioned in the 1970s by the Assistance League of Seattle are labeled ALS; those commissioned for the 1989 Washington State Centennial are labeled WSC. See maps (M1, M2, M3) on pages 180–182 for locations. (For example, M1-1 indicates Map 1, location 1.)

Marker/Plaque	Year	Original and Current Location (unless noted)
First Post Office (Ch. 2)	1905	First Ave. and Marion St., M2-9
First School House (Ch. 2)	1905	First Ave. and Madison St., M2-10
Block House (Ch. 2)	1905	Foot of Cherry St. (missing)
Yesler's Sawmill (Ch. 2)	1905	MOHAI, M2-17
Second Block House (Ch. 2)	1905	Occidental Ave. and Main St., M2-16
First Cabin (Ch. 2)	1905	Second Ave. and Cherry St., M2-7
*Carnegie Library, dedication of main library	1906	Central Library first floor
Alaska Yukon Pacific Exposition (Ch. 4)	1909	University of Washington campus
Louisa Boren (Ch. 2)	1914	East Interlaken Blvd., Interlaken Park, M1-19
Battle of Seattle (Ch. 6)	1916	City Hall Park, M2-2
Puget Sound Lake Washington Waterway (Ch. 10)	1916	Chittenden Locks Administration Building
First location University of Washington (Ch. 12)	1924 & 1984	Olympic Hotel; University St. between Fourth and Fifth Aves., M3-14
Kerry Park (Ch. 12)	1927	Kerry Park; Queen Anne
Boeing Field (Ch. 6)	1928	Boeing Field Admin. Building parking lot
Arthur Denny Homestead (Ch. 2)	1933	Second Ave. and Union St. (missing)
Will Rogers and Wiley Post (Ch. 8)	1937	Boeing Field Admin. Building lobby (missing)

Marker/Plaque	Year	Original and Current Location (unless noted)
First White Settlers in King County (Ch. 2)	1940	Boeing Field Admin. Building parking lot, M1-7
Old Central School (Ch. 2)	1940	Third Ave. and Madison St.
*Judge William Long, founder of Camp Long, in West Seattle	1941	Camp Long Lodge
*Rainier Beach WWII heroes, neighborhood residents who died during the Second World War	1946	57th Ave S, Fletcher St., and Waters Ave., M1-22
*First Service Station, site of the first gas station in 1907	1947	2225 East Marginal Way South
*Samuel Maple (Mapel) Claim Site (see First White Settlers King County)	1950	Boeing Field Admin. Building parking lot, M1-7
Chinese American Soldiers (Ch. 9)	1950	Hing Hay Park, M2-4
Great Seattle Fire (Ch. 12)	1952	First Ave. and Madison St., M2-11
Spanish–American War (Ch. 7)	1953	Volunteer Park
*Alex Shults, *Seattle Times* sports writer	1954	Green Lake Park
*Jacob Umlauff, Seattle parks head gardener	1956	Leschi Park
Ton of Gold from steamer *Portland* (Ch. 10)	1957	Pier 58, M3-13
Seattle's First Ferry Boat *City of Seattle* (Ch. 10)	1958	Alaska Way and Madison St., M2-8
Sloop-of-war *USS Decatur* (Ch. 10)	1959	Alaska Way and Yesler Way
Hospital Ship *Idaho* (Ch. 10)	1960	Alaska Way and Washington St., M2-13
Fishermen Lost at Sea (Ch. 10)	1961	7500 block of 34th Ave. NW, M1-8
The Great White Fleet (Ch. 10)	1961	North of Piers 62 and 63 overlooking Bell Street Marina, M3-7
*First Commercial Monorail, location of the northern terminus of the monorail for the World's Fair	1962	Seattle Center Monorail Station
First Home Site at Alki (Ch. 2)	1962	63rd Ave. SW and Alki Ave. SW
Willapa, first Alaska Steamship Company vessel (Ch. 10)	1962	Pier 58 (missing)
U.S. Coast Guard Cutter *Bear* (Ch. 10)	1963	Alaska Way and Seneca St., M3-3
Yesler's Sawmill, Wharf, and Cookhouse (Ch. 10)	1964	Alaska Way and Yesler Way, M2-17
Battleship USS *Nebraska* (Ch. 10)	1965	Elliott Bay Trail, south of King St., M2-3
*Lake City WWII heroes, private marker to neighborhood veterans	1965	12356 Lake City Way NE

Marker/Plaque	Year	Original and Current Location (unless noted)
Colman Ferry Terminal (Ch. 10)	1966	Seattle Ferry Terminal/Colman Dock, foot of Marion St., M2-5
B-17 Flying Fortress Crew Memorial (Ch. 9)	1966	Fourth Ave. between Cherry and James Sts. (missing)
United Parcel Service founding site (Ch. 12)	1967	Second Ave. S and S Main St., M2-18
Chittenden Locks (Ch. 10)	1967	Chittenden Locks, Ballard, M1-4
*WWI U.S. Naval Training Station Seattle	1967	NW corner of the Medical Center building; UW Medical Center
First Hospital (Ch. 2)	1967	1010 Fifth Ave., M3-5
Miike Maru, first regular freight service to Japan (Ch. 10)	1968	Between Piers 57 and 58, M3-15
Skinner & Eddy Shipyards (Ch. 10)	1969	Elliott Bay Trail, south of King St., M2-3
*Mutual Life Building, 1897 (ALS plaque)	1970s	First Ave. and Yesler Way
*Maynard Building, 1892 (ALS plaque)	1970s	S First Ave. and S Washington St.
*Merchant's Café, 1889 (ALS plaque)	1970s	109 Yesler Way
Pioneer Square Information Booth (ALS plaque) (Ch. 12)	1970s	Occidental Park
Silk Trains and Ships *Dakota* and *Minnesota* (Ch. 10)	1970	Pier 88 (missing)
Mosquito Fleet Steamer *Flyer* (Ch. 10)	1971	Seattle Ferry Terminal, M2-5
Harbor Island (Ch. 10)	1972	Terminal 18 Public Access Park; Harbor Island, M1-11
Sinking of the Steamer *Dix* (Ch. 10)	1973	Duwamish Head, M1-26
Carl S. English (Ch. 10)	1974	Chittenden Locks
Ferryboat *San Mateo* (Ch. 10)	1974	Ferryboat San Mateo (missing)
Joshua Green (Ch. 10)	1975	Pier 58, M3-10
*Holyoke Building, 1889	1975	First Ave. and Spring St.
*Giuseppe Desimone, prominent Pike Place Market figure	1975	Pike Place Market
Thomas H. Petersen (Ch. 10)	1976	Commodore Park, M1-30
*USA Bicentennial	1976	Waterfront Park
Smith Cove (Ch. 10)	1978	Smith Cove Park, M1-27
*Richard Mohn, Port executive 1963–1978	1978	Smith Cove Park
Lake Washington Ferries (Ch. 10)	1979	Leschi moorage, M1-17

Marker/Plaque	Year	Original and Current Location (unless noted)
First Modern Freight and Passenger Terminal (Ch. 10)	1980	1519 Alaskan Way S, M1-6
Ainsworth & Dunn Dock (Ch. 10)	1981	Pier 70 (missing)
Colonial Hotel (Ch. 12)	1982	1119 First Ave.
Elliott Bay Harbor (Ch. 10)	1982	Pier 56
Ballast Island (Ch. 10)	1983	Alaska Way, just south of the Washington St. Boat Landing, M2-1
Fireboat *Duwamish* (Ch. 10)	1984	Lake Union, M1-5
Savoy Hotel (Ch. 12)	1984	University St. between Second and Third Aves.
*Smith and Squire Buildings, 1900	1984	80 South Jackson St.
Salmon Bay Terminal (Ch. 10)	1985	Fishermen's Terminal, M1-23
*Captain George Vancouver, British explorer who visited Puget Sound in 1792	1986	Marshall Park, 1191 Seventh Ave. W, M1-3
*Ballard/Howe House, 1904	1986	22 West Highland Drive
Great Northern Railway Tunnel (WSC plaque) (Ch. 4)	1989	S Main St. and Fourth Ave. S
*Interurban Building, 1890 (WSC)	1989	Yesler Way and Occidental Way
*King Street Coal Wharf, Skinner & Eddy Shipyard, and Hooverville (WSC)	1989	Alaskan Way South and South King St.
King Street Station (WSC) (Ch. 4)	1989	S King St., east of Second Ave. S
Madame Lou Graham's Sporting House (WSC) (Ch. 12)	1989	S Washington St. and Third Ave. S, M2-14
*Pioneer Building, 1889 (WSC)	1989	Pioneer Square Park
*Schwabacher's Store, 1890 (WSC)	1989	S First Ave., south of Yesler Way
*Smith Tower, 1914 (WSC)	1989	Second Ave. and Yesler Way
*Yesler's Pavilion, 1865 (WSC)	1989	Cherry St., east of First Ave.
*Goldmark Family, dedicated to a family of four who were murdered in 1985	1992	Madrona Drive and Lake Washington Blvd.
*Luna Park, amusement park open from 1907 to 1913	1999	37 Alki Trail; West Seattle
Pioneer Square Pergola (Ch. 12)	2002	Pioneer Square Park, M2-15
Michael E. Fleming (Ch. 10)	2004	Chittenden Locks
Panama Hotel (Ch. 12)	2006	605½ S Main St.
*Pike Place Market	2007	Market's north side, open-air breezeway, east of the Pike Place Fish Company

Marker/Plaque	Year	Original and Current Location (unless noted)
United Parcel Service 100th Anniversary (Ch. 12)	2007	Second Ave. S and S Main St., M2-18
*Bataan/Corregidor Memorial, Second World War monument	2012	Dr. Jose Rizal Park, 12th Ave. S, M1-3
*Riverside Memorial to Croatian Immigrants	2012	17th Ave. SW and West Marginal Place
The Brooklyn Building, 1891 (Ch. 12)	Unknown	1212 Second Ave.
*Exchange Building, 1930	Unknown	Second Ave. and Marion St.
White Chapel District (Ch. 12)	Unknown	206 Third Ave. S, M2-19

Map 1. Seattle

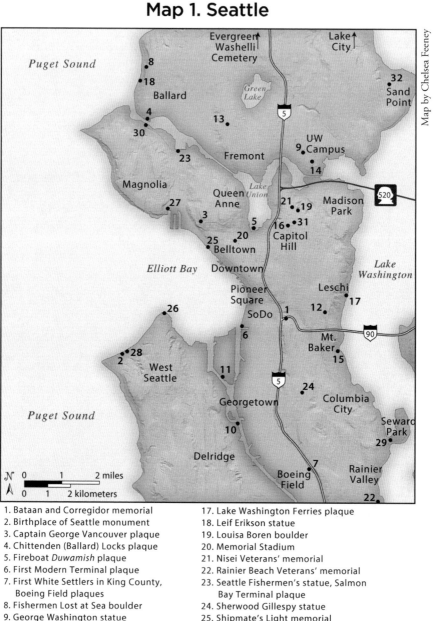

Puget Sound

Evergreen
Washelli
Cemetery

Lake
City

8

18

Ballard

Green
Lake

32
Sand
Point

4

13

30

5

23

Fremont

UW
9 Campus

14

Magnolia

Lake
Union

Queen
Anne

27

21
19

Madison
Park

3

5

16 31

25
20

Belltown

Capitol
Hill

Elliott Bay

Downtown

Lake
Washington

Pioneer
Square

Leschi

26

1

12

17

SoDo

6

Mt.
Baker

90

15

28

2

West
Seattle

11

5

24

Georgetown

Columbia
City

Puget Sound

10

Seward
Park

29

Delridge

0   1   2 miles

0   1   2 kilometers

7
Boeing
Field

Rainier
Valley

22

Map by Chelsea Feeney

1. Bataan and Corregidor memorial
2. Birthplace of Seattle monument
3. Captain George Vancouver plaque
4. Chittenden (Ballard) Locks plaque
5. Fireboat *Duwamish* plaque
6. First Modern Terminal plaque
7. First White Settlers in King County,
   Boeing Field plaques
8. Fishermen Lost at Sea boulder
9. George Washington statue
10. Gorst Field plaque
11. Harbor Island plaque
12. Henry Yelser medallion
13. Hiker statue, Woodland Park
14. James J. Hill bust
15. Japanese lantern
16. Judge Thomas Burke statue,
   Luther B. Youngs plaque

17. Lake Washington Ferries plaque
18. Leif Erikson statue
19. Louisa Boren boulder
20. Memorial Stadium
21. Nisei Veterans' memorial
22. Rainier Beach Veterans' memorial
23. Seattle Fishermen's statue, Salmon
   Bay Terminal plaque
24. Sherwood Gillespy statue
25. Shipmate's Light memorial
26. Sinking of *Dix* plaque
27. Smith Cove plaque
28. Statue of Liberty
29. Taiko Gata lantern and boulders
30. Thomas Petersen plaque
31. William Seward statue
32. World Flyers shaft

Map 2. Pioneer Square

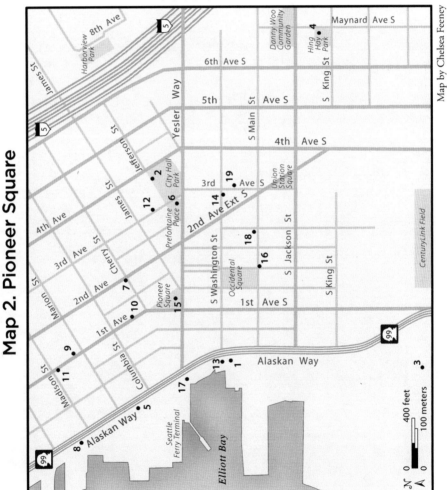

1. Ballast Island plaque
2. Battle of Seattle boulder
3. Battleship USS *Nebraska*, Skinner & Eddy Shipyards plaques
4. Chinese-American memorial
5. Early Ferry Terminal, Mosquito Fleet Steamer *Flyer* plaques
6. Father Prefontaine fountain
7. First Cabin plaque
8. First Ferry Boat, *City of Seattle* plaque
9. First Post Office plaque
10. First School House plaque
11. Great Fire plaque
12. Henry Yesler plaque
13. Hospital ship *Idaho* plaque
14. Madame Lou Graham's Sporting House plaque
15. Pioneer Square Totem Pole, Chief Seattle bust, Pergola
16. Second Blockhouse plaque
17. Sloop-of-War *Decatur*, Yesler's Sawmill plaques
18. UPS founding site plaques
19. White Chapel District plaque

Map by Chelsea Feeney

Map 3. Downtown Seattle

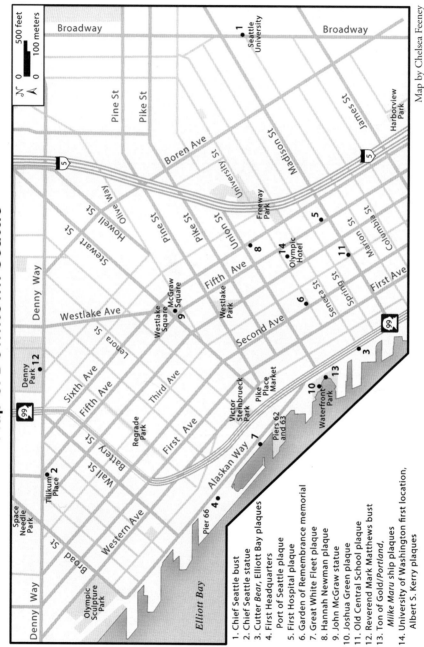

1. Chief Seattle bust
2. Chief Seattle statue
3. Cutter *Bear*, Elliott Bay plaques
4. First Headquarters
   Port of Seattle plaque
5. First Hospital plaque
6. Garden of Remembrance memorial
7. Great White Fleet plaque
8. Hannah Newman plaque
9. John McGraw statue
10. Joshua Green plaque
11. Old Central School plaque
12. Reverend Mark Matthews bust
13. Ton of Gold/*Portland*,
    Mike Maru ship plaques
14. University of Washington first location,
    Albert S. Kerry plaques

Map by Chelsea Feeney

NOTES

Preface

1. Greg Dickinson, Carole Blair, and Brian L. Ott, eds., *Places of Public Memory: The Rhetoric of Museums and Memorials* (Tuscaloosa: University of Alabama Press, 2010), 7.
2. Paul A. Shackel, ed., *Myth, Memory, and the Making of the American Landscape* (Gainesville: University Press of Florida, 2001), 9.
3. Erika Doss, *Memorial Mania: Public Feeling in America* (Chicago: University of Chicago Press, 2010), 30.
4. Carlos A. Schwantes, *The Pacific Northwest: An Interpretive History* (Lincoln: University of Nebraska Press, 1998).
5. Kirk Savage, "History, Memory, and Monuments: An Overview of the Scholarly Literature on Commemoration" (paper commissioned by the Organization of American Historians and the National Park Service, 2006).
6. "The whole point of Confederate monuments is to celebrate white supremacy," *Washington Post*, August 16, 2017.

Chapter 1: The Pioneer Square Totem Pole

1. Murray Morgan, *Skid Road: An Informal Portrait of Seattle* (New York: Viking Press, 1951), 163.
2. Ken Chowder, "North to Alaska," *Smithsonian Monthly*, June 2003; Paige Williams, "The Tallest Trophy," *New Yorker*, April 20, 2015; "A Tale of Two Totem Poles," *Washington Post*, September 17, 2004; Thomas S. Litwin, *The Harriman Alaska Expedition Retraced: A Century of Change, 1899–2001* (New Brunswick, NJ: Rutgers University Press), 2005; Frederic Gleach, "From Cape Fox, Alaska to Cornell University: The Changing Meanings of a Totem Pole," paper presented at the American Society of Ethnohistory, 1995; "Two Poles, One Story," NAGPRA in the Museum Galleries, www.peabody.harvard.edu/node/313.
3. Walter A. McClure "As a Matter of Fact: The Totem Pole." *Seattle Daily Times*, April 4, 1928, 6.
4. Viola Edmundson Garfield, *Seattle's Totem Poles* (Bellevue, WA: Thistle Press, 1996), 9.
5. Kate C. Duncan, *1001 Curious Things: Ye Olde Curiosity Shop and Native American Art* (Seattle: University of Washington Press, 2000), 162.
6. Stephen Langdon, email message to author, March 22, 2017.
7. "Totem Pole Stands at Last Unveiled," *Seattle Post-Intelligencer*, October 19, 1899, 1–2.
8. H. E. Jamison, "Giant Totem Pole has Seen and Helped in the Making of History," *Seattle Star*, January 25, 1936.
9. *Northwest Magazine* XX, no. 6, June 1902, 1–2.
10. Robin K. Wright, "How Did Totem Poles Become a Symbol of Seattle?," Burke Museum, November 19, 2015, www.burkemuseum.org/blog/how-did-totem-poles-become-symbol-seattle.
11. "Totem Pole Damage May Be Repaired," *Seattle Daily Times*, October 24, 1938, 1; James A Wood, "Speaking for the Times, It Would Be Missed," *Seattle Daily Times*, October 25, 1938, 6.
12. "U.W. Anthropologist Urged As Arbiter on Totem Pole," *Seattle Daily Times*, November 7, 1938, 3.
13. Duncan, *1001 Curious Things*, 165–66.

14. B. Frank Heintzleman to C. M. Archbold, August 18, 1939; U.S. Forest Service, Alaska Division, Juneau, Alaska to C. M. Archbold, September 27, 1945.
15. "Landmark Totem Rededicated," *Seattle Daily Times*, August 22, 1972, E6.

Chapter 2: Founders, Firsts, and a Statue of Liberty

1. Coll Thrush, *Native Seattle: Histories from the Crossing-over Place* (Seattle: University of Washington Press, 2007), 144.
2. Knute Berger, *Pugetopolis: A Mossback Takes on Growth Addicts, Weather Wimps, and the Myth of Seattle Nice* (Seattle: Sasquatch Books, 2009), 101.
3. William C. Speidel, *Sons of the Profits: Or, There's No Business Like Grow Business: The Seattle Story 1851–1901* (Seattle: Nettle Creek Publishing, 1967), 31.
4. Roger Sale, *Seattle, Past to Present* (Seattle: University of Washington Press, 1976), 11.
5. Thrush, *Native Seattle*, 19.
6. "City's Birthday Impressively Observed," *Seattle Daily Times*, November 13, 1905, 1; "Observe City's 54th Birthday," *Seattle Post-Intelligencer*, November 14, 1905, 1.
7. Sale, *Seattle, Past to Present*, 11.
8. Stuart Eskenazi, "Settling Seattle Again," *Seattle Times*, November 14, 2001.
9. "Seattle's Lady Liberty Gets a Bath," *Seattle Post-Intelligencer*, June 25, 1986, D1.
10. Kery Murakami, "Sea Scout Leader Recalls Unveiling of Alki's Lady Liberty," *Seattle Post-Intelligencer*, March 29, 2005.
11. "City's Birthday Impressively Observed"; "Observe City's 54th Birthday."
12. Sale, *Seattle, Past to Present*, 11.
13. Harold F. Osborne, "Sic Transit Gloria—Where Are Markers That Are 'for All Time'?," *Seattle Daily Times*, April 30, 1951, M3.
14. "Son Will Unveil Tablet at Denny Homestead Site," *Seattle Daily Times*, May 21, 1933, 7; "Denny Homestead Honored," *Washington Historical Quarterly* 24, no. 3 (July 1933): 240.
15. "Old Central School Plaque Is Dedicated," *Seattle Daily Times*, December 11, 1940, 19.
16. Janice Krenmayr, "Foot-loose in Seattle No. 39—Sweetbriar Bride Has Her Own Park," *Seattle Daily Times*, August 19, 1962, M2.

Chapter 3: Images of Chief Seattle

1. Thrush, *Native Seattle*, 41.
2. "Local Sculptor Casts Old Chief," *Seattle Post-Intelligencer*, July 31, 1907, 1. Frank Lynch, "Seattle Scene; Pygmalion and Chief Seattle," *Seattle Post-Intelligencer*, September 11, 1951.
3. "Proposed Statue Cause of Comment," *Seattle Post-Intelligencer*, August 1, 1907, 20.
4. "Panels for Base of Chief Seattle Statue," *Seattle Post-Intelligencer*, July 5, 1908, M8. "Says Statue Is of Wrong Indian," *Seattle Post-Intelligencer*, July 8, 1908, 5.
5. Sally Hayman, "Looking Back on the Creation of a Landmark…Sculptor James Wehn Remembers How it Was," *Seattle Post-Intelligencer*, May 13, 1973, 12–13.
6. Thrush, *Native Seattle*, 127.
7. "Tilikums to Unveil Statue of Seattle," *Seattle Daily Times*, November 10, 1912, 20.
8. Thrush, *Native Seattle*, 129.
9. "Statue Dedicated to Chieftain Who Guarded Pioneers," *Seattle Post-Intelligencer*, November 13, 1912, 1.
10. Ibid.
11. Fred Poyner IV, *The First Sculptor of Seattle: The Life and Art of James A. Wehn* (CreateSpace, 2014).
12. Robert Haslach, "Relics of the Bronze Age," *The Argus*, May 18, 1973, 5.
13. "Statue Dedicated to Chieftain Who Guarded Pioneers," 1.

14. Paul Scolari, "Indian Warriors and Pioneer Mothers: American Identity and the Closing of the Frontier in Public Monuments, 1890–1930" (PhD diss., University of Pittsburgh, 2005).

15. Dora Dean, "Last Wooden Indian Goes, Chief Seattle Statue Lingers," *Seattle Daily Times*, November 22, 1925, 25.

16. "Relics of Barbarism on Seattle's Streets," *Seattle Daily Times*, January 10, 1926, 6.

17. "Chief Seattle's Statue Sought by Seattle U.," *Seattle Daily Times*, February 21, 1957, 9.

18. "New Site for Chief Seattle Statue Urged," *Seattle Daily Times*, January 12, 1959.

19. "Chief Seattle Still Greets Newcomers," *Seattle Daily Times*, February 24, 1962, magazine section, 2.

20. "Chief Seattle Statue Unveiled for Second Time," *Seattle Times*, December 9, 1975, D4.

21. John Hahn, "Chief Seattle Gets a Needed Scrubbing," *Seattle Post-Intelligencer*, May 4, 1989, C2.

22. Gil Bailey, "As Seattle's Early Settlers Knew, the Old Chief Has a Heart of Gold," *Seattle Post-Intelligencer*, May 25, 1989, B3.

23. "No Horses; No Fountains Needed: Do We Hear $20," *Seattle Post-Intelligencer*, August 30, 1934, 10.

24. Thrush, *Native Seattle*, 179–80.

25. Leonard Garfield, Karin Murr Link, Marc K. Blackburn, and Dana Cox, *Pioneer Square: Seattle's Oldest Neighborhood* (Seattle: Pioneer Square Community Association/University of Washington Press, 2005), 154.

26. Poyner, *First Sculptor of Seattle*.

Chapter 4: Monuments of the A-Y-P Exposition

1. Harry C. Bauer, "U. of W.'s Patriotic Shrine," *Seattle Daily Times*, February 21, 1960, magazine section 3.

2. "Honor to Be Paid First President," *Seattle Daily Times*, February 10, 1924, club section.

3. J. M. Goode, *The Outdoor Sculpture of Washington, DC: A Comprehensive Historical Guide* (Washington, DC: Smithsonian Institution Press, 1974).

4. O. H. Sample, "New Sculptural Conceptions of Washington and Lincoln," *Pacific Monthly*, February 1910, 136.

5. "George Washington," americanart.si.edu/collections/search/artwork/?id=9575 Search Collections: Horatio Greenough.

6. "Campus Statue Praised by Critic," *Seattle Post-Intelligencer*, February 4, 1908, 5.

7. "Bronze Statue to Be Unveiled," *Seattle Post-Intelligencer*, June 13, 1909, sec. II, 12.

8. O. H. Sample, "New Sculptural Conceptions of Washington and Lincoln," *Pacific Monthly*, February 1910, 136.

9. Eliza Ferry Leary, "As A Matter of Fact; the Statue of Washington," *Seattle Daily Times*, April 9, 1928, 6.

10. C. T. Conover, "Letter to the Editor," *Seattle Daily Times,* April 13, 1928, 6.

11. "Washington Goes for a W.P.A. 'Ride'," *Seattle Daily Times*, August 9, 1938, 5.

12. "George Washington's Feet Too Big for Ten-Foot Base," *Seattle Daily Times*, October 12, 1930, 11.

13. Kurt E Armbruster, *Orphan Road: The Railroad Comes to Seattle, 1853–1911* (Pullman, WA: Washington State University Press, 1999), 173–85.

14. "Gophers Plan a Statue of Hill," *Seattle Post-Intelligencer*, January 17, 1909, section II, 4.

15. "Pacific Northwest Commerce," *Seattle Journal of Commerce*, July 1909, 36.

16. M. P. Malone, *James J. Hill: Empire Builder of the Northwest* (Norman, OK: University of Oklahoma Press, 1996), 274.

17. "Plan to Honor Great Norwegian," *Seattle Post-Intelligencer*, September 2, 1917, 11.

18. "Declared Fitting to Honor Seward Here," *Seattle Post-Intelligencer*, November 8, 1906, 1.
19. "Seward Monument Committee Named," *Seattle Post-Intelligencer*, November 4, 1906, 4.
20. "Ministers Favor Seward Monument," *Seattle Post-Intelligencer*, November 5, 1906, 5.
21. "Seward Monument Committee Named," 4.
22. "Alaska Governor Favors Monument," *Seattle Post-Intelligencer*, November 7, 1906, 20.
23. "Favors Monument in Alaska Capital," *Seattle Post-Intelligencer*, November 25, 1906, 11.
24. "Brooks to Make Seward Statue," *Seattle Post-Intelligencer*, March 10, 1907, 14.
25. "Close Terms for Seward Statue," *Seattle Post-Intelligencer*, June 18, 1907, 4.
26. "Statue of Buyer of Golden North Unveiled at Fair," *Seattle Post-Intelligencer*, September 11, 1909, 1.
27. "Hill Site for Seward Statue," *Seattle Post-Intelligencer*, November 3, 1909, 1.
28. Ibid.
29. Ibid.
30. "Japan's Industrial Giant Sees Lamp He Gave City," *Seattle Daily Times*, March 5, 1936.
31. Donald N. Sherwood, "Mount Baker Park," Seattle.gov. www.seattle.gov/parks/history/sherwood.html.
32. "Historic Earthquakes." Historic Earthquakes. earthquake.usgs.gov/earthquakes/world/events/1923_09_01.php.
33. "Japanese Lantern, Good-Will Token Given to Seattle," *Seattle Daily Times*, June 15, 1931.
34. "Japanese Arch To Be Placed In Seward Park," *Seattle Times*, August 25, 1934.
35. "Seward Park Torii Story." Seward Park Torii. www.sewardparktorii.org/home/seward-park-torii-story.
36. "Rock of Great Friendship." *Seattle Post-Intelligencer*, May 25, 1976.

Chapter 5: Recognizing Seattle's Own

1. Clarence Bagley, *History of Seattle from the Earliest Settlement to the Present Time, Vol. 2* (Chicago: S.J. Clarke, 1916), 698.
2. "Memorial to Former Governor Unveiled," *Seattle Daily Times*, July 23, 1913, 19.
3. Knute Berger, "Let's Hear It for the Mayor's Incrementalism!" Crosscut, June 6, 2014.
4. John Caldbick, "Yesler, Henry L. (1810?–1892)," HistoryLink, August 1, 2014, www.historylink.org/File/286.
5. "About the Douglass-Truth Branch," Seattle Public Library, www.spl.org/locations/douglass-truth-branch/dth-about-the-branch.
6. Martin Pool, "Jefferson Park Golf Course—a Centennial Celebration," Washington State Golf Association, February 6, 2015, thewsga.org/jefferson-park-golf-course-a-centennial-celebration.
7. *A Volume of Memoirs and Genealogy of Representative Citizens of the City of Seattle and County of King, Washington, including Biographies of Many of Those Who Have Passed Away* (New York: Lewis Publishing Company, 1903).
8. David Wilma, "Jefferson Park Municipal Golf Course (Seattle) Opens on May 12, 1915," HistoryLink, February 24, 2001, www.historylink.org/File/3014.
9. Mark Holland and Mira Latoszek, "The Vanishing History of Jefferson Park Golf, Part II: Dreamers and Builders," Beacon Hill Blog, August 25, 2012, beaconhill.seattle.wa.us/2012/08/25/the-vanishing-history-of-jefferson-park-golf-part-ii-dreamers-and-builders.
10. "Place Golf Memorial on Municipal Links," *Seattle Post-Intelligencer*, April 28, 1915; "Nielson's Medallion of Sherwood Gillespy," *Seattle Post-Intelligencer*, May 2, 1915.
11. Wilma, "Jefferson Park Municipal Golf Course (Seattle) Opens."
12. David Wilma and Catherine Hinchliff. "Jefferson Park Municipal Golf Course (Seattle)." HistoryLink, February 24, 2001, www.historylink.org/File/3015.

13. William L. Wilton, "The WAC Plaque." *Puget Soundings*, Spring 1982, 18–21.
14. John Emmett Berns Collection of "Packer Jack" Newman Photographs, University of Washington Libraries, December 15, 2015, digital.lib.washington.edu/findingaids/view?docId=BernsJohnPHColl504.xml.
15. Wilton, "The WAC Plaque."
16. John Emmett Berns Collection, University of Washington Libraries.
17. "Mollie Walsh Park," Alaska.org, www.alaska.org/detail/mollie-walsh-park.
18. Wilton, "The WAC Plaque."

Chapter 6: The Twenties

1. Lowell Thomas, *The First World Flight* (New York: Houghton Mifflin Company, 1925), 316.
2. For more about the World Flyers: Carol Glines, *Around the World in 175 Days* (Washington, DC: Smithsonian Institute Press, 2001); Spencer Lane, *First World Flight* (U.S. Press, 2011); Ernest A. McKay, *A World to Conquer* (New York: Arco Publishing Company, 1981).
3. Display, *Boeing Field History*, King County Airport Main Building, Seattle, WA, viewed October 2015.
4. "City Put on Air Map by Opening of Boeing Field," *Seattle Daily Times*, July 27, 1928.
5. Display, *Boeing Field History*.
6. Lange, Greg. "U.S. President Warren G. Harding Makes His Last Speech in Seattle on July 27, 1923." HistoryLink. February 10, 1999, www.historylink.org/File/878.
7. "Members of Elks Lodges, Who Assisted in Raising Funds for Park Bandstand, In Charge of Ceremonies." *Seattle Daily Times*, March 22, 1925.
8. "Political Scene a Real Zoo." *Seattle Post-Intelligencer*, February 19, 1978.
9. Junius Rochester, "Prefontaine, Father Francis Xavier (1838–1909)," HistoryLink, December 2, 1998, www.historylink.org/File/3633.

Chapter 7: Early War Memorials

1. "Memorial Stone is Dedicated by D.A.R. President," *Seattle Post-Intelligencer*, August 16, 1916, 28.
2. C. T. Conover, *Mirrors of Seattle* (Seattle: Lowman & Hanford Co., 1923), 169; Thrush, *Native Seattle*, 49.
3. "Mrs. Story, D.A.R. Head, Arrives On Tour of Coast," *Seattle Post-Intelligencer*, August 15, 1916, 6.
4. Lorado Taft, *The History of American Sculpture* (New York: Macmillan Company, 1924), 570.
5. Jennifer Wingate, *Sculpting Doughboys: Memory, Gender, and Taste in America's World War I Memorials* (Florence, KY: Routledge, 2013).
6. Gervais Reed and Joan H. Nilsson, *Art in Seattle's Public Places: Five Urban Walking Tours* (Seattle: Seattle Public Library, 1977).
7. "American Doughboy," *Seattle Daily Times*, December 10, 1922.
8. Louis Fiset, "World War I Memorial Is Moved to Seattle's Evergreen-Washelli Cemetery on November 11, 1998," HistoryLink, May 17, 2001, www.historylink.org/File/3294.
9. Louis Guzzo, "Doughboy, Requiescat in Peace," *Seattle Daily Times*, January 31, 1961.
10. William R. Hunt, "It's That Kook Again, Talking to Statues," *Seattle Post-Intelligencer*, August 31, 1980, 11.
11. Fiset, "World War I Memorial Is Moved."
12. "It Is Bestial and Unheroic Charges Gould," undated newspaper clipping, Alonzo Victor Lewis file, Hugh and Jane Ferguson Seattle Room, Central Library, Seattle.

Chapter 8: Great Depression, Modest Monuments

1. Sarah Truax Albert, "Seattle Monuments," *The Argus* (Seattle), July 11, 1955, 8.
2. Sale, *Seattle, Past to Present*, 63.
3. Ibid, 67.
4. "Thomas Burke Papers, 1875–1925," University of Washington Libraries, archiveswest. orbiscascade.org/ark:/80444/xv77651.
5. Paul Dorpat, "A Hidden Memorial," *Seattle Times*, March 22, 1992, Pacific Magazine sec. 23.
6. "Burke Memorial, Soon to Be Dedicated, Viewed by Artist," *Seattle Daily Times*, March 27, 1930, 5.
7. Ibid.
8. "Club's Gift Will Honor J. D. Ross," *Seattle Daily Times*, April 18, 1935, 12.
9. "Seattle Honors Rogers' Memory," *Seattle Daily Times*, July 27, 1936, 14.
10. "Rogers' Memorial Gets Tot's Mite," *The Spokesman-Review* (Spokane), August 23, 1935.
11. Alan J. Stein, "Sicks' Stadium (Seattle)," HistoryLink, August 22, 1999, www.historylink.org/File/1501.
12. Dale Soden, "Matthews, Reverend Mark (1867–1940)," HistoryLink, January 13, 2007, www.historylink.org/File/8049; Margaret Bendroth, "Bendroth on Soden," review of *The Reverend Mark Matthews: An Activist in the Progressive Era*, H-SHGAPE, December 2002, net works.h-net.org/node/20317/reviews/21418/bendroth-soden-reverend-mark-matthews-activist-progressive-era.
13. "Denny Park Site Chosen for Statue," *Seattle Daily Times*, December 5, 1941, 16.

Chapter 9: Memorializing the Second World War

1. James R. Warren, *The War Years: A Chronicle of Washington State in World War II* (Seattle: History Ink/University of Washington Press, 2000), 18.
2. "A Fitting Memorial to Our War Heroes Is Deserving of Some Careful Thought," *Seattle Daily Times*, February 27, 1944.
3. "Seattle Honors Name of Marine," *Marine Corps Chevron* 3, no. 36, September 1, 1944, 1; Warren, *The War Years*, 132.
4. "Strolling Around the Town," *Seattle Daily Times*, April 19, 1945, 18. "Shrine, Sadly Neglected, No Honor to War Dead," *Seattle Daily Times*, April 29, 1945, 6.
5. "Two Who Lost Son Proud in V Celebration," *Seattle Daily Times*, August 16, 1945, 21.
6. "Victory Square Plans Shouldn't Wait Too Long," *Seattle Daily Times*, August 29, 1945, 6.
7. "75-Ft. Shaft to Replace Wood Pylon," *Seattle Daily Times*, September 7, 1945, 1.
8. "Many Approve of Memorial Plan…Parks, Gymnasium Named as Alternatives," *Seattle Daily Times*, September 10, 1945, 15.
9. Ibid.
10. "Can—And Should—Victory Square Be Transplanted?," *Seattle Daily Times*, September 11, 1945, 6.
11. Nora Burton, "Times Readers Have Their Say," *Seattle Daily Times*, December 14, 1948, 6.
12. "Son Lives!," *Seattle Daily Times*, September 25, 1945, 4.
13. "Can—And Should—Victory Square Be Transplanted?," 6.
14. Pat O'Donnell, "Times Readers Have Their Say," *Seattle Daily Times*, December 1, 1946, 6.
15. "Regents Turn Down Request for Memorial," *Seattle Daily Times*, February 11, 1948, 1.
16. Patrick O'Reardon, "Times Readers Have Their Say," *Seattle Daily Times*, December 7, 1947, 6.
17. "Thoughts While Reading the Times," *Seattle Daily Times*, January 12, 1949, 6.
18. Kathy Mulady, "Memorial Wall Could Become Just a Memory," *Seattle Post-Intelligencer*, May 28, 2006, www.seattlepi.com/local/article/Memorial-wall-could-become-just-a-memory-1204709.php.

19. Dickinson, Blair, and Ott, eds., *Places of Public Memory*, 156.
20. "Thoughts While Reading the Times," *Seattle Daily Times*, October 23, 1947, 6. "Hope Is Renewed for Perpetuation of Victory Square," *Seattle Daily Times*, October 30, 1947, 6.
21. Mulady, "Memorial Wall Could Become Just a Memory."
22. "City to Tear Down Victory Square Pylon," *Seattle Daily Times*, January 11, 1949, 11.
23. "Listing County Dead Long, Hard Job," *Seattle Daily Times*, March 3, 1949, 1.
24. "MacArthur Welcomes Korea Vets," *Seattle Daily Times*, November 14, 1951, 9.
25. Ed Guthman, "Monument Dedicated to 55 Fighting Nisei," *Seattle Daily Times*, May 31, 1949, 4.
26. Doss, *Memorial Mania: Public Feeling in America*, 192.
27. "Bainbridge Island Japanese American Memorial—Introduction," Bainbridge Island Japanese American Community, www.bijac.org/index.php?p=MEMORIALIntroduction.

Chapter 10: Maritime Memories

1. Four of the temporary markers were not made permanent: the Moran Brothers shipyard where gold rush steamers were built at Pier 42; the clipper sailing ship *Windward* buried in the landfill at Western Avenue near Colman Dock; the steamship *George S. Wright* which provided regular service between Seattle, the Columbia River, and San Francisco, located between Pier 53 and the fire station; and the berth at Pier 91 where the ship *Roosevelt*, in which Admiral Robert E. Peary discovered the North Pole in 1909, was docked.
2. Thrush, *Native Seattle*, 22-23.
3. "Plaque to Mark Landing of Gold Ship," *Seattle Daily Times*, May 19, 1957, 36.
4. David Suffia, "Yesler Better Remembered for Mill Than His Ill-fated Lottery Venture," *Seattle Times*, December 24, 1972, A13.
5. Morgan, *Skid Road*, 5.
6. "Exile to Ballast Island," Duwamish Tribe, www.duwamishtribe.org/ballastisland.html.
7. George Blomberg, email message to author, February 15, 2016.
8. *Maritime Seattle*, 63.
9. Scott Boyd and Laura James, "SS *Dix* Expedition," OceanGate, www.oceangate.com/expeditions/dix-expedition.
10. *Maritime Seattle*, 22.
11. "Area's First Battleship Recalled," *Seattle Daily Times*, May 20, 1965, 19.
12. Greg Lange, "Skinner & Eddy Shipyard Begins Ship Construction in Seattle on February 3, 1916," HistoryLink, January 24, 1999, www.historylink.org/File/749.
13. "Shipyard Commemorated," *Seattle Times*, May 23, 1969, 34.
14. Mike McKinley, "Cruise of the Great White Fleet," Naval History and Heritage Command. April 1, 2015, www.history.navy.mil/research/library/online-reading-room/title-list-alphabetically/c/cruise-great-white-fleet-mckinley.html.
15. "About the Port: 1911–1919," Port of Seattle, www.portseattle.org/About/History/Pages/1911-1919.aspx.
16. Susan Gilmore, "Honoring Those Taken by the Sea," *Seattle Times*, November 1, 1987, B4.
17. "$50,000 Prize Set for Best Design of Memorial to Lost Fishermen," *Seattle Times*, May 1, 1986, B6.
18. Gil Bailey, "A Choice With a Price: Loved Ones Lost at Sea Remembered at Service," *Seattle Post-Intelligencer*, April 2, 1990, B1.
19. "Sharing Our History," *Norwegian American Weekly*, December 29, 2011, www.na-weekly.com/featured/sharing-our-history.

Chapter 11: Heroes, Leaders, and Legends

1. "Leif Erikson Statue Site Still Debated," *Seattle Daily Times*, March 10, 1959, 3. Louis R Guzzo, "Site Remains Problem in Erikson-Statue Plan," *Seattle Daily Times*, March 13, 1959, 49.

2. Don Duncan, "Controversial Erikson Model Unveiled," *Seattle Daily Times*, February 21, 1961, 2.

3. Kristine Leander, "Seattle Statue," Leif Erikson International Foundation, 2005, www.leiferikson.org/Seattle.htm.

4. John Hinterberger, "Columbus Rejected," *Seattle Daily Times*, December 11, 1976, A9.

5. Wayne Johnson, "Political Hot Potatoes Juggles by Commission," *Seattle Daily Times*, November 3, 1976, D2.

6. "Christopher Columbus Comes to Seattle to Stay," *Seattle Daily Times*, October 6, 1978, downtown Seattle Discovery Sale section.

7. Chet Skreen, "Doug Bennett and Seattle's Statuary 'War'," *Seattle Daily Times*, April 14, 1979, magazine section; Rae Tufts, "Donations: When It Comes to Public Art, Some Gift Horses Should Remain in Stable," *Seattle Times*, July 1, 1984, D10.

8. Hinterberger, "Columbus Rejected," A9.

9. Susan Gilmore, "Douglas Bennett, Who Sculpted Columbus at Pier 57, Dies at 90," *Seattle Daily Times*, July 20, 2010.

10. Brandi Kruse, "Full Restoration for Columbus Statue after Years of Vandalism," My Northwest.com, May 22, 2013, mynorthwest.com/11/2279605/Full-restoration-for-Columbus-statue-after-years-of-vandalism.

11. Paul Dorpat, "Haglund, Ivar (1905–1985), HistoryLink, June 20, 2000, www.historylink.org/File/2499.

12. "Our Story," Ivar's Seafood Restaurants & Chowder, www.ivars.com/our-story; "Donations Are Sought to Build Ivar Statue," *Seattle Times*, June 5, 1987; Richard Beyer, "Ivar Feeding the Gulls, 1988," City of Seattle Arts Collection, www9.seattle.gov/arts/collection/permanent/permanent.asp?cat=9.

13. Mary T. Henry, "Martin Luther King Jr. Arrives for His Sole Seattle Visit on November 8, 1961," HistoryLink.org, January 8, 1999, www.historylink.org/File/673.

14. "Seattleites Propose a Monument to Dr. King," *Seattle Post-Intelligencer*, July 8, 1983; Susan Gilmore, "Sculptor Vows to Honor King," *Seattle Times*, July 25, 1983.

15. Anne Christensen, "Backers of Martin Luther King Memorial Try Again." *Seattle Times*, December 14, 1987.

16. Gilmore, "Sculptor Vows to Honor King"; Dick Lilly, "Money Drive for King Memorial Boosted by Major Corporations, *Seattle Times*, March 24, 1989.

17. Christensen, "Backers…Try Again"; Dick Lilly, "Fundraising for King Memorial Picks Up," *Seattle Times*, April 10, 1990; John Marshall, "They Have a Dream," *Seattle Post-Intelligencer*, December 6, 1990.

18. "Donations Sought for Rev. King Tribute," *Seattle Times*, June 13, 1988; Lilly, "Money Drive for King Memorial Boosted"; Lilly, "Fundraising for King Memorial Picks Up"; "Granite for King Memorial Arrives," *Seattle Times*, September 21, 1990.

19. Constantine Angelos, "Work to Begin on Memorial to Slain Civil-Rights Leader," *Seattle Times*, May 24, 1991. Neil Modie, "Site for King Memorial Challenged," *Seattle Post-Intelligencer*, May 11, 1991.

20. Robert Jamieson, "Memorial to Dr. King Is Readied," *Seattle Post-Intelligencer*, November 11, 1991.

21. Dee Norton, "King Memorial Park Done at Last," *Seattle Post-Intelligencer*, November 17, 1991.

22. "Seattle Area's Many Jimi Hendrix Memorials," *Seattle Times*, August 14, 2011.

23. Charles E. Brown, "New Memorial A Tribute to Fallen Firefighters," *Seattle Times*, June 4, 1998; Casey McNerthy, "Wednesday Marks Anniversary of Deadly Seattle Fire," Seattle Post-Intelligencer, January 5, 2011, blog.seattlepi.com/seattle911/2011/01/05/wednesday-marks-anniversary-of-deadly-seattle-fire.

24. "Firefighter Memorial," Seattle.gov, Seattle Fire Department, www.seattle.gov/fire/about-us/fallen-firefighter-memorial.

Chapter 12: Remembering Places

1. Morgan, *Skid Road,* 9.

2. Garfield et al., *Pioneer Square: Seattle's Oldest Neighborhood,* 96.

3. "A Red Light History of Seattle," *Seattle Met,* January 29, 2010, www.seattlemet.com/articles/2010/1/29/red-light-history-0210.

4. Greg Lange, "Seattle's Great Fire," HistoryLink. January 16, 1999, www.historylink.org/File/715.

5. "Plaque Found to Mark Great Fire," *Seattle Daily Times,* June 6, 1952, 6. "Iron Pergola and Totem Pole—Seattle, Washington: A National Register of Historic Places Travel Itinerary," National Parks Service. www.nps.gov/nr/travel/seattle/s26.htm.

6. Priscilla Long, "Truck Accidentally Destroys Seattle's Historic Pioneer Square Pergola," HistoryLink, January 15, 2001, www.historylink.org/File/2944; Priscilla Long, "Seattle's Pioneer Square Pergola Re-opens on August 17, 2002," HistoryLink, August 19, 2002. www.historylink.org/File/3920.

7. "U.P.S.: Under Public Sidewalk." *Seattle Times,* June 21, 1967, 44.

8. "Our History," Historic Panama Hotel Bed and Breakfast, www.panamahotel.net/history.

9. "Plaque to Be Unveiled in Hotel." *Seattle Daily Times,* November 16, 1924, 9.

Chapter 13: What Might Have Been

1. Poyner, *First Sculptor of Seattle.*

2. Virgil Gay Bogue, *Plan of Seattle: Report of the Municipal Plans Commission, Submitting Report of Virgil G. Bogue, Engineer, 1911* (Seattle: Lowman & Hanford, 1911), 68–69.

3. "Statue for Mothers Proposed Monument May Rise Above Bay," *Seattle Daily Times,* December 10, 1935.

4. David Suffia, "Some Monuments That Never Were," *Seattle Times,* January 14, 1973, 12.

5. "Big Monument to Peace Urged for Puget Sound." *Seattle Daily Times,* November 3, 1951, 4.

6. "400-Foot Tower Urged as Seattle's 'Statue of Liberty'," *Seattle Daily Times,* March 1, 1957, 16.

7. Louis Guzzo, "Why Not Make Seattle a City of Fountains?," *Seattle Daily Times,* May 23, 1958, 23.

8. "The Gold Seeker," *Seattle Post-Intelligencer,* August 21, 1927; Stanton H. Patty, "Famed Sculptor's Sourdough Soon to Come Out of Hiding," *Seattle Times,* February 22, 1981, H11.

9. "Tribute to Sculptor: Work of A. V. Lewis Symbolized a State," *Seattle Times,* November 1, 1981, B21.

SELECTED SOURCES

Armbruster, Kurt E. *Orphan Road: The Railroad Comes to Seattle, 1853-1911.* Pullman, WA: Washington State University Press, 1999.

Bagley, Clarence. *History of Seattle from the Earliest Settlement to the Present Time, Vol. 2.* Chicago: S.J. Clarke Pub., 1916.

Berger, Knute. *Pugetopolis: A Mossback Takes on Growth Addicts, Weather Wimps, and the Myth of Seattle Nice.* Seattle: Sasquatch Books, 2009.

Bogue, Virgil Gay. *Plan of Seattle: Report of the Municipal Plans Commission, Submitting Report of Virgil G. Bogue, Engineer, 1911.* Seattle: Lowman & Hanford, 1911.

Dickinson, Greg, Carole Blair, and Brian L. Ott, eds. *Places of Public Memory: The Rhetoric of Museums and Memorials.* Tuscaloosa: University of Alabama Press, 2010.

Dorpat, Paul. *Seattle Now & Then.* Seattle, WA: Tartu Publications, 1989.

_____. *Seattle Waterfront: An Illustrated History.* Seattle, WA: Seattle City Council, 2006.

Doss, Erika. *Memorial Mania: Public Feeling in America.* Chicago: University of Chicago Press, 2010.

Duncan, Kate C. *1001 Curious Things: Ye Olde Curiosity Shop and Native American Art.* Seattle: University of Washington Press, 2000.

Fleming, Samuel Edgar. *Civics (supplement) Seattle, King County.* Seattle: Seattle Public Schools, 1922.

Fleming, Samuel Edgar, and Noah Cleveland Davenport. *Government in Seattle: City, County, State, National.* Seattle, WA: Seattle Public Schools, 1935. Appendix A: Memorial Monuments, Statues, and Tablets in Seattle and Vicinity.

Garfield, Leonard, Karin Murr Link, Marc K. Blackburn, and Dana Cox. *Pioneer Square: Seattle's Oldest Neighborhood.* Edited by Mildred Tanner Andrews. Seattle: Pioneer Square Community Association in Association with University of Washington Press, 2005.

Garfield, Viola Edmundson. *Seattle's Totem Poles.* Bellevue, WA: Thistle Press, 1996.

Goode, J. M. *The Outdoor Sculpture of Washington, D.C.: A Comprehensive Historical Guide.* Washington, DC: Smithsonian Institution Press (Publication No. 4829), 1974.

Hitchman, Robert. "Historical Markers in Seattle." 1951. MS, Hugh and Jane Ferguson Seattle Room, Seattle Central Library, Seattle.

John Emmett Berns Collection of "Packer Jack" Newman Photographs. University of Washington Libraries. digital.lib.washington.edu/findingaids/view?docId=BernsJohnPHColl504.xml.

"Leif Erikson Dedication Set for June 17." *Marine Digest*, March 24, 1962.

Litwin, Thomas S. *The Harriman Alaska Expedition Retraced: A Century of Change, 1899-2001*. New Brunswick, NJ: Rutgers University Press, 2005.

Malone, M. P. *James J. Hill: Empire Builder of the Northwest*. Norman, OK: University of Oklahoma Press, 1996.

Mattox, Jeremy. "Historical Site Location Researched by Mattox." *Marine Digest* 63, no. 24 (January 19, 1985): 2-23.

Miles, Charles, and Ottis Bedney Sperlin. *Building a State: Washington, 1889-1939*. Tacoma, WA: Washington State Historical Society, 1940. Chapter XV Monuments and Markers

"Mollie Walsh Park." Alaska.org. www.alaska.org/detail/mollie-walsh-park.

Morgan, Murray. *Skid Road: An Informal Portrait of Seattle*. New York: Viking Press, 1951.

Murakami, Kery. "Sea Scout Leader Recalls Unveiling of Alki's Lady Liberty," *Seattle Post-Intelligencer*, March 29, 2005.

"National Maritime Day." MARAD—Maritime Administration. www.marad.dot.gov/education/national-maritime-day.

Ochsner, Jeffrey Karl. *Shaping Seattle Architecture: A Historical Guide to the Architects*. Seattle: University of Washington Press in Association with the American Institute of Architects Seattle Chapter and the Seattle Architectural Foundation, 1994.

Potts, Ralph Bushnell. *Seattle Heritage*. Seattle: Superior Publishing Company, 1955.

Poyner, Fred, IV. *The First Sculptor of Seattle: The Life and Art of James A. Wehn*. CreateSpace, 2014.

Puget Sound Maritime Historical Society, *Maritime Seattle*. Chicago: Arcadia Publishing (Images of America), 2002.

"A Red Light History of Seattle." *Seattle Met*, January 29, 2010.

Reed, Gervais, and Joan H. Nilsson. *Art in Seattle's Public Places: Five Urban Walking Tours*. Seattle, 1977.

Sale, Roger. *Seattle, Past to Present*. Seattle: University of Washington Press, 1976.

Sayre, J. Willis. *This City of Ours*. Seattle: Seattle School District No. 1, 1936.

Schwantes, Carlos A. *The Pacific Northwest: An Interpretive History*. Lincoln: University of Nebraska Press, 1998.

Scolari, Paul. "Indian Warriors and Pioneer Mothers: American Identity and the Closing of the Frontier in Public Monuments, 1890-1930." PhD diss., University of Pittsburgh, 2005. d-scholarship.pitt.edu/7029/1/SCOLARI2005_etd.pdf.

"Seattle Landmarks." *Seattle Times*, September 23, 1945.

"Seattle's Lady Liberty Gets a Bath." *Seattle Post-Intelligencer*, June 25, 1986.

"Seward Park Torii Story." Seward Park Torii Story. www.sewardparktorii.org/home/seward-park-torii-story.

Shackel, Paul A., ed. *Myth, Memory, and the Making of the American Landscape*. Gainesville: University Press of Florida, 2001.

Sherwood, Jessie C. "Robert Bridges." Pacific Northwest Features. November 19, 2009. pnwblog.wordpress.com/tag/robert-bridges/.

Speidel, William C. *Sons of the Profits: Or, There's No Business Like Grow Business: The Seattle Story 1851-1901*. Seattle: Nettle Creek Publishing, 1967.

Stein, Alan J. *The Olympic: The Story of Seattle's Landmark Hotel since 1924*. Seattle, WA: University of Washington Press, 2005.

Stein, Alan J., and Paula Becker. *Alaska-Yukon-Pacific Exposition: Washington's First World's Fair: A Timeline History*. Seattle, WA: History Ink/HistoryLink, 2009.

Taft, Lorado. *The History of American Sculpture*. New York: Macmillan Company, 1924.

Thrush, Coll. *Native Seattle: Histories from the Crossing-over Place*. Seattle: University of Washington Press, 2007.

"A Timeline of Leif Ericson Statues." Leif Erikson International Foundation. www.leiferikson.org/Timeline.htm.

A Volume of Memoirs and Genealogy of Representative Citizens of the City of Seattle and County of King, Washington, including Biographies of Many of Those Who Have Passed Away. New York: Lewis Publishing Company, 1903.

Warren, James R. *The War Years: A Chronicle of Washington State in World War II*. Seattle: History Ink, in Association with the University of Washington Press, 2000.

Wehn, James A. File. Central Library, Hugh and Jane Ferguson Seattle Room, Seattle.

"West by Water: Maritime History of West Seattle." Southwest Seattle Historical Society. www.loghousemuseum.info/exhibits/west-by-water-maritime-history-of-west-seattle.

Wilton, William L. "The WAC Plaque." *Puget Soundings*, Spring 1982, 18-21.

Wingate, Jennifer. *Sculpting Doughboys: Memory, Gender, and Taste in America's World War I Memorials*. Florence, KY: Routledge, 2013.

Newspapers

The Argus (Seattle)
Capitol Hill Times
Ellensburg Daily Record
Norwegian American Weekly
International Examiner

Seattle Daily Journal of Commerce
Seattle Daily Post-Intelligencer
Seattle Post-Intelligencer
Seattle Star
Seattle Daily Times
Seattle Times (1966–present)
Seattle Weekly
The Spokesman Review (Spokane, WA)
West Seattle Herald

Websites

Pacific Coast Architecture Database, pcad.lib.washington.edu
Seattle Parks and Recreation, www.seattle.gov/parks
Seattle Department of Neighborhoods; Seattle Historical Sites, web6.seattle.
    gov/DPD/HistoricalSite
Port of Seattle, www.portseattle.org
Seattle Public Library, www.spl.org
Seattle Public Schools, www.seattleschools.org
University of Washington Libraries, digitalcollections.lib.washington.edu
HistoryLink, www.historylink.org

INDEX

197